SOGO SHOSHA

The Vanguard of the Japanese Economy

SOGO SHOSHA

The Vanguard of
the Japanese Economy

YOSHIHARA KUNIO

Tokyo
OXFORD UNIVERSITY PRESS
Oxford New York Melbourne

Oxford University Press

Oxford London Glasgow
New York Toronto Melbourne Auckland
Kuala Lumpur Singapore Hong Kong Tokyo
Delhi Bombay Calcutta Madras Karachi
Nairobi Dar es Salaam Cape Town

and associates in
Beirut Berlin Ibadan Mexico City Nicosia

© *Oxford University Press 1982*

First published 1982
Third impression 1983

ISBN 0 19 582534 9 (boards)
ISBN 0 19 582500 4 (limp)

Printed in Japan
by Akatsuki Art Printing Co., Ltd.
Published by Oxford University Press K.K.
Enshu Building, 3-3-3 Otsuka
Bunkyo-ku, Tokyo 112

To Ben Haggott

Preface

THROUGH my research on foreign investment and industrialization in South-East Asia in the mid-1970s, I was able to gain a better understanding of sogo shosha which were often participants in industrial joint ventures. At that time, however, my knowledge was confined only to their industrial activities in that region, and was thus far from complete. It was my intention to undertake a more comprehensive study of sogo shosha at some later date, but I first wanted to complete a study on economic development which I had been doing off and on for the past several years. This priority was changed, however, in the second half of 1978. In the middle of that year Professor Ishikawa of Hitotsubashi University asked me if I would write a report on sogo shosha for the ILO office in Bangkok, Thailand. It turned out that ILO was interested in the role trading companies could play in the export-led industrialization of South-East Asian countries. And so, I decided to put off my research on economic development for several months and write this report. Then a few months later I met Messrs. Kawawaki Tatsuo and John Nicholson of Oxford University Press—the publisher of an earlier work of mine—who asked me whether I would write a book on this topic. Since there was no urgency in finishing the work on economic development, I decided to make a fairly comprehensive study of sogo shosha by extending for two more years the work I had been doing for ILO.

As for my method of research, I first examined all the printed materials I was able to find and obtain. I searched the major weekly and monthly magazines for articles on trading companies. In most cases, I did not go back to pre-war issues, except in the case of *Ekonomisuto, Toyo Keizai,* and *Daiya-mondo.* I perused all the pre-war issues of these three major economic weeklies that were available at the library of the Faculty of Economics at Kyoto University. Next, I studied all the company magazines, which turned out to be a gold mine of firsthand information on trading companies. Since they were not available in public or university libraries, I asked the sogo shosha if I could either borrow or read their magazines at their offices in Osaka or Kyoto. Finally, I went through books, mimeographed papers, articles in academic journals, and other printed materials which dealt with trading companies. These are listed in the bibliography.

I supplemented my reading with interviews, which were conducted over a two-year span beginning in August 1978. The first series of interviews were conducted in Tokyo in connection with my work for ILO. These interviews were concerned with questions relating to South-East Asia—their operations and their perceptions of trading companies in the region (including Korea and Taiwan). The later interviews were conducted to discuss the questions which were either not taken up or were ambiguous in the printed materials. During these two years, I met over a hundred persons including some who are now retired. Some of them had worked for companies which were once active but are now non-existent or obscure. Also, by meeting people who worked at banks and at the Ministry of International Trade and Industry I was able to gain a different perspective on trading companies. Some of the people I interviewed wanted to remain anonymous, and so, when I used their explanations, I presented them as my own personal conjecture. Otherwise, the names of those interviewed are given whenever I quote or rely upon their ideas.

The major source of information on the statistical data of sogo shosha is their securities reports. Whenever I used these reports, if the years for the data are clearly indicated, I have not provided a specific note of reference. Data from other sources, however, are documented. Among these are journalistic writings, but since they often neglected to indicate where they received their information, they cannot be regarded as fully reliable. But when no other source is available, I have used them to give a rough numerical idea.

Much of what sogo shosha do is reflected in the statistics of their securities reports. When I rely on these statistics, my discussion is on a fairly firm basis; but to rely only on statistics would indeed result in a very boring book. My concern, then, is centred on the way in which the sogo shosha were able to attain the results indicated by the statistics. For this, it was sometimes imperative for me to impose subjective judgement.

Here, I am reminded of the story of the three blind men and the elephant. When asked to identify the animal, each man gave a different answer depending on which part of the elephant he touched (for example, the one who touched the trunk said that it was a snake). By going beyond what the statistics show, I may make a similar mistake. As I explained earlier, however, I consulted other writings and conducted interviews, in order to be as objective as possible, but subjective judgement could not be avoided. This book should be considered as the perception of sogo shosha that I arrived at after having read printed materials and conducted interviews.

Otsu, Japan   Yoshihara Kunio
October 1980

Contents

Tables

Figures

Author's Notes

1. In this work, Japanese names appear in the normal Japanese order: surname first and given name second.

2. Mitsubishi Shoji, Mitsui Bussan, and Sumitomo Shoji have English names (Mitsubishi Corp., Mitsui & Co., and Sumitomo Corp., respectively), but the English names are not used in this work since they tend to give the impression that they are holding companies of the respective enterprise groups.

Abbreviations commonly used in Japan are Shoji for Mitsubishi Shoji, Bussan for Mitsui Bussan, and Sumisho for Sumitomo Shoji, but these abbreviations are not used in this work since they rarely appear in English publications. Alternative abbreviations are Mitsubishi for Mitsubishi Shoji, Mitsui for Mitsui Bussan, and Sumitomo for Sumitomo Shoji, but when they are discussed together with other Mitsubishi, Mitsui, and Sumitomo companies, such abbreviations become confusing. Thus, although it seems slightly repetitive, the full names are always used.

3. The yen is the unit of Japanese money in the modern period. In the early 1870s, ¥1 was roughly equivalent to US$1. By 1897, the yen had devalued to ¥2 per US dollar. From then until 1931, the exchange rate remained at about the same level (although in the early 1920s, there was a tendency for the yen to devalue). In 1932, the yen devalued sharply, and the rate remained for the rest of the 1930s at approximately ¥4 per US dollar. In the post-war years, the exchange

rate was set at ¥360 to the dollar (in 1949), and it remained at that level until December 1971. The yen then revalued to ¥308 to the dollar, and this rate was maintained until February 1973. Since then, the exchange rate has been floating. The trend has been toward the revaluation of the yen. At the time of this writing (October 1980), US$1 is worth about ¥210.

4. If the name of a publisher is missing in a reference, the work cited is a privately printed one. If the name of a Japanese publisher is given but the place of publication is omitted, the work cited was published in Tokyo. Japanese titles are translated in the bibliography, but not in the footnotes.

1

Introduction

THE 'sogo shosha fever' seems to have spread throughout the world. Brazil, Mexico, Korea, Thailand, and Taiwan have set up their own versions of sogo shosha, while the United States, Malaysia, and several other countries are considering doing the same. Their motives for replicating the Japanese organization are, however, varied. In the case of industrial countries, such as the United States, there is a need to create organizations to link small and medium-sized companies to the export market, whereas in the case of developing countries, the focus is on bringing foreign trade which has been dominated by foreign companies under their control, and increasing exports. But both the industrial and the developing countries agree on one point—the sogo shosha are efficient conduits of international trade.

Foreign journals are also lavish in their praise of sogo shosha. For example, a British weekly, *The Economist*, has published articles on Japanese trading companies from time to time since the mid-1960s, and has attributed the success of Japanese export drive to the existence of sogo shosha. *Forbes*, an American business journal, wrote complimentary reports in 1972 and 1978. The most recent praise came from the *Far Eastern Economic Review*, which wrote

If one factor had to be singled out for the explosive growth of Japan's economy since World War II, it would undoubtedly be the nation's unrivalled virtuosity in foreign trade. At the center of this worldwide web of trading, marketing and financial operations sit the nine giant sogo shosha (general trading companies), which orchestrate Japan's complex and diverse international commerce.[1]

The road to eminence was an uphill struggle for the sogo shosha. In Western countries, although trading companies were important in the period before the Industrial Revolution, their relative importance declined as manufacturing companies grew in size. Thus, when Western companies were approached by Japanese trading companies, they often regarded the Japanese trading companies as unnecessary intermediaries, who were trying to make money by taking advantage of their ignorance. Since Western companies normally conducted their dealings directly, their reaction was understandable. But many of them changed their views as they learned more about the operations of sogo shosha, which included taking risks, giving large credits, collecting information pertinent to business, and undertaking numerous other activities. In other words, these sogo shosha did not serve simply as intermediaries.

In the West, there are some large trading companies. In grain trade, companies such as Continental Grain, Cargill, Bunge, etc., cannot be considered merely as intermediaries. European trading companies such as East Asiatic, Sime Darby, Inchcape, and Jardine Matheson play an important role in trade with Asia by performing many of the functions of sogo shosha. They, too, cannot be said to be simple intermediaries. But are these companies sogo shosha? They are not: for to be a sogo shosha, a trading company must have a world-wide network, handle numerous commodities, and account for a large share of the foreign trade in the country of its domicile.

The sogo shosha is a unique Japanese organization. For example, Mitsui Bussan, the second ranking sogo shosha in Japan, accounts for about 10 per cent of Japan's exports and imports, employs more than 13,000 people, maintains a network of 181 offices in the major cities of the world, and handles such diverse products as iron and steel, non-ferrous metals, chemicals, textiles, foodstuffs, and machinery. Such a large and diversified trading company exists in no other country.

The sogo shosha is Japan's organizational innovation—an innovation necessitated by the problems the country faced in international trade.

How many sogo shosha are there in Japan today, and how do they differ from other trading companies? These are the major questions discussed in Chapter 2. The next two chapters review the evolution of the trading companies which are today called sogo shosha, describe their positions *vis-à-vis* their competitors at various points in time, and explain why they have been more successful than others. The primary purpose of these two chapters is to give not only a historical dimension to the sogo shosha of today, but also to provide a basis for discussion in the subsequent chapters.

In the Western press, Japan's success is often attributed to the government. The question of why Japan developed sogo shosha is often explained in a similar manner. Without doubt, the interventionist government played a part, but it was not the major factor. The basic reason for the growth of sogo shosha is that there was a market need for them in the Japanese economy. Why that was the case in Japan and not in Western countries is the major focus of discussion in Chapter 5.

The following chapter examines the role trading companies played in Japan's industrialization. A typical approach to this question is to list the industrial companies set up by trading companies and discuss their subsequent growth. The emphasis in this chapter, however, is mainly on their role as intermediaries. As marketing and financial intermediaries, trading companies reduced market imperfection and contributed to greater efficiency in the allocation of resources.

What is a trading company? The best answer would be that it is people and money. Since the importance of money is discussed in Chapter 5, Chapter 7 focuses its attention on people. Such questions as: what sort of people were needed by trading companies; what type of training did they give; what sort of commitment did they expect from their people and what did they give in return; how are they organized and why; what problems did they encounter in increasing the size of their

operation; and what role did the family enterprise play in the
evolution of trading companies, are the major issues discussed
in Chapter 7.

In the 1970s, as sogo shosha attracted greater attention
abroad as organizations fit to promote international trade
(particularly export), in Japan they faced severe criticism from
journalists, intellectuals, leftist politicians, and the government's Fair Trade Commission. They were accused of corner-
ing the market, causing inflation, destroying the competitive
framework of the economy, and corrupting the political process. A great part of the public's critical outcry was based on
the values of the Japanese élite who looked down on trading—
a remnant of the feudal value system. But trading companies
must carry, for a long time to come, the stigma that they have
been part of the trinity of Japan's corrupt politics (the other
two being politicians and bureaucrats), an accusation which is
hard to deny in view of various recent revelations. This does
not mean that political involvement was a *sine qua non* for the
emergence of sogo shosha. Even if the political system had
been clean, the sogo shosha would have emerged anyway.
What supported their growth was essentially a market need
for them; and possibly, they would have preferred to act
in a *laissez-faire* environment. Chapter 8 discusses their political involvement and other activities for which they are
criticized.

From the viewpoint of historical particularism, we could
argue that since sogo shosha developed in the Japanese institutional environment, they cannot be transplanted in other
countries. If so, are the attempts by other countries to set up
their own sogo shosha futile? Should countries which are considering whether to replicate the Japanese experience drop
the idea? Undoubtedly, we have to look carefully at the Japanese environment in which sogo shosha developed, but we
need not be too pessimistic, in view of the progress Korea
has made in this endeavour. The concluding chapter first
reiterates major points in the preceding chapters and then,
it discusses what lessons can be drawn from the Japanese

experience, and attempts to provide a guide for governments which want to develop their own sogo shosha or for the top management who want to make their companies sogo shosha in the future.

1. *Far Eastern Economic Review*, February 1980, p. 39.

2

The Trading Industry

1. TRADING COMPANIES

IF trading companies are defined as those which are engaged in wholesale activities, there are innumerable trading companies in Japan, ranging from a giant company which employs over 10,000 people and has offices all over the world to a one-man company whose major asset is a telephone in a shared office. In order to eliminate the small companies, if we stipulate that we want to consider only those companies engaged in foreign trade, we will be disappointed, for there are about 6,000 such companies, most of which are very small.[1]

Sogo shosha form the top strata of this large group of companies. In the mid-1970s, they were, in order of sales, Mitsubishi Shoji, Mitsui Bussan, Marubeni, C.Itoh, Sumitomo Shoji, Nissho-Iwai, Toyo Menka, Kanematsu-Gosho, Ataka, and Nichimen. Since Ataka was merged with C.Itoh in 1977, there are only nine today.

How do they differ from other trading companies? In order to investigate this question, the sales of all trading companies listed on stock exchanges and major unlisted companies were obtained for 1973–5, and the top thirty companies were selected. The result is shown in Table 2.1.

The first question to be asked about this Table would be why Nichimen is a sogo shosha and why Toyota Motor Sales is not. In the past several years, Toyota's position has risen, and it has become comparable to Nissho-Iwai in sales, so that

TABLE 2.1

The Average Annual Sales of the
Top Thirty Trading Companies in 1973–1975
(Unit: billion yen)

Company Name	Sales	Company Name	Sales
Mitsubishi Shoji	8,677	Toshiba Shoji	388
Mitsui Bussan	7,815	Okura	378
Marubeni	5,254	Shinko Shoji	348
C.Itoh	5,036	Mitsubishi Motor Sales	348
Sumitomo Shoji	5,014	Okaya	345
Nissho-Iwai	3,819	General Sekiyu	320
Toyo Menka	2,223	Sumikin Bussan	316
Kanematsu-Gosho	2,179	Matsushita Electric Trading	298
Ataka	1,902	Hitachi Sales	286
Nichimen	1,780	Hanwa	283
Toyota Motor Sales	1,718	Kinsho-Mataichi	267
Kawasho	638	Kokubu	255
Chori	569	Japan Pulp & Paper	244
Toshoku	453	Nagase	235
Toyoda Tsusho	396	Osaka Kozai	234

Source: *Kaisha Nenkan: Jojo Kaisha-ban*, Nihon Keizai Shinbun-sha, and *Kaisha Sokan: Mijojo Kaisha-ban*, Nihon Keizai Shinbun-sha.

today, it has even a better claim to be referred to as a sogo shosha. Previously, the size of sales was a convenient criterion to determine whether a company was a sogo shosha or not, because there used to be a large gap between the smallest sogo shosha and other trading companies. This criterion is still valid in differentiating Nichimen from Kawasho and those listed below it, for the decline of sales, which is gradual from Mitsubishi Shoji to Nichimen, becomes abrupt from Nichimen to Kawasho.

Ordinary trading companies differ from sogo shosha in other respects. For one thing, some of them are the subsidiaries of manufacturing companies. Table 2.2 lists eight such companies. Toyota Motor Sales is a subsidiary of Toyota Motor; Kawasho, Kawasaki Steel; Toshiba Shoji, Tokyo Shibaura Electric; Shinko Shoji, Kobe Steel; Mitsubishi Motor Sales,

TABLE 2.2
Independent Trading Companies *v.* Manufacturers'
Subsidiaries

Independent Companies	
Mitsubishi Shoji	Toyoda Tsusho
Mitsui Bussan	Okura Shoji
Marubeni	Okaya
C.Itoh	General Sekiyu
Sumitomo Shoji	Hanwa
Nissho-Iwai	Kokubu
Toyo Menka	Nagase
Kanematsu-Gosho	_ _ _ _ _ _ _ _
Ataka	Kinsho-Mataichi
Nichimen	Japan Pulp & Paper
Chori	Osaka Kozai
Toshoku	

Manufacturers' Subsidiaries	
Toyota Motor Sales	Mitsubishi Motor Sales
Kawasho	Sumikin Bussan
Toshiba Shoji	Matsushita Electric Trading
Shinko Shoji	Hitachi Sales

Mitsubishi Motor; Sumikin Bussan, Sumitomo Metal Industries; Matsushita Electric Trading, Matsushita Electric Industrial; and Hitachi Sales, Hitachi. Among these, Toshiba Shoji was absorbed by its parent company, and is non-existent today.

Among those which were not manufacturers' subsidiaries, three companies (Kinsho-Mataichi, Japan Pulp & Paper, and Osaka Kozai) were not quite independent companies. Kinsho-Mataichi and Osaka Kozai often functioned as the satellite companies of Mitsubishi Shoji, and Japan Pulp & Paper as a sales outlet for former Oji companies. Although Mitsubishi Shoji exerted considerable influence in the affairs of Kinsho-Mataichi and Osaka Kozai, and although former Oji companies influenced Japan Pulp & Paper, these trading companies were not subsidiaries in a typical sense for they retained a considerable degree of freedom. They were, however, not completely independent either.

Next, among the top 30 companies, 19 companies are left as independent trading companies. As seen from Table 2.2, the 19 companies consist of 10 sogo shosha and 9 ordinary trading companies. How do the two groups differ? As already pointed out, one difference was size. Chori, which had the largest sales among the nine, fell far short of Nichimen in sales (about a third). Another difference was that the sales composition of an ordinary trading company was unbalanced. In the case of Chori, textiles accounted for a large part of its sales (about three-quarters); Toshoku and Kokubu, foodstuffs; Toyoda Tsusho and Okura Shoji, metals and machinery; Okaya and Hanwa, steel; Nagase, chemicals; General Sekiyu, petroleum products. In addition, the share of foreign trade was small for most of these companies. If foreign trade was an important factor, it was always in terms of either export or import; there was never a case where the two were balanced.

The one picture which emerges from the analysis of these nine trading companies is that they developed as specialized dealers, and undertook foreign trade as long as it was a necessary extension of that specialization. They have, of course, never been fully satisfied as specialized trading companies. They have tried to diversify, and to some extent, they have been successful, but progress has been slow.

2. SOGO SHOSHA

In the pre-war period, the term 'sogo shosha' did not exist. Mitsui Bussan, Mitsubishi Shoji, and other major trading companies were called *boeki shosha* (foreign trading companies), and were differentiated from other *shoji kaisha*, or for short, *shosha* (both mean 'trading companies') which were not engaged in foreign trade. When there was a need to emphasize that a company was handling a variety of goods, it was called a general merchant. For some time even in the post-war period, all major trading companies continued to be called *boeki shosha* or general merchants.

It is difficult to pin-point exactly when the word, 'sogo shosha', began to be used, but it must have been around 1954. In the securities report of Mitsubishi Shoji, which was submitted on 30 June 1954, the word, 'sogo shosha', appears at a place where the merger plan is discussed. Then, the government used this word in a communiqué issued on 16 July.[2] In company magazines, the word first appeared in the August 1954 issue of *C.I. Monthly* and then in the January 1955 issue of *Marubeni*.

Around this time, there was no exact definition of what was meant by the term 'sogo shosha', but people who used the word seemed to know roughly what it meant. For a trading company to be a sogo shosha, it had to deal with many products (not concentrating in one product group, such as textiles or steel), engage in both export and import, have offices in various parts of the world, and wield considerable power in the spheres of marketing and finance. These criteria still serve as a rough guide to differentiate sogo shosha from ordinary trading companies.

There are problems, however. Marubeni, for example, was essentially a textile trader in the early 1950s, but then diversified into machinery, steel, and other products. Today, it is generally regarded as a sogo shosha. When did Marubeni become a sogo shosha? Mitsui Bussan started as 'Jack of all trades' in the early Meiji era, and grew to become a sogo shosha within the next several decades, but exactly when did it cease to be an ordinary trading company and become a sogo shosha? Today, nine companies are generally regarded as sogo shosha, but this number is disputed by those arguing that only Mitsubishi Shoji and Mitsui Bussan can be called sogo shosha. Others do not go that far, but argue against the inclusion of the bottom three companies (Toyo Menka, Kanematsu-Gosho, and Nichimen) in the class of sogo shosha.

These questions cannot be adequately answered, because the criteria suggested above are qualitative. A more elaborate list of criteria has been suggested by several people.[3] In addition to meeting the criteria listed above, for a trading company to become a sogo shosha, it has to be engaged in offshore trade, undertake various activities (such as warehousing, transportation, resource development, manufacturing, etc.) to complement its trading activities, command large financial resources, play a leadership role in industrialization, etc. But these are also qualitative criteria, and are not of much help in answering our questions.

One might try to devise a quantitative index of sogo shosha to answer those questions, but this would be futile. Perhaps, the best alternative would be to keep in mind that there are three dimensions to a sogo shosha (the number of commodities, geographical spread, and economic power), and try to answer those questions to our best ability. This approach would make it imperative to impose subjective judgements and to leave a great deal of 'grey area', but it would serve most purposes, and often make more sense than to try to construct a quantitative index of sogo shosha.

3. TOWARDS A CONGLOMERATE

In 1971, Mitsubishi Shoji changed its English name from Mitsubishi Trading Co. to Mitsubishi Corp., because it felt that 'the old name no longer adequately expresses the company's current activities'.[4] Does this mean that the sogo shosha is no longer a trading company?

A look at the British company, Jardine Matheson, whose headquarters is in Hong Kong, should give us some insight into this problem. Jardine Matheson started out as a trading company more than a century ago, and became a large company because of its success in trading.[5] At present, however, it cannot be called a trading company. Besides trading, it is engaged in light industry, shipping, tourism, insurance, merchant banking, leasing, real estate, resource development, engineering, and construction. According to the 1979 annual report, 30 per cent of its profits came from trading and light industry, 29 per cent from service activities, 12 per cent from financial service, 6 per cent from natural resource development, and 23 per cent from property. From the report it is not clear how much of a contribution trading alone made to the company's profits. What is clear, however, is that trading is only one of several major activities, and that Jardine Matheson is no longer a trading company.

Jardine Matheson is not an exception. The Danish company, East Asiatic, started to export teak from Thailand to Europe in the late nineteenth century, and became one of the most successful European trading companies operating in Asia.[6] But today, it is no longer a trading company. Besides trading, it is engaged in shipping, industry, forestry, and plantation. In 1979, trading accounted for only 20 per cent of total profits; industry accounted for 45 per cent, shipping 15 per cent, forestry 17 per cent, and others 3 per cent. The breakdown by sales does not change the picture much. In 1977, trading accounted for only 29 per cent of total sales.

Are not sogo shosha like these European companies? They are also engaged in various activities that one does not expect from a trading company. For one, every sogo shosha has a construction division, and though these do not actually undertake construction, they do architectural designs, act as prime contractors, and initiate projects at their own risk.[7] Also, every sogo shosha has a large number of subsidiaries, through which they are engaged in various activities, such as manufacturing, resource development, shipping, warehousing, packaging, leasing, merchant banking, and travel agency. Marubeni, for example, had 172 affiliated companies (*kankei kaisha*) in Japan in mid-1975, and held the equity of 213 companies abroad in early 1976.[8]

Although sogo shosha have undertaken many such activities outside trading, they differ from Jardine Matheson and East Asiatic in one important respect: that is, trading is still the centre of their activities. Many investments in industry, shipping, warehousing, and resource development were undertaken either to protect the trade channels already established or to create new ones. When Mitsubishi Shoji changed its English name from Mitsubishi Trading Co. to Mitsubishi Corp., 70 to 80 per cent of its profits still came from trading.[9]

Yet, Jardine Matheson and East Asiatic suggest a direction in which sogo shosha may evolve in the future. As pointed out above, sogo shosha are engaged in a number of activities which are not directly related to trading, though these have not become significant. There is a possibility that such activities will gain in importance in the future. Also, the activities which are, at present, undertaken in connection with trading may become important on their own account. When such eventualities occur, trading will no longer be the central activity of sogo shosha, and the word, conglomerate, will become the most appropriate appellation. This has not taken place yet. In this book, sogo shosha are considered trading companies because trading is still the linchpin of their major activities.

1. Ministry of International Trade and Industry, *Boeki Gyotai Tokei-hyo 1977*, p. 13.

2. *Daiyamondo*, 11 August 1954, p. 33.

3. For example, see Togai Yoshio, *Mitsui Bussan no Keiei-shi teki Kenkyu*, Toyo Keizai Shinpo-sha, 1974, pp. 11–13; and Morikawa Hidemasa, 'Sogo Shosha no Seiritsu to Ronri', in Miyamoto Mataji *et al.* (eds.), *Sogo Shosha no Keiei-shi*, Toyo Keizai Shinpo-sha, 1974, pp. 43–78.

4. *Tokyo Newsletter*, May 1976, p. 6.

5. For a brief outline of the evolution of Jardine Matheson, see Jardine, Matheson & Co., *Jardine, Matheson, & Co.: An Historical Sketch*, Hong Kong, n.d.

6. A historical sketch of East Asiatic appeared in the *Reader's Digest*, Hong Kong edition, February 1979.

7. For a detailed discussion of the evolution and present activities of the construction division of sogo shosha, see *Boeki no Nihon: Tokushu—Ote Shosha Kensetsu Bumon*, December 1976.

8. Marubeni, *Kankei Kaisha Yoran 1975* (unpublished), July 1975; and *Kaigai Jigyo Yoran 1976* (unpublished), June 1976.

9. Mainichi Shinbun-sha (ed.), *Nippon no Shosha—Mitsubishi Shoji*, Mainichi Shinbun-sha, 1973, p. 120.

3

Historical Evolution: The
Pre-war Period

1. MITSUI BUSSAN

THE BIRTH OF THE COMPANY

IN 1874, the House of Mitsui, known for over a century as an influential apparel dealer and banker, decided to expand its horizons and establish a general wholesaling company.[1] This company, which it called Kokusan Kata (National Products Co.), operated from its headquarters in Tokyo and Yokohama. The Tokyo office handled raw silk, rice, and rail cargo on the newly established line between Yokohama and Tokyo. The Yokohama office handled the tea and raw silk traded to foreign merchant houses located there. Parallel to this was the creation of the Mitsui Clothing Store (the present-day Mitsukoshi Department Store) to handle its apparel business. With the establishment of these two companies, the main branch of the Mitsui House was able to devote its energies exclusively to banking.

In the early 1870s, the general wholesaling business offered opportunities for large profits, particularly in rice trading and in exports. The rice trading business had entered a new phase in 1873 due to a new land tax which required peasants to pay their taxes in cash. But for this to work, the rice had first to be sold in central markets. Mitsui, which served as exchequer to the new government, had interest-free government deposits in twenty-seven locations around the country which it was able to put to use in the rice trade.[2] As a result, local purchasing offices were set up by this new Mitsui trading branch, Kokusan Kata.

Foreign trade must also have looked promising to Mitsui. Soon after trade with the West had started, at the end of the Tokugawa period, Mitsui set up a store in Yokohama to sell silk and tea to foreign merchants. This business was taken over by the Yokohama office of Kokusan Kata which, in addition, handled rice exports. Rice exports were entered into partly to conform with the government export promotion policy (to reduce trade deficits and stop specie outflow), but more importantly because they were necessary for Mitsui's overall rice dealings.

Kokusan Kata was a successful operation, earning, for example, profits of ¥7,855 in the second half of 1875.[3] Nevertheless, Mitsui, in 1876, acquired another trading company called Senshu Kaisha, and merged it with Kokusan Kata to establish a new company, Mitsui Bussan. This decision was based partly on political considerations. Okuma Shigenobu, Minister of Finance at that time, urged Mitsui to get into direct trade, since he felt that foreign trading companies would not meet the government's goals for export promotion. Government assistance and protection was offered to willing merchants.[4] Though direct foreign trade was enticing to Mitsui, Kokusan Kata did not have the qualified personnel to undertake it, so Minomura Rizaemon, general manager of Mitsui at this time, consulted on this matter with Mitsui's political patron, Inoue Kaoru, who happened also to be the owner of Senshu Kaisha.[5] Inoue set up this company in 1873 when he resigned from the Ministry of Finance in protest over what he regarded as an unfair budget allocation, and since then, had left its management to Masuda Takashi, one of his most competent subordinates and one of the few Japanese of his time who had had dealings with foreigners.

With the establishment of Mitsui Bussan, Mitsui committed itself to foreign trade, but only to a limited extent in the beginning. Since there was a great deal of uncertainty, Mitsui had to take precautions to prevent the potential failure of Mitsui Bussan from affecting the main line of its activities, banking. Thus, initially, a ¥50,000 line of credit from the Mitsui Bank and the small assets held by two sons (not the first) of the Mitsui family who lent their names to Mitsui Bussan were the extent of the wealth the Mitsui family pledged. Of course, Mitsui was willing to increase the investment as things turned successfully, for foreign trade appeared to offer opportunities to diversify and hedge the risk of putting all of its capital in banking.[6]

THE GROWTH OF THE COMPANY

The growth of Mitsui Bussan in subsequent years is well reflected in the increase of its capital. In 1876 when the company was born, the amount of capital was ¥50,000, which increased to 1 million yen in 1893, 20 million yen in 1909, 100 million yen in 1918, and 150 million yen in 1936.[7] This dramatic increase in capital was not from the infusion of capital by the Mitsui family or the public, but from the accumulation of profits. Business seemed off to a good start when, during the 1877 Satsuma Rebellion, Mitsui Bussan earned large profits as the official purveyor to the Army. Despite such an auspicious beginning, however, Mitsui Bussan's business stagnated in the following years, and it even made a loss in 1881. The Matsukata deflation (in the first half of the 1880s) can be blamed in part, but a more fundamental cause was at work. During this early period, the Japanese economy as a whole was going through a massive transition, and industrialization did not really begin until the second half of the 1880s.

In subsequent years Mitsui Bussan made enormous profits. It acted as an agent for Japanese producers who wanted raw materials (such as cotton) and machinery (for example, spinning machines), and for many of those who wanted to sell their products abroad, it served as a pioneer in exports. By paying careful attention to the fluctuations in demand

and productivity both in Japan and abroad, Mitsui Bussan promptly made all the necessary adjustments. This accounts for the large profits it made after the Japanese economy took-off.

Mitsui Bussan's profits during the First World War were phenomenal. In 1917, for example, when the amount of capital was 20 million yen, it earned 32 million yen. During the boom years of 1915–19, altogether it earned over 100 million yen. Such large profits enabled Mitsui Bussan to increase its capital from 20 million yen to 100 million yen in 1918.

Mitsui Bussan was not the only one to earn large profits during the boom years. Practically all trading companies enjoyed this prosperity and were able to enlarge. What is unique about Mitsui Bussan, however, is that it continued to earn substantial profits even in the 1920s when other trading companies were either severely crippled or going bankrupt. While the crash in the spring of 1920 caused large losses to many other trading companies, Mitsui Bussan was not severely affected, and though there was a slight drop in profits in 1921, its profits increased again in the following years. In fact, there were no years when losses were recorded. Its success in avoiding a crisis in the 1920s can be attributed to the precautionary measures it took in anticipating the possible economic reversal which follows a boom—experience it had gained in its forty-year history.

The growth of Mitsui Bussan is also reflected in the spread of its overseas offices. The first overseas office was set up in Shanghai in 1877, and as of September 1939, there were ninety-one offices spanning the globe (see Table 3.1 for their regional distribution).

The Shanghai office was set up mainly for the purpose of selling coal. As will be explained later in more detail, Mitsui Bussan was the exclusive agent for the Miike coal mine in Kyushu, and actively marketed its coal abroad as bunker fuel. The establishment of the offices in Hong Kong in 1886, Tientsin in 1888, and Singapore in 1891 were largely for the same purpose. Before the Sino–Japanese War (August 1894 to April

TABLE 3.1
Mitsui Bussan: Offices Abroad (As of September 1939)

	1876–1894.8	1895.4–1904.2	1905.9–1913	1914–1939.9	Total
Taiwan		2	2	1	5
Korea		2	1	10	13
Manchuria		2	3	7	12
China	3	5	1	8	17
South-East Asia	1	2	3	9	15
South Asia	1		1	2	4
The Middle East				4	4
Africa				3	3
Europe	1	1	1	4	7
U.S.A.		2		2	4
Latin America				4	4
Oceania		1		2	3
Total	6	17	12	56	91

Source: Mitsui Bussan, *Mitsui Bussan Shoshi*, 1951, pp. 175–7; and Matsumoto Hiroshi, 'Nihon Shihon Shugi Kakuritsu-ki ni okeru Mitsui Bussan Kaisha no Hatten', *Mitsui Bunko Ronso*, 1973, pp. 119–23.

1895), Mitsui Bussan also set up offices in Bombay and London: the Bombay office to import raw cotton from India, and the London office to purchase machinery and arms which could not be produced in Japan.

In the period between the Sino–Japanese War and the Russo–Japanese War (February 1904 to September 1905), seventeen offices were set up abroad.[8] Two were in Taiwan, 2 in Korea, 2 in Manchuria, 5 in China, 2 in South-East Asia, 1 in Europe, 2 in the United States and 1 in Oceania. In this period, Mitsui Bussan began to get extensively involved in East Asia, backed up by Japanese military power. As soon as Taiwan became Japan's colony, Mitsui Bussan started investing there in cooperation with the Japanese government which wanted to develop Taiwan's economy. It also became interested in Manchuria, and expanded its network there, with Ying-kow as the base. In China proper, Mitsui Bussan took advantage of greater freedom made possible by Japan's victory in the Sino–Japanese War, and set up offices not only along the coast but also inland, at Hankow.

In general, once an office is set up for handling a particular product (say, coal), it can start dealing in other products. The Shanghai office, set up for coal, began around 1886 to buy large quantities of raw cotton for Japanese spinners. The Surabaya office was set up in 1901, to buy Indonesian sugar needed for the Singapore office which was looking for a suitable return cargo for its coal ships from Kyushu. The New York office was set up in 1896 primarily for the export of silk from Japan, but a few years later, started handling the purchase of raw cotton for Japanese spinners.

In the period from the Russo–Japanese War to the First World War, about twenty offices were set up, bringing the total, by the First World War, to forty. Nevertheless, Mitsui Bussan's offices were still concentrated mainly in Asia. By that time, the company had developed a fairly extensive sales network in Asia, especially in East Asia. Offices outside Asia handled exports from Japan to some extent (especially, the New York office which handled silk exports), but their more important function was purchasing. The London office was a typical example.

The expansion of Mitsui Bussan's offices outside Asia took place largely after the First World War. As shown in Table 3.1, nineteen of the twenty-five offices outside Asia were set up in this period. It was also in this period that offices were set up for the first time in the Middle East, Africa, and Latin America. This regional spread was largely a reflection of the growth of the Japanese economy which required the presence of Mitsui Bussan's offices at new regions where both the demand for Japanese goods existed and raw materials were available. At the same time, however, it is important to note that anti-Japanese feelings played some role in forcing Mitsui Bussan to penetrate new regions. This was especially true for the 1930s when such feelings became strong in Asia and the West.[9]

MAJOR COMMODITIES

Since its founding, Mitsui Bussan was a general trader. The number of goods it could handle was limited, particularly in the beginning when its capital was small, and it could not handle as many goods as it wished, but the policy was to be open to any commodity which looked promising. It seems to have wished to become a 'wholesale department store'. As the amount of capital increased in subsequent years, the number of goods it handled increased, and by the end of the pre-war period, it had certainly fulfilled its ambition. In fact, the goods it handled had by then become so diverse that it is difficult to think of a commodity it did not handle.

This diversity does not imply that capital and human resources were spread equally over the goods handled. Mitsui Bussan had always key commodities to which it allocated the bulk of its capital and manpower, and which earned most of the profits. In the beginning, rice was the most important.[10] Rice was replaced by raw cotton in the mid-1890s and, except for several years in the next few decades, raw cotton maintained the top position. In the early 1900s, coal temporarily surpassed raw cotton, but in subsequent years, raw cotton regained the leading position.[11] In the early 1920s, when raw cotton together with cotton products (especially fabric whose sales at the time had been rapidly increasing and closely following those of raw cotton) were separated out from Mitsui Bussan and handed over to its subsidiary, Toyo Menka, silk became the number one product.[12]

Rice, which was the corner-stone of the Tokugawa economy, became merely an important commodity in the Meiji era. At times, when the price of rice became too low because of an abundant crop, or too high because of poor harvest, Mitsui Bussan exported or imported rice. Nevertheless, the larger part of rice transactions was domestic. Since it was the most important food in the Japanese diet, the absolute amount of rice sales remained substantial for Mitsui Bussan throughout the period before the First World War. As late as 1919, rice was the fourth most important commodity, accounting for 7.4 per cent of total sales.[13]

Coal, though not the most important commodity in terms of sales in Mitsui's first fifteen years, was the basis for Mitsui Bussan's later expansion to Asia. The Meiji government, which acquired the Miike mine in Kyushu (which turned out to be one of the richest coal mines in Japan), wanted to sell coal abroad in order to reduce trade deficits. Mitsui Bussan was appointed as the exclusive sales agent for the Miike mine, and in 1877, Mitsui Bussan set up the office in Shanghai to sell Miike coal as bunker fuel to merchant vessels. In the following ten-year period, Mitsui Bussan succeeded in selling coal not only in Shanghai but also in Hong Kong, Singapore, Swatow, Cheefoo and Foochow.[14] In 1878, the Hong Kong office (set up at first for money exchange but closed a few years later for lack of business) was re-opened for selling coal.

In 1888, the Mitsui House bought the Miike mine from the government, an investment valuable not only in the short-run coal trading, but as the basis for Mitsui's subsequent diversification into industry. Coal was the energy base for Japan's rapid industrialization which started in the middle of the Meiji era, so its domestic demand sharply increased. Furthermore, in China, where industrialization was just beginning, an increasing amount of coal was sold to factories and railroads. As early as 1887, these concerns were already more important buyers than shipping companies.[15] The Miike mine alone could not meet these demands (though its production increased under Mitsui's management), so Mitsui Bussan became an agent for independent coal mines and started handling their coal in the 1890s.

Masuda Takashi, who headed Mitsui Bussan in its formative years, stated that although profits from coal were small, it was important because it laid the foundation for overseas expansion.[16] There is no record of profits before 1900, so there is no way to verify his statement, but it is likely that in the early years costs involved were quite substantial, and not much profit was made. To oust the coal that British trading companies (such as Jardine Matheson) had been shipping from Australia and Wales, a considerable amount of promotion and sales costs were likely to have been incurred. But, by 1900 at the latest, coal seems, finally, to have become a profitable business. From 1900 to the first half of 1903, coal earned on the average ¥340,000 per half year.[17]

The cotton industry was another important business focus. This industry was the vanguard of industrialization in Japan, becoming a leading sector of the economy in the pre-war period. Mitsui Bussan imported textile machinery (primarily spindles) and raw cotton, and later exported cotton yarn and fabric. As the Japanese machinery industry developed and textile machinery began to be produced in Japan, the import of textile machinery declined in importance, but the import of raw cotton and the export of cotton products increased and became so important a part of Mitsui Bussan's overall activities that, as mentioned above, they were separated out in 1920 and handed over to Toyo Menka, a subsidiary created for this purpose. After that (because the financial statement was not consolidated) raw cotton and cotton products virtually disappeared from Mitsui Bussan's list of major commodities.

Mitsui Bussan's first business in the cotton industry was the import of spindles from a British company called Platt Brothers & Co. In 1883, a large spinning company (Osaka Boseki) was established, and Mitsui Bussan purchased Platt Brothers' spindles for this company through its office in London.[18] In 1886, it became the exclusive agent for Platt Brothers in Japan. How important this business was cannot be ascertained since there is no record, but it must have been substantial, especially from the late 1880s when spinning companies mushroomed in Japan. By 1895, the number of spindles had surpassed 500,000 and by 1898, one million. A significant number of the spindles imported were Platt Brothers' products handled quite profitably by Mitsui Bussan.

Mitsui Bussan became interested in importing raw cotton from China soon after it set up the Shanghai office in 1877. In the next ten years, however, the cotton sent to Japan by the Shanghai office was largely for distribution to spinning companies as samples, and thus sales remained at an insignificant level. The first large order came from Osaka Boseki (Osaka Spinning) in 1886 when it decided to import Chinese cotton to make up for the deficiency in domestic production.[19] Within a couple of years, Mitsui's business with Osaka Boseki was virtually terminated since another trading company (Naigai Wata) was formed to handle the import of raw cotton. Nevertheless, the increase of spinning mills in this period boosted Mitsui Bussan's import of cotton. In 1892, Mitsui Bussan became a purchasing agent in India for three large spinning mills to import raw Indian cotton, and established its Bombay office in 1893 for this purpose.[20] With this, India became a more important supply source: in 1893, Mitsui Bussan imported ¥660,000 worth of raw cotton from India, ¥273,000 from China, and ¥142,000 from the United States.

As Japanese spinning mills began to produce high quality yarn, long fibre cotton became necessary, and American cotton, which could meet this requirement best, increased in importance in the following years.[21] The New York office, set up to handle silk exports from Japan, began also to act as a purchasing agent for Japanese spinners. In the second half of the 1890s, the import of cotton from the United States increased rapidly, and by 1898, it had become comparable to that from India.[22]

A further boost to Mitsui Bussan's handling of raw cotton was brought about by a contract signed with Kanegafuchi Boseki in 1901.[23] This spinning company agreed to purchase at least 70 per cent of the raw cotton it would require from Mitsui Bussan in return for Mitsui Bussan's extension of credit, quality inspection, and other services. Kanegafuchi was one of the major spinners (and the company rapidly increased in size in the subsequent years), and this contract greatly boosted the volume of cotton sales. Within a few years, cotton surpassed coal to become Mitsui Bussan's most important product, and remained so in most years after that until 1920 when it was taken over by Toyo Menka.

From 1897 when it accounted for about 30 per cent, there are data on Mitsui Bussan's share of cotton imports. Before this (especially after the Bombay office was set up in 1893), Mitsui Bussan's share may have been higher, since it pioneered cotton import from India. Unfortunately, however, there is no way to verify this. After 1897, Mitsui Bussan's share declined gradually, and by 1920, when Toyo Menka took over the cotton business, its share was down to about 20 per cent. In the next fifteen-year period, Toyo Menka maintained roughly this level.[24] The gradual decline before 1920 was possibly due to the increase of competition from Japanese trading companies which followed Mitsui Bussan's path to China, India, and the United States. Some of these (for example, Naigai Wata) had the strong backing of large spinners who would have liked to establish supremacy over the large trading companies like Mitsui Bussan.

For spinners to establish such supremacy was not simple, however, since they depended on trading companies to market their products overseas. By the mid-1890s, the prospect of yarn export had become promising enough that Mitsui Bussan decided to make it a strategic commodity and invest in its export promotion. As part of this, it invited influential merchants in Shanghai and Tientsin to Japan and let them observe the Japanese spinning industry.[25] It also made efforts to reduce distribution costs by dispensing with Chinese compradores; and from the mid-1890s to the early 1900s, expanded its sales network by establishing offices in new places in China and Korea.

These sales efforts proved to be successful. In 1894, cotton yarn was an insignificant commodity for Mitsui Bussan, with sales amounting to about ¥670,000 (about 2 per cent of total sales).[26] A few years later, in 1897, however, yarn exports jumped to about 4 million yen to become the third most important commodity.[27] Two years later (1899), yarn became the second most important commodity,[28] and from 1897 to 1914, cotton yarn appeared often in the list of Mitsui's five major commodities.[29] In the following years, cotton yarn was replaced by cotton fabric, and its exports declined, relatively at first and absolutely later on.

By 1897, the year when the time series records of sales by commodity begins, Mitsui Bussan had been exporting cotton fabric, but at this time, it was still an insignificant commodity.[30] It was only after the Russo–Japanese War that exports of cotton fabric began to increase at a rapid rate. In 1910, Mitsui Bussan's fabric exports reached the 10 million yen level for the first time, and the increasing trend continued throughout the First World War. In 1917, exports of cotton fabric amounted to 34 million yen, and it became the second most important commodity.[31] This position was maintained in the following years until Toyo Menka was set up.

Production of cotton fabric increased rapidly late in the first decade of this century, and part of this was exported abroad, especially to the Asian continent. The increase in Mitsui Bussan's fabric exports must be looked at within this overall change. One important development around this time was the technical improvement and cost reduction of power-looms produced in Japan. Another was the increase of electric power supply. These two developments made it possible to start weaving with a small amount of capital, as a consequence of which a number of weaving centres emerged. Up to this point, weaving was done either in households by hand-looms, or at factories by large spinners which had integrated operations.

Basically, the maturing of the cotton textile industry, especially its weaving sector, accounts for the rapid increase of fabric exports after the Russo–Japanese War. Nonetheless, some credit has to be given to Mitsui Bussan for its pioneering role in the early years. In 1907–10, it accounted for 40 to 50 per cent of Japan's fabric exports.[32] This dominant position was possible largely because it was an agent for the cartels formed for exports to Korea and especially to Manchuria. It organized the large Japanese spinners who were also engaged in weaving, and set up in 1906 an export cartel called Nippon Menpu Yushutsu Kumiai (Association of Cotton Fabric Exporters of Japan). Through its offices in Dairen, Yingkow, Harbin and Changchun, Mitsui Bussan dumped fabric into Manchuria. In 1905, a year before the cartel was formed, American cotton fabric dominated the Manchurian market, and Japanese exports amounted to only ¥390,000. Six years after the cartel, exports jumped to 33 million yen, and Japanese fabric dominated the market.[33] Soon after this, after the cartel accomplished its mission to oust American and other foreign fabric, it was disbanded. The cartel's dissolution did not, however, put an end to Mitsui Bussan's contribution to fabric exports, for it continued to play an organizing role. In particular, its organization of small manufacturers in different parts of Japan to help them export their products was an important contribution to fabric exports.

Silk was Japan's most important export from the beginning of the Meiji era until the early 1930s when it was overtaken by cotton fabric, but for Mitsui Bussan, it was not important for many years. As late as 1890, it was insignificant compared with rice, coal, raw cotton, and machinery, amounting to only a few per cent of total sales. By the mid-1890s, the situation had improved a little, but not much.[34] In subsequent years, however, its importance gradually increased. In 1903, it became the fifth most important commodity, accounting for 6.7 per cent of Mitsui Bussan's total sales. In 1914, it became the most important commodity, accounting for 15.5 per cent of total sales. Throughout most of the 1910s, raw cotton and coal occupied the top position, but in the 1920s when coal entered its declining phase and raw cotton was taken over by Toyo Menka, silk became the most important commodity.[35]

Mitsui Bussan started handling silk exports relatively early and set up its office in New York in 1879 for this purpose. It was evidently still difficult for Mitsui Bussan to make inroads into foreign control of silk exports, and the office was closed after three years. In the 1890s, it tried again, this time with success. The reason for the re-entry was the acquisition of filatures by the industrial department of the Mitsui zaibatsu. In 1893, a modern filature at Tomioka was purchased from the government, and another (at Oshima) was acquired by fore-closure. In the next year, the industrial department established two more filatures, one at Nagoya and the other at Mie.[36] It was around this time that Mitsui Bussan began emphasizing the silk business, apparently in order to market the products of these four factories. In 1896, the New York office was re-opened for this purpose. In the following years, by using loans as an inducement, Mitsui Bussan obtained its supply of silk both from independent filatures and wholesalers, and steadily increased silk exports. In 1907, surpassing Siber, Wolff & Co. (then the largest foreign silk dealer in Japan), Mitsui Bussan became the country's largest silk dealer.[37]

MITSUI ZAIBATSU

Since Mitsui Bussan did not receive the full support of the Mitsui family in the beginning and had to prove itself to be a worthy member of the zaibatsu,[38] one tends to get the impression that it grew up independently of other Mitsui companies. Certainly, Mitsui Bussan's growth was of its own making to a great extent, and this differentiates it from Mitsubishi Shoji, which grew up more or less as a purchasing and sales agent for Mitsubishi's industrial companies. Although Mitsui Bussan formed one of the three pillars of the Mitsui zaibatsu (the other two being the Mitsui Bank and Mitsui Mining; see Figure 3.1) and occupied a far more important position in its zaibatsu than Mitsubishi Shoji, one should not forget that Mitsui Bussan was also dependent in many ways for its growth on the other Mitsui companies.

Important help came from the Mitsui Bank. At the beginning of Mitsui Bussan's history, the only help it obtained was a ¥50,000 line of credit. In the 1890s, as the company earned profits and was brought as a full-fledged member into the Mitsui zaibatsu, the Mitsui Bank began to function as the main financier of its operations. This gave Mitsui Bussan a tremendous advantage since the Mitsui Bank, in 1903–15, was the largest in Japan in terms of deposits. In the 1920s and 1930s, the Yasuda and Mitsubishi Banks grew so rapidly that the Mitsui

FIGURE 3.1
The Mitsui Zaibatsu in the Early 1930s

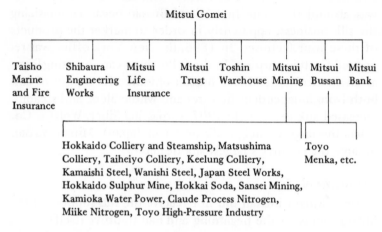

Source: Mitsui Gomei Kaisha, *The House of Mitsui*, 1933, various pages.

Bank declined in relative importance, but it remained as one of the top ranking banks throughout the pre-war period.[39]

Mitsui Bussan used the ample funds provided by the Mitsui Bank to increase its transactions. It gave loans and advances to producers as means of becoming their exclusive sales agent, or to help them step up production of the goods it had been marketing. To its customers, Mitsui Bussan offered credits making it easier for them to buy the goods it handled. This financial assistance would not have meant much if other traders had been able to obtain funds on an equal basis, but since the capital market was quite imperfect, there was a great deal of variation in the interest rate borrowers had to pay. Needless to say, Mitsui Bussan could borrow money at the prime rate from the Mitsui Bank.

The importance of Mitsui Mining to Mitsui Bussan is another factor in its growth that cannot be over-emphasized. When the government decided in 1888 to sell the Miike mine (which provided the basis for Mitsui Bussan's overseas operations), Mitsui Bussan was faced with the choice of either acquiring the mine, or withdrawing from China (Shanghai and Hong Kong). At this time, it was in no position to raise single-handedly the necessary capital to buy the mine, and without the assistance of the Mitsui Bank, could not have bought the mine.[40]

In the early 1890s, however, the Miike mine was separated from Mitsui Bussan, and its management was handed over to a newly set up company called Mitsui Mining Co. This company, with the help of the Mitsui Bank, invested a large sum of money in the machinery and equipment needed to modernize the mine, and succeeded in making it one of the most productive mines in Japan. Although the company later acquired other mines and produced copper, lead, silver, gold and several other metals, coal remained its major product, and it continued to be marketed by Mitsui Bussan.

By the mid-1930s, the Mitsui zaibatsu had numerous companies spread over various industries. Besides mining, banking and wholesaling, they covered such industries as public utilities, life insurance, shipping, warehousing, agriculture, and manufacturing. These companies all helped Mitsui Bussan's growth since it functioned as their sales agent.

The Mitsui zaibatsu's manufacturing investment began in the 1890s under the direction of Nakamigawa Hikojiro. During his relatively brief control (about ten years), he bought one filature, re-possessed another, and established two new ones. He also acquired Kanegafuchi Boseki, Oji Paper Co., and the Shibaura Engineering Works. The filatures provided a large part of the silk Mitsui Bussan marketed in the United States in that decade. As noted above, Kanegafuchi Spinning concluded an agreement with Mitsui Bussan in 1901 to buy from them at least 70 per cent of the raw cotton it would use, and contributed to the increase of Mitsui Bussan's cotton sales. In a way, the relationship with Kanegafuchi Spinning corresponded to that with Mitsui Mining in coal.

After Nakamigawa, Masuda Takashi took over the overall management of the Mitsui zaibatsu, and tried to divest Mitsui's manufacturing investments, but found them to be indispen-

sable for Mitsui's growth. In subsequent years, Mitsui bought
Toyo Koatsu Industries and also set up such companies as
Electro-Chemical Industrial and the Japan Steel Works. These
investments made it possible for Mitsui Bussan to diversify
into heavy industrial products which were gaining importance
in the 1920s and 1930s.

Although the growth of Mitsui Bussan depended on other
Mitsui companies, a great deal of credit has to be given to its
own initiative and strategy, especially considering that Mitsui's
industrial companies were not as strong as Mitsubishi's. Although the Mitsui zaibatsu came to possess various industrial
companies over time, its industrial sector remained weak compared with Mitsubishi's. Mitsui's strength lay rather in commerce and finance. Consequently, Mitsui Bussan played a more
important role in undertaking industrial ventures than expected of trading companies in other zaibatsu.

This fact is reflected in a large number of investments Mitsui
Bussan undertook. Some of the companies which it established
or took over through investment are listed in Table 3.2. Most
notable among them were Toyo Rayon and Onoda Cement
which were then Japan's representative manufacturing companies. Toyo Menka was the third largest trading company,
ranking immediately below Mitsubishi Shoji. By the late 1930s,
Tama Shipyard had been added to this list. In 1940, Mitsui Bussan held equity shares in 253 companies spreading

TABLE 3.2

Mitsui Bussan's Major Subsidiaries in the Early 1930s

Toyo Menka	Kyokuto Condensed Milk
Toyo Rayon	Santai Oil Mills
Taisho Marine and Fire Insurance	Sanki Kogyo (Engineering)
Taiwan Sugar Manufacturing	Toyo Carrier Engineering
Yuasa Storage Battery Manufacturing	Toyo Otis Elevator
Onoda Cement Manufacturing	Toyo (Babcock)
	Toyo Card Clothing

Source: Mitsui Gomei Kaisha, *The House of Mitsui*, 1933, pp. 40–2.

over 14 industries, and amounting to 275 million yen (about 90 per cent of its paid-up capital).[41] Thus, by this time, Mitsui Bussan had become a holding as well as trading company.

In the early years of Mitsui Bussan, however, Masuda Takashi set down a policy to avoid investment in industrial enterprises.[42] He evidently felt that the primary role of the company was to promote foreign trade, and that capital at hand should be used to establish its distribution network both within and without the country and to meet its need for working capital. In the face of mounting competition from other trading companies, however, the policy had to be changed. The change seems to have begun in the early 1920s and accelerated in the next decade.

It would have been ideal if industrial investments had not been necessary, since this tied down capital and reduced the flexibility of the trading company. In fact, such thinking was behind Masuda's doctrine of commercialism, but since other trading companies (such as Mitsubishi Shoji) started to threaten the position of Mitsui Bussan in various fields, the original policy had to change. In order to maintain its advantage over others, it became necessary to nurture industrial companies or to take over their management by acquiring stock shares and becoming their exclusive agent. For example, the establishment of Toyo Rayon (the present Toray), which became a major rayon manufacturer in the 1930s, was a result of this new investment policy.

In the 1930s, especially towards the end of the decade, Mitsui Bussan stepped up industrial investment. This was to cooperate with the government which was pushing heavy industrialization as part of military build-up. Since Mitsui Bussan was accused of being too commercially oriented and thus not meeting the national needs (one of which was heavy industry), it was under pressure to move into heavy industry. It was under such circumstances that Mitsui Bussan invested in companies producing construction machinery, machinery parts, arms, automobiles, and instruments. Furthermore, in

order to cooperate with the military, it stepped up investment
in Manchuria and South-East Asia.

Industrial investment under pressure from the military was
an aberration from its history as a trading company, but the
necessity for Mitsui Bussan to undertake such investment was
not. It is an inevitable outcome of competition among trading
companies, and all sogo shosha today have numerous industrial
companies as subsidiaries or affiliates. Yasukawa Yunosuke,
who managed Mitsui Bussan from the early 1920s to the early
1930s, noticed the change in the position the company occupied in the trading industry, and initiated a new policy to
get Mitsui Bussan more actively involved in the formation
and management of industrial companies. Though this may
have reduced the earning capacity of the company, it enabled
sales increase and maintenance of its leading position throughout the rest of the pre-war period.[43]

2. MITSUBISHI SHOJI[44]

Mitsubishi Shoji was established in 1918 by its holding company, Mitsubishi Goshi Kaisha (Mitsubishi & Co.). From the
very beginning of its corporate life, it was already a fairly large
company with 15 million yen in capital, 900 employees, 18
branch and representative offices in Japan, branches in Hankow, Shanghai and Hong Kong, and representative offices in
Dairen, Taipei, Canton, Haiphong, Peking, Tientsin, Tsinan,
Vladivostok, and Singapore. Within the company, there were
divisions of coal, metals, shipping and miscellaneous goods, in
addition to one for general affairs.

The year 1918 cannot be taken, however, as the beginning
of Mitsubishi's trading activities. Exactly when trading began
is more difficult to determine than in the case of Mitsui, which
set up Mitsui Bussan relatively early as a separate entity. The
actual origins of Mitsubishi Shoji go back to the period when
it was a trading department within the parent company, and
in order to understand the context in which trading activities
began, one must look first at the founding period of the Mit-

subishi zaibatsu and the establishment of the trading department.

THE MITSUBISHI ZAIBATSU IN THE EARLY YEARS

The year 1870 is regarded as the beginning of Mitsubishi.[45] In this year, its founder, Iwasaki Yataro established a shipping company (called Tsukumo Shokai) in Osaka, with the help of the Tosa provincial government. At this point, the company was semi-public, and Yataro was, technically speaking, an employee of the Tosa provincial government. But the abolition of fiefs, the establishment of prefectures, and other political and social changes in the subsequent few years made the Tosa government withdraw from the company, and Yataro took over the company in a private capacity. In 1873, he renamed the company Mitsubishi Shokai (Mitsubishi Trading Co.), and adopted the famous 'three diamond' symbol as the trade mark of Mitsubishi.

Through good service to customers, ingenuity, and political manoeuvring, Yataro made his shipping business immensely prosperous in the following several years. Through his connections with Meiji leaders such as Okubo Toshimichi and Okuma Shigenobu, he was able to obtain financial help and protection from the government. Furthermore, he was able to become the major shipping agent for the government at the time of the Taiwan expedition (1874) and the Satsuma Rebellion (1877), and made large profits. This enabled Mitsubishi not only to become the largest shipping company in Japan, but also to drive out from the country foreign shipping companies. Pacific Mail and P & O had made substantial gains (taking advantage of Japanese inexperience in shipping caused by the Tokugawa seclusion policy), but, from the mid-1870s to the early 1880s, Mitsubishi was so successful that hardly any competitors were left.

In the early 1880s, the situation began to change rapidly. The pro-Mitsubishi government fell, and Mitsui and others indignant at Mitsubishi's domination of the shipping business, succeeded in persuading the new government to establish a

new shipping company as a counterbalance. Mitsubishi fought
back, and the two companies became entangled in a life or
death struggle for a few years. Finally, because competition
was threatening the infant shipping industry, the government
decided to merge the two and establish a new company called
Nippon Yusen Kaisha (N.Y.K.) as a 'national policy' company.

This merger of 1885 was an important turning point for
Mitsubishi, for now that it lost its monopoly over the shipping
business, it had to find a way out into other fields. Fortunately,
in the preceding fifteen-year period, Mitsubishi had been engaged in various peripheral businesses relating to shipping
(banking, marine insurance, warehousing, shipbuilding and repairing), and also bought mines with the money made in shipping. These businesses were brought together under the aegis
of a new company called Mitsubishi-sha (Mitsubishi & Co.)
established in 1886.[46] At this point, Mitsubishi began to assume a new shape: from a one-industry company, Mitsubishi
had become a conglomerate.[47]

Most of Mitsubishi's businesses from 1885 to the late 1910s
were not given separate corporate entities, but merely constituted departments of the parent company (see Figure 3.2).
Although the number of departments varied somewhat, in the
early 1910s there were shipbuilding, banking, trading and real
estate departments.[48] Among these departments, mining was
most important in terms of both assets and profits. From 1894
to 1899, it accounted for about 45 per cent of Mitsubishi's
total assets and 60 per cent of its total profits.[49] In the period
1905–8, it accounted for about 75 per cent of Mitsubishi's
total profits.[50]

Trading activities began as an appendage to mining. During
Yataro's reign (1870–85), two important mines were bought:
the Takashima coal mine in Nagasaki, and the Yoshioka copper
mine in Okayama. During the period 1885–93 when Yanosuke
(Yataro's younger brother) was president, over a dozen coal
and other mines were added. Among them, coal mines at the
Chikuho coalfield in Fukuoka (northern Kyushu) were a par-

FIGURE 3.2

Organizational Changes in the Mitsubishi Zaibatsu in the Late 1910s

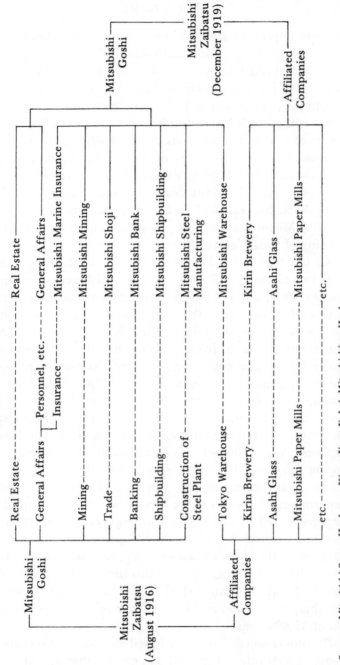

Source: Mitsubishi Sogyo Hyakunen Kinen Jigyo Iinkai, *Mitsubishi no Hyakunen*,
1970, p. 94; and Iwasaki Koyata Den Hensan Iinkai, *Iwasaki Koyata Den*,
1957, pp. 23—7.

ticularly important addition. In the next period, 1893–1916, when Kyuya (Yataro's son and Yanosuke's nephew) was president, Mitsubishi bought the Sado gold mine and the Ikuno silver mine from the government and also took over private coal mining companies in Hokkaido. With these acquisitions, in the early 1900s Mitsubishi became one of the largest producers of coal and non-ferrous metals. Trading activities began in order to market products of the mining department, particularly coal. It was primarily in connection with selling coal as bunker fuel that Mitsubishi established offices in Hong Kong, Shanghai and Hankow in 1906, and Singapore in 1917. As with Mitsui Bussan, coal played an important role in the opening of offices abroad.

At the time when Mitsubishi Shoji was established, there were two divisions which were not related directly to mining— one was shipping. For smooth operation of trading activities, it was often necessary that the company has its own ships. At the time when the shipping line, N.Y.K., was established, Mitsubishi withdrew from shipping, but it went back again under the trading department to meet its own shipping requirements (not as a common carrier). In 1900, Mitsubishi obtained a contract from newly-created Yahata Steel to bring back iron ore from Ta-yeh in China. With this as leverage, Mitsubishi started building up a shipping fleet. The Russo–Japanese War (1904–5) gave this additional impetus, and during this time Mitsubishi bought three ships made abroad. In 1912, a shipping section was created within the trading department. Soon after, the First World War brought about unprecedented profits to the shipping section, and though it was not possible to order many ships because of the large backlog in the shipbuilding industry, the company managed to purchase several new ships at this time. In 1918, when Mitsubishi Shoji was established, the shipping section became the shipping division and it took over fifteen ships, totalling about 37,000 tons.

The other main division established was that of miscellaneous goods—goods other than coal and metals (that is, non-mining goods). For the first several years after the trading department was set up, these goods were insignificant, and it was not until after the Russo–Japanese War that they became of significance. The trading department exported products of the Mitsubishi Paper Mills, Asahi Glass, and the Kirin Brewery—companies which were set up either by the Iwasaki family or with its help. It also marketed pitch, coal tar, and other coal derivatives which were produced as by-products at the coke manufacturing plant in northern Kyushu. In 1910, the Shanghai office began dealing in raw cotton and cotton yarn.[51] The handling of miscellaneous goods further increased during the First World War which cut the supply route from Europe and helped Japan become the major supply centre for Asia. In the report Mitsubishi submitted to the Ministry of Agriculture and Commerce in 1916, it is stated that chalcanthite was exported to Australia, India and Europe; sheet glass to Vladivostok, China, England and Indo-China; paper products to China; tung oil to the United Kingdom, the United States, and Australia; and grain from China to Europe and the United States. In 1917, the trading department set up the section of miscellaneous goods. The Kobe office took charge of the section, and promoted exports of miscellaneous goods to Manchuria, China and South-East Asia. It is also reported that numerous miscellaneous goods (agricultural products, oils and fats, fertilizer, fishery products, textiles, construction materials, chemicals, etc.) were handled around 1918.

DEVELOPMENT UNDER KOYATA

As shown in Figure 3.2, the establishment of Mitsubishi Shoji in 1918 was part of the overall organizational restructuring. About a year after Iwasaki Koyata (son of the second president, Yanosuke) became the fourth president of Mitsubishi, he made the shipbuilding department independent and established Mitsubishi Shipbuilding as a limited company. At the same time, he set up the Mitsubishi Steel Manufacturing Co. for the plant Mitsubishi had been constructing in Korea. In the following year, the mining department became Mitsubishi

Mining, the trading department became Mitsubishi Shoji, and
Tokyo Warehouse Ltd. (which was under the parent company
as a separate entity) was re-named Mitsubishi Warehouse. In
1919, the insurance section of the general affairs department
became Mitsubishi Marine Insurance, and the banking department, the Mitsubishi Bank. These seven companies were made
branch companies (*bunkei kaisha*) of the parent company
which, now without any operating divisions left, became a
holding company. In 1918, its capital was doubled to 30 million yen.[52]

There were at least three important developments under
the presidency of Koyata. The major development was the
building up of heavy industry for which Mitsubishi later became famous (particularly aircraft). When Koyata became
president, shipbuilding was the only activity of Mitsubishi
which could be regarded as heavy industry. Although by the
mid-1910s Mitsubishi had three modern shipyards (Nagasaki,
Kobe and Shimonoseki) and were building 10,000-ton ships,
progress in the subsequent period is even more remarkable.
The level of technology rose (for example, Mitsubishi could
manufacture diesel engines on its own), and there was a large
increase in the tonnage of ships built. By the late 1930s, it
was ready to build a 72,000-ton battleship, the Musashi. In a
twenty- to twenty-five-year period, Mitsubishi caught up with
the level of shipbuilding in the West and was able to produce
submarines, carriers and battleships which were fully comparable to what the Allies had during the Pacific War.

In addition, Koyata set up Mitsubishi Electric, which became an important producer of heavy electric machinery, and
Mitsubishi Internal Combustion Engine Manufacturing, which
became Mitsubishi Aircraft in 1928. This company merged
with Mitsubishi Shipbuilding in 1934, to become Mitsubishi
Heavy Industries. It was from around the mid-1930s that Mitsubishi's aircrafts began to be known internationally. In 1935,
carrier fighters (type 96) and bombers (type 96) were produced,
and in 1939, Zero fighters.[53]

Mitsubishi had also a steel manufacturing plant in Korea,

but this company merged with Yahata Steel and some other private steel manufacturing companies to become Nippon Seitetsu (Japan Steel Manufacturing) in 1934. Thus, after 1934, steel production ceased to be part of Mitsubishi's manufacturing activities. The only company in the steel industry which remained under Mitsubishi after 1934 was a company called Tokyo Steel Materials which processed steel into various steel products. In aluminium, Mitsubishi participated in the establishment of Nippon Aluminium Co. in 1935, and a few years later, brought it under its control.

Mitsubishi's entry into the chemical industry was relatively late, but it was built up at a rapid rate in the 1930s. Until then, Asahi Glass, which was producing soda ashes (a raw material for glass production) was the only company in that industry. In 1931, Mitsubishi set up Mitsubishi Oil with an American company (Associate Oil Co.), and went into petroleum refining. In 1934, it set up Nippon Tar Industry (a few years later renamed Mitsubishi Chemical), and began to produce various coal derivatives (cokes, dye, and ammonium sulphate being three major products). Furthermore, Asahi Glass started manufacturing caustic soda in the early 1930s. Mitsubishi also participated in the management of a rayon manufacturing company.[54]

Another development was the expansion of banking activity. Mitsubishi's banking started relatively early, but still, in 1916 when Koyata took over the parent company, its banking department functioned primarily as a bank for the other departments in Mitsubishi, and had only four branches throughout Japan.[55] Yataro wanted to make Mitsubishi's banks public institutions, and started emphasizing open banking. In the 1920s and 1930s, the Mitsubishi Bank grew rapidly (partly by merging with smaller banks) and became one of the most dynamic banks in Japan. By 1934, it had about 170 branches, and employed about 6,900 people.

THE GROWTH OF MITSUBISHI SHOJI

The third major development under Koyata was entry into

general trading. During the First World War, there was a large increase in foreign trade. The increase of exports in particular brought about unprecedented prosperity and a new international outlook in business. It was under this general economic setting that Yataro decided to make foreign trade a main pillar of Mitsubishi Shoji's business. He felt that since the size of the domestic market was limited, a large company like Mitsubishi Shoji must look outside for expansion.[56] For this, it was necessary to increase the transactions of non-mining products (that is, miscellaneous goods) since these goods had been growing most rapidly.

It was neither wise nor practical to deal in every commodity, so a strategy for diversification had to be laid down. What Mitsubishi Shoji decided was to deal in major exports and imports and to confine itself to large transactions only. That is, the handling of miscellaneous goods meant not to handle many minor products for the sake of diversity (a certain branch was handling shoe strings and umbrella frames), but to select several strategic products whose transactions were large. In order to make inroads into such goods, close relations (such as exclusive agency agreements) had first to be established with manufacturers, and Mitsubishi Shoji was willing to give financial assistance to aid establishment of such relations.

Its major area of trading was, of course, foreign trade. This is reflected in the fact that it was one of the three programmes (public service, fair play and promotion of foreign trade) first enunciated by Yataro in the meeting of branch managers in 1920 and which wero adopted in 1934 as official policy.[57] This does not mean, however, that Mitsubishi Shoji did not engage in domestic trade. In fact, at the time when the strategy for diversification was laid down, it was decided that the company would handle domestic transactions which were either related to foreign transactions or were too large for average companies to handle.

In general, diversification was successful, though problems were encountered in the beginning. Of the miscellaneous goods handled previously, machinery, oils and fats, wood, and raw cotton were made into four new divisions in early 1920. In the following four years, however, the last two divisions suffered large losses and were abolished. Furthermore, the division of coal was abolished in 1924, and the exclusive agency right of mining products was returned to the ailing Mitsubishi Mining Co.

It was from the mid-1920s that diversification began to go fairly smoothly, and three new divisions were created: the division of fuel (which took over the export business of the coal division but directed its major efforts to petroleum), the division of grain and fertilizer (which took over the main business of the division of oils and fats), and the new division of food. In 1930, the food division was divided into agricultural and fishery products divisions, and the grain and fertilizer division became the fertilizer division (grain was handed to the agricultural division). Thus, in 1930, there were six commodity divisions (metals, machinery, fuel, agricultural, fishery products, and fertilizer) in addition to the division of miscellaneous goods which remained, as always, the division for goods not handled by the independent commodity divisions. In 1936, a division for silk was created, and in 1939, one for cotton textiles. Thus, around 1940, there were eight commodity divisions (not counting the division of miscellaneous goods).

Progress in diversification is reflected in the increase of sales. In 1920, the first year for which sales data are available, the amount of sales was below 100 million yen. In the following years, there were ups and downs, but the overall trend was up. In particular, the increase from the early 1930s was spectacular. In 1932, sales exceeded 400 million yen, but in 1940 they had leaped to 2,200 million yen. Because of such rapid increase, the gap between Mitsubishi Shoji and Mitsui Bussan was considerably narrowed. Mitsui Bussan's sales still exceeded Mitsubishi Shoji's by two to three times in the early 1930s, but in 1939–40, the difference was half that.

By the time the Pacific War broke out, although it could not catch up with Mitsui Bussan, Mitsubishi Shoji had become a large trading company. In 1941, its capitalization amounted to 100 million yen, and it employed about 6,500 persons. As for the number of offices, in addition to those in Japan and its colonies (Taiwan and Korea), there were 27 offices in Asia, 5 in Europe, 8 in America, 2 in Australia, and 4 in Africa: altogether 46 outside of Japan.[58]

Mitsubishi Shoji's growth cannot be divorced from the overall growth of the Mitsubishi zaibatsu. Without the support from other Mitsubishi companies, it is inconceivable that it could have grown to become such a large general trading company within such a short period. For one thing, Mitsubishi Shoji was dependent on the Mitsubishi Bank for a large part of the capital it used to undertake direct investment or to supply credits to obtain agency rights and other concessions from manufacturers whose products it wanted to market.[59] The Mitsubishi Bank ceased to be a purely internal financial organization, but remained the major bank for Mitsubishi Shoji and other Mitsubishi companies. Furthermore, Mitsubishi Shoji could increase its transactions by using its political connections. For example, the agency rights of the mines operated by the South Manchurian Railroad, the financial privileges accorded by Japan's 'national policy' banks such as the Yokohama Specie Bank, appointment by the military as a major supply agent in China, cooperation with the military both within and without Japan, and its privileged position when mobilization measures began to be implemented in 1937—all these worked for the rise of Mitsubishi Shoji's position in the trading industry. Some of these connections were possibly made on its own, but since political activities were handled by the parent company, in many cases it used the political connections established by the parent company to enhance its business interests.

As pointed out in the preceding section, Mitsui Bussan also depended on the Mitsui zaibatsu, and thus, the feature is not unique to Mitsubishi Shoji, but there is a difference in degree. Mitsubishi Shoji's dependency was possibly much greater, since it grew, to a large extent, as a purchasing and marketing agent for other Mitsubishi companies whose production rapidly increased as heavy industrialization was pushed in the 1920s and 1930s.

As for marketing, Mitsubishi Mining, Mitsubishi Electric, Mitsubishi Shipbuilding (later Mitsubishi Heavy Industries), Mitsubishi Steel Manufacturing, Mitsubishi Paper Mills, and Asahi Glass gave Mitsubishi Shoji agency rights. In the case of Mitsubishi Mining, which began to face troubles in the early 1920s, the agency rights within Japan were handed back, but the rights for marketing abroad were retained. Also in the case of the Mitsubishi Paper Mills and Asahi Glass, the agency rights were restricted to foreign countries. In the case of Mitsubishi Steel Manufacturing, all sales to non-Mitsubishi companies were handled by Mitsubishi Shoji. Mitsubishi Shipbuilding, however, was not dependent on Mitsubishi Shoji except when it supplied pipes, boilers, and other products for instalment of generators produced by Mitsubishi Electric, in which event the order had to go through Mitsubishi Shoji. Mitsubishi Electric, which claimed an important position in the field of heavy electrical machinery (especially thermal power generators), gave exclusive agency rights to Mitsubishi Shoji from the very beginning. In fact, this rescued the division of machinery from collapse in the early 1920s—a fate two other divisions failed to avoid, as described earlier.

Mitsubishi companies were also important as the source of demand. Mitsubishi Shoji became the major purchasing agent for Mitsubishi Shipbuilding which needed a large quantity of steel as a raw material. In the 1920s, since Japan still depended on foreign countries for 25 to 50 per cent of its steel consumption, Mitsubishi Shoji's offices in the West, the London office in particular, played an important role in securing the supply of steel for Mitsubishi Shipbuilding. In addition, the fact that Mitsubishi Shoji was the major agent for such a large source of demand as Mitsubishi Shipbuilding was one of the factors which made it possible for it to become an authorized agent of Yahata Steel within the several years after its establishment. Furthermore, the fact that Mitsubishi Shoji was a member of the Mitsubishi zaibatsu worked in its favour when it negotiated with foreign companies for distribution rights in Japan. For example, when it negotiated with Aluminium Co. of America, the presence of Mitsubishi Shipbuilding and Mitsubishi Internal Combustion Engine Manufacturing within the zaibatsu (large buyers of aluminium) was of great help. Furthermore, in the case of machinery, Mitsubishi Shipbuilding and several other Mitsubishi companies, which depended often on import for the machinery used, helped Mitsubishi Shoji become a distributor for major machinery producers in the West (such as Krupp and Vickers) and increase the sales of machinery in Japan.

Without the backing of other Mitsubishi companies, Mitsubishi Shoji could not have grown to become such a large, diversified trading company in 1940 as to have sales of over 2 billion yen and capital of 100 million yen. At the same time, however, such growth would have been unlikely had it remained simply a purchasing and marketing agent of the Mitsubishi zaibatsu. Some credit has to be given to its dynamism as a trading company, though this was probably not as powerful a factor as in the case of Mitsui Bussan.

One example of the company's dynamism was the diversification into light industrial products (such as soybeans, fishery products, silk, raw cotton, and wool), goods which other Mitsubishi companies neither produced nor required as raw materials. Consider the case of silk. In line with the policy laid down by Yataro to handle major exports and imports, Mitsubishi Shoji started dealing in silk soon after establishment. It tied up with a large wholesaler (Ono Shoten), and started silk exports to the United States. The Japanese wholesaler took care of purchasing in Japan, and Mitsubishi Shoji of marketing in the United States through its New York office. This tie-up was not, however, successful, and Mitsubishi Shoji decided to go into the silk business by itself, taking over in 1924 a well-known silk trading firm which was facing financial trouble.[60] Through this company, Mitsubishi Shoji established a firm footing in the silk trade, and became one of the three largest silk traders in the 1930s. In 1936, it absorbed the company and established the silk division.

Another example of Mitsubishi Shoji's dynamism was its entry into petroleum in the early 1920s. Around this time, petroleum consumption began to increase in Japan, and for trading companies dealing in coal as the major fuel, this development could not be overlooked. Then, in 1924, when the exclusive agency rights for Mitsubishi Mining were lost, petroleum acquired additional importance. In this year, the coal division was abolished, and in its place, the fuel division was created. Mitsubishi Shoji's basic strategy in this new field was to tie up with a major oil company in the West and become its agent in Japan. Standard Oil and Shell had already started marketing on their own in Japan, so they had to be ruled out. Its choice became an American company named Associate Oil and it became, in 1924, the exclusive agent for this firm's crude oil and various petroleum products. In 1927, in order to broaden the range of petroleum products it handled (particularly high quality lubrication oil), Mitsubishi Shoji tied up also with Associated Oil's parent company, Tidewater Oil. Then, in 1931, in accordance with the government policy to promote petroleum refining in Japan, Mitsubishi Shoji established a joint venture with Associated Oil (Mitsubishi Oil), and became the exclusive agent of the new company. Even after this, it continued to import from Associated Oil petroleum products which could not be produced in Japan or were in short supply, as well as crude oil needed in Japanese refineries. Through the agency rights and joint venture, Mitsubishi Shoji became a major trader of petroleum, and at the same time, made the Mitsubishi zaibatsu aware of the importance of petroleum and petrochemicals.

Mitsubishi Shoji was a sogo shosha already before the Pacific War broke out. Its beginnings can be traced back to the late 1890s, but real growth began in the 1910s, and within a twenty- to twenty-five-year period, it grew into a large company. The growth was dependent on that of other Mitsubishi companies, for which it acted as a purchasing and marketing agent, but that was not the whole reason for its success. Mitsubishi Shoji utilized the financial resources of the Mitsubishi Bank and close ties with other Mitsubishi companies, to generate new trade. To do this, the company had to study new businesses, make plans, and implement them by investing resources and assuming risk. Thus, even in the case of Mitsubishi Shoji, which was fairly securely on the track of success from its beginning, there was an undeniable element of commercial dynamism.

3. C.ITOH AND MARUBENI[61]

ITOH CHUBEI

C.Itoh's history begins in 1858 when Itoh Chubei started a travelling wholesale business.[62] Chubei was born in 1842 at Toyosato in the province of Omi, which is the birthplace of the so-called Omi merchants who occupied an important position in Tokugawa commerce. They took textile and other local products to distant places and brought back goods from those places to Kyoto and Osaka. Many of those who made money in this trade bought stores in Kyoto, Osaka and the other major commercial cities, and became resident merchants there. After settling down, some amassed large fortunes in trading and financing, and became influential merchants. In general, Omi merchants were famous for their business acumen.

Chubei, however, was born into a family engaged in both agriculture and commerce. Since he was the second son, he was destined in any case to leave the family and become independent. At 16, he joined his uncle who had been engaged in the travelling wholesale business, and in the following fourteen-year period, by hard work and good business sense, made trade between northern Kyushu and his birthplace a profitable operation.

In 1872, he decided to give his market in northern Kyushu to his elder brother, and with the money he had saved, started a wholesale store in Osaka. At this time, it was one of many small-scale *gofukuya* (stores which dealt in kimono material) in the city. He had only two employees, and his assets amounted to no more than ¥20,000. However, by 1903, the year when he died, he had become a wealthy merchant with four stores employing around 100 people. His personal wealth is estimated to have amounted to over one million yen.

Chubei was an innovator. He started as a kimono cloth merchant, but unlike other such traders, he did not stick just to kimono cloth, but was willing to deal in any textile products for which demand was expected to rise.

The diversification into other textile products was made possible by his success in handling kimono cloth. Since this is a centuries-old commodity, it might be thought that he was just a traditional merchant, but the way in which he handled this traditional good, showed him to be an innovator. During his time, few Osaka merchants placed much importance on the Tokyo area as a source of supply. Consequently, the silk cloth of Tokyo which came to Osaka went through a number of intermediaries, and the distribution margin was high. Chubei decided to make it the major source of supply for his business, and sent purchasing agents there to stay on a long-term basis. This made it possible not only to reduce the distribution margin but also get to know who were good weavers and with whom to establish long-term contacts. The purchasing network was extended to other weaving areas as Chubei's business expanded.

Two important factors in becoming a successful merchant are knowing what the market demands and who can supply it as cheaply as possible. Chubei studied what patterns of silk cloth were popular and then experimented with a new supply source. For example, he took a certain established pattern of a famous weaving centre to relatively unknown weaving areas and succeeded in obtaining an 'imitation' at a much lower price.[63] The constant search for better and cheaper cloth was a contributing factor in his success.

In the ten-year period after Chubei's death, there were three important developments. One was the further strengthening of the position of the head store in the distribution of kimono cloth. The purchasing network extended from the Kanto district to Hokuriku and several other districts, and now covered most of the important weaving districts in Japan at the time. Furthermore, the store began to play a leadership role in distribution. It made a number of weavers its subcontractors by providing capital and necessary materials, and had them weave according to its specifications. In the case of weavers and weaving areas which had established names, it obtained agency rights for some of their products.

Another development of the head store was diversification into wide-width cloth. Originally, imported fabrics were of a wider width than the traditional cloth, but this wide-width cloth came also to be produced in Japan. In 1910, the store set up a department to handle Western cloth. It was heresy for a kimono dealer to handle such a product, but in order to nurture a new business, Chubei's firm could not afford to wait until others changed their way of business. This decision led to the handling of serge, cotton flannel and mousseline, and made it possible to capture part of a growing demand for wide-width cloth brought about by changes in life-style under Western influence. In 1915, when a branch store (West Store) was merged by the head store, its business of woollen cloth was taken over by the head store, and wide-width cloth (woollen cloth in particular) acquired further importance.

The third development was the beginning of an export business. The head store began engaging in export in the late 1890s, but for the next several years, it was confined to sales to foreign traders in Japan. In 1906, since manufacturers had begun dealing with them directly, the head store decided to set up an export department and deal directly with traders abroad. In line with this policy, it set up liaison offices in Seoul and Shanghai in 1907, and sent a representative to the Philippines in 1909. In 1910, the export department was made independent, and the Export Store established. The main export was cotton cloth, the production of which had been increasing rapidly thanks to the spread of power-looms.

REORGANIZATION

In the 1910s, Chubei's son, the second Chubei, introduced two major innovations. One was to modernize the organizational structure of the family business. Thus far, it had been a proprietorship, and since there was no superstructure covering different stores to which different family members were assigned, there was a tendency for the family wealth to disperse. In order to pool the family wealth as well as to coordinate the activities of different stores, he set up, in 1914, an unlimited partnership called C.Itoh & Co., capitalized at 2 million yen. In 1918, capital was raised to 20 million yen, and it had two operating subsidiaries, C.Itoh & Co., Ltd., and Itohchu Shoten, Ltd. (see Figure 3.3).

The second innovation was to split the business into foreign trade and domestic trade. In 1914, when the unlimited partnership was set up, the Yarn Store took charge of trade with the Asian continent, the Kobe Store handled trade with other regions, and all other stores specialized in domestic wholesale trade. During the First World War, there was a rapid increase in foreign trade, and the volume of C.Itoh's foreign trade became comparable to that of its domestic trade. Thus, in 1918, when C.Itoh & Co., Ltd. was established, foreign trade was made independent and became one of the two pillars of the family business. The other company, Itohchu Shoten, Ltd., took over the operation of the stores which had handled domestic wholesale.

In March 1920, a crash occurred in Japan. Prices, which had been rapidly increasing due to the war boom, suddenly collapsed, and this caused a severe blow to many companies, especially textile-related companies. Since they had been confident that the price increase would continue, they had bought textile goods at high prices in the futures market. They now had to sell the same goods in a depressed market and incur large losses. C.Itoh lost heavily in cotton yarn, and Itohchu Shoten in fabric. The losses of the former amounted to 175 million yen, and that of the latter to 30 million yen. These

50

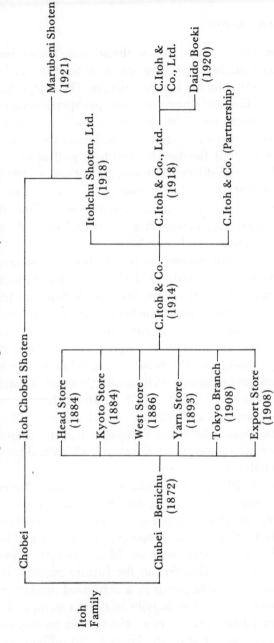

FIGURE 3.3
Organizational Changes in the Itoh Family's Business

Source: Itohchu Shoji, *Itohchu Shoji Hyakunen,* 1969, various pages.

losses surpassed even the capital of the parent company, C.Itoh & Co.

A crisis was averted by the sacrifice made by the Itoh family and a great effort at reorganization. The family gave all of its disposable wealth to pay for losses, but even this was not enough to maintain the two companies as they were. C.Itoh & Co., Ltd., decided to confine operations to trade with the Asian continent and to reduce the scale of its operation. Trade with other regions was handed to a newly-created firm, called Daido Boeki. Itohchu Shoten was merged with the financially sound Itoh Chobei Shoten (the store of the elder brother, Itoh Chobei), to become Marubeni Shoten (see Figure 3.3).[64]

Like his younger brother, the first Itoh Chubei, Chobei discontinued the travelling wholesale business and set up a store (Itoh Chobei Shoten) at Hakata in Kyushu to engage in the wholesaling of kimono cloth. In the next several decades, he and his son-in-law built the family business to a considerable size by conservative business methods. In the late 1910s, they had stores in Kyoto and Osaka for purchasing, and their marketing network extended to Hiroshima on the east and Korea on the west. Because Chobei's son-in-law maintained his predecessor's conservative business policy and abstained from speculation, the store was in a financially sound position, even after the crash of March 1920.

C.ITOH

The first several years of the 1920s were a period of retreat for C.Itoh. Its capital, which was 10 million yen before the crash, dwindled down to 7 million yen in 1922 and then to 5 million yen in 1928. In employment, a similar decline took place. In 1920, there were 426 workers, but in 1926, the number was down to 161. The only consolation was that since only the young and energetic ones remained, labour productivity was higher and the company had more flexibility.[65]

In the last few years of the 1920s, C.Itoh began to show signs of recovery, and paid out dividends in 1930 for the first time since the panic of 1920. In the second half of the 1931 financial year, it recorded small losses, and dividends were not paid out in that year. In the following years, however, the company enjoyed a spell of profitable years. In 1932, dividend payments were renewed, and in 1933, 40 per cent extra dividends were paid. With increase in profits, the amount of capital was raised to 6.2 million yen in 1934, 7.5 million yen in 1935, and 12.5 million yen in 1937.

There were three important developments in C.Itoh during the 1920s and 1930s. The first is that it became an integrated textile trading company. The traditional business of C.Itoh was cotton yarn and fabric—the business it took over from the old Yarn Store. Its first major diversification into other textile areas was the handling of raw cotton. In the mid-1920s, the company considered a plan to handle raw cotton, starting with a spinning company named Toyama Spinning, in whose establishment C.Itoh had participated. But there was strong opposition within the company, since this was generally believed to be a risky business and unsuitable for a reputable trading company to undertake. One way to avoid speculation in raw cotton transactions was to engage in so-called basis transactions and to become a commission merchant. By persuading spinners of the merits of such transactions, C.Itoh started in the raw cotton business.

The next important diversification was into rayon. C.Itoh's handling of rayon began when it became an agent for Teikoku Jinken (the present Teijin) in 1924. From the middle of the 1920s, rayon production rapidly increased, and the 1930s were the golden decade of the rayon industry. In this, trading companies played an important role. C.Itoh brought rayon fabric from the West and gave encouragement to weavers to experiment with it. When their products improved in quality and the costs of production declined, they were exported to the Chinese market. In the 1930s, C.Itoh also handled exports of rayon products to Indonesia and other South-East Asian countries.

Another major diversification was into wool products. The

wool industry needed more time to mature than the cotton industry, and it was not until the early 1930s that the stage of import substitution ended. As the wool industry grew in importance, C.Itoh began emphasizing the handling of woollen yarn, woollen fabric, and raw wool. Structurally, the wool industry was similar to the cotton industry. Spinning and weaving were done separately, and trading companies such as C.Itoh bought yarn from spinners, sold it to weavers, and bought fabric for either domestic wholesaling or export. C.Itoh also began handling the import of raw wool and sent representatives to Australia and South America.

The second major development in C.Itoh during the 1920s and 1930s was the establishment of an extensive marketing network on the Asian continent. In 1926, when C.Itoh's fortunes were at rock bottom, it had only two branches and two representative offices in China: in Shanghai and Tientsin, and Tsingtao and Hankow, respectively. In the following five-year period, new offices were set up in Tsinan, Seoul, Harbin, and Mukden. The offices in Manchuria (Mukden and Harbin) were established primarily to find an outlet for the export of Japanese textiles which had begun to stagnate because of the progress of import substitution in China, and secondly, to back up the policy of the Japanese government to develop Manchuria. By the middle of the 1930s, C.Itoh had established two more offices in Manchuria: one in Hsin-ching (present Changchun) and the other in Antung. In the second half of the 1930s and the early 1940s, the network in Manchuria and China was further extended. In 1941, C.Itoh had 1 branch and 7 representative offices in Manchuria and 2 branches and 21 representative offices in China.

MARUBENI

The history of Marubeni in the pre-war period is less colourful. There were no violent ups and downs as in the case of C.Itoh. In forty-two financial periods, Marubeni suspended dividend payments only twice (in the first and the fortieth periods). In the remaining periods, it paid 8 to 15 per cent dividends. With such steady profit records, capital was raised from 5 million to 7.5 million yen in 1934, to 8.5 million yen in the following year, and to 10 million yen in 1937.

Marubeni's steady growth in the 1920s is somewhat puzzling in view of the fact that most companies were in distress. This is in sharp contrast especially with its sister company, C.Itoh, which had to reduce both the size of its capital and the number of its employees. One reason for this must be that since before Itohchu Shoten merged it had worn off the 'surplus fat' accumulated during the boom years, the new company did not have to inherit excess workers. Also, the fact that the losses of Itohchu Shoten were settled by either the Itoh Chobei family or the unlimited partnership, C.Itoh & Co., made it possible for Marubeni to start without accumulated losses. In the case of C.Itoh & Co., Ltd., however, accumulated losses had to be made good by writing off part of its capital.

That the merger had revitalizing and modernizing effects is also important in accounting for Marubeni's steady growth. Since the well established network of Itohchu Shoten was combined with Itoh Chobei Shoten's ample funds, the merger produced something like a synergetic effect. Also, the fact that management was left to a competent man named Furukawa Tetsujiro, a professional manager from the ranks of Itohchu Shoten, made it possible for the new company to make better use of its potential. Neither the seventh Itoh Chobei, who became president of Marubeni representing the interests of the Chobei family, nor Itoh Chuzo (husband of a sister of the second Chubei) who became its vice-president representing the interests of the Chubei family, interfered much in the way in which Furukawa restructured and managed the company. In view of the important role Furukawa played in the growth of Marubeni, the separation of management from ownership was an important contributing factor in the success of the company.

Marubeni's main business was domestic wholesaling of textile products. The major product it handled was silk cloth, which was the traditional commodity of both Itohchu Shoten and Itoh Chobei Shoten. In this business, Marubeni had established a dominant position. After the Kanto Earthquake of 1923, Marubeni increased its sales in eastern Japan (the Kanto and Tohoku areas) by taking over business from Tokyo-based wholesalers who had been hit severely by the earthquake.

In the 1930s, Marubeni developed close relations with the wool and rayon industries. The role it played in the distribution of woollen and rayon textiles was similar to that of C.Itoh in the distribution of cotton. In place of spinners and rayon manufacturers, who did not go beyond their respective fields in production, trading companies such as C.Itoh and Marubeni acted as organizers for the fragmented downstream. They bought woollen yarn and rayon, sold them to weavers, and bought back their output (cloth) for domestic wholesaling or export.

In 1918 when Itohchu Shoten and C.Itoh were established as separate companies, the former was to undertake domestic wholesaling and the latter, foreign trade. This functional division was retained to a considerable extent even after the restructuring in the early 1920s, with Marubeni replacing Itohchu Shoten. Thus, even as late as 1940, Marubeni was basically a domestic wholesaler, and C.Itoh a foreign trader.

This does not mean, however, that C.Itoh did not handle domestic trade. From the beginning, C.Itoh was involved in the domestic distribution of cotton products. Also, in such new products as rayon and woollen textiles, it was involved in the various facets of their distribution in Japan. Marubeni, similarly, did not stay away completely from foreign trade. From around 1934, it began dealing directly with foreign countries, and in 1940, it had about 80 employees abroad (in such places as Mukden, Dairen, Harbin, Tientsin, Peking, Shanghai, and Bombay).

There was something like a gentleman's agreement between Marubeni and C.Itoh, which was related to the situation in the late 1910s and early 1920s. Cotton yarn and fabric were a preserve for C.Itoh, and silk fabric for Marubeni; but there was no agreement between the two concerning rayon and woollen textiles, which became important in subsequent years. In these areas, Marubeni went into foreign trade, and C.Itoh expanded domestic operations.

4. IWAI[66]

IWAI BUNSUKE

In 1862, a man named Iwai Bunsuke opened a store in Osaka to engage in the indent business of Western merchandise. Bunsuke was born in 1842 in a village in the northern part of present Kyoto Prefecture, and when he was about 10 years old, left for Osaka to be apprenticed to a store dealing mainly in imported Chinese products. In the late 1850s, Japan reluctantly started trading with Western countries, and around this time, the store to which he was apprenticed seems to have begun dealing in Western goods as well. Seeing great opportunity in this new trade, in 1862 he rented a house with a small amount of capital he had saved to open his store. The store was called Kagaya, a popular name among the stores dealing in Chinese goods, and also the name of the store at which he

had originally worked. The trade mark, ⟨KB⟩ , of Iwai & Co. is derived from the K of Kagaya and the B of Bunsuke.

Bunsuke became a successful merchant. By 1868, the year of the Meiji Restoration, he had made enough money to buy a house, and used part of it as his store. Around this time, he was dealing in glass, woollen yarn, oil, Western liquor, matches, and drugs. In 1878, he had about 7 employees, and his capital amounted to about ¥10,000. Though this is a very small operation by today's standards, other stores dealing in Western goods were not probably much bigger. He was one of the fourteen prominent Western goods dealers in the Chamber of Commerce and Industry which was established in that year. A few years later, he became the deputy head of his trade association.

From the late Tokugawa to the early Meiji era, there were

two kinds of Japanese merchants who dealt with foreign merchants, *urikomiya*, and *hikitoriya*. *Urikomiya* can be regarded as exporters, and *hikitoriya* as importers, but with the possible exception of Mitsui Bussan, Japanese 'exporters' and 'importers' did not have direct contacts abroad and were satisfied to deal with foreign merchants in Yokohama and Kobe, the major ports of Japan. In the above classification, Bunsuke was a *hikitoriya*, an importer.

Bunsuke's business was to act as a middleman between Japanese merchants (wholesalers and retailers) and foreign merchants. Foreign merchants were often uncertain about how large the demand would be for the goods they had in stock, and needed the assistance of Japanese merchants. On the other hand, Japanese merchants, especially retailers and wholesalers in local cities, needed intermediaries who would buy Western goods from foreign merchants and distribute them in smaller quantities. Since it was possible to enter into this business with fairly little capital, competition was tough. Bunsuke, who did not have a particular advantage in language skill, succeeded largely due to his ability to judge the profitability of new Western goods.

GROWTH

By the early 1890s, the number of employees had increased to thirty and the amount of capital to ¥500,000. At the same time, the products he dealt in diversified. In the mid-1880s, the list of the goods he handled included oil, Western liquor, canned goods, condensed milk, fabric, woollen yarn, blankets, towels, lamps, paper, and matches. Among them, lamp oil (kerosene) was particularly important. In the process of Westernization in the Meiji era, the lamp became a popular product replacing the candle and this obviously brought about a rise in demand for kerosene. Bunsuke started handling it relatively early in his career, and established a firm footing in this business.

Iwai's real growth began in the mid-1890s. After twenty years of trial and error under the Meiji government, indus-

trialization finally began to bear fruit and the vanguard industry, spinning, had completed import substitution and become
ready for export. As industrialization progressed further, both
exports and imports increased in absolute terms and also diversified. Furthermore, the concessions Japan obtained as a
victor in the Sino–Japanese War (1894–5), Russo–Japanese
War (1904–5), and First World War (1914–18) facilitated
Japanese foreign trade. Iwai's growth was related to the overall growth of Japanese industry as well as the increase of its
political power.

In 1912, Iwai became a limited company capitalized at 2
million yen, and for the first time, Iwai & Co. was adopted as
its official English name. Then, in 1918, thanks to the large
profits it made during the unprecedented boom during the
First World War, the amount of capital was increased to 10
million yen. The profits, which were about ¥40,000 in the
first half of 1914, increased to ¥80,000 in the second half
of the year, and to ¥240,000 in the first half of the following
year. In the following periods, profits continued to rise, peak-
ing in the first half of 1918 when about 1.8 million yen was
earned. During the war boom years, altogether about 6 million
yen was made, marking an increase of three times over the
capital of 1912.

The 1920s was a difficult decade for Iwai. The first shock
came in early 1920 when prices began to plummet. In the
one-year period from mid-1920, the company incurred large
losses, which amounted to about half of the profits made
during the boom years. Then, the Kanto Earthquake of 1923
rendered an additional blow by damaging property and merchandise and inflicting damage on customers to whom credits
were extended. Furthermore, industrial investments undertaken during the boom years became burdens which required
additional injection of capital. Despite these problems, Iwai
managed to tide over this difficult decade, and started expanding again in the 1930s when business conditions became favourable. In 1935, the amount of capital was raised to 13 million
yen, and in 1939, to 15 million yen. Volume of sales, around

9 million yen in 1905, increased by the end of the 1930s to 300 million yen.

As the size of operation increased, the activities of Iwai changed. Unlike in the period up to the early 1890s, Iwai was no longer a *hikitoriya*. It imported directly from foreign countries through its own offices abroad or agents. Furthermore, its activities were not confined to imports: exports and domestic trade were also handled. As Japanese economic development attained the capability to manufacture the products (especially heavy-chemical products) that Iwai had been importing, it became necessary to undertake industrial investments to maintain its domestic market position. These investments made it necessary for Iwai to get involved in domestic transactions and also in export as an extension of this.

Iwai's network became fairly extensive by the late 1930s. In October 1939, its head office was in Osaka (this had been the case throughout), branches in Tokyo, Kobe and Nagoya, and representative offices in Yokohama, Fukui, Yahata, and Shizuoka. Abroad, there were offices in Shanghai, Seoul, Dairen, Mukden, Hsin-ching, Tientsin, Hankow, Tsingtao, Peking, Canton, Manila, New York, London, Bombay, Sydney, Melbourne, and Buenos Aires. Then, within the next two years before the Pacific War started, Iwai established offices in Johannesburg, Surabaya, Santiago, Saigon, Haiphong, Bangkok, and Batavia.

IWAI KATSUJIRO

The man behind Iwai's growth from the mid-1890s was Bunsuke's cousin, Katsujiro. He was born in a village west of Kyoto (which is part of Kameoka city today) in 1863, a year after Bunsuke opened his store. In 1876, when Katsujiro was 13 years old, he went to Osaka to work for Bunsuke. Then, in 1889, he married Bunsuke's daughter and became his adopted son. In the period from the mid-1890s until his death in 1935, he converted Iwai from an inward looking import store to a trading company which had operations in many countries of the world.

Katsujiro started direct trade with foreign countries. In the late 1890s, since Mitsui Bussan was trading directly in Osaka, Katsujiro was not the first to start direct trade, but he was one of its pioneers. The first contact was made with a London trading company named William Duff & Co., which Katsujiro came to know through industrialists in Osaka who had been importing chemicals from it. In 1897, by appointing Duff as Iwai's agent, Katsujiro began the first direct trade.

In 1900, Katsujiro went to Europe for the first time. His main purpose was to see the exhibition in Paris, but during his five-month stay, he observed business conditions in Europe and pondered over a strategy to expand direct trade. It was after his return that Iwai stepped up direct import activities. In 1902, one employee was sent to Duff in order to strengthen relations with the English company and at the same time develop the import trade from Germany, which was then just emerging as an industrial nation. Relations with Duff remained beneficial to Iwai, but during the First World War, since the son of the owner and other male employees joined the military service, adversely affecting Duff's business activities, it became necessary for Iwai to do business on its own. Thus, in 1917, a representative office was set up, and in 1921, it was promoted to a branch office.

The New York office was established in 1915. As the war progressed, the increasing difficulty of importing from Europe necessitated a search for alternative sources of supply. The United States, whose industry had been rapidly growing and had already surpassed Britain's in a number of fields, was the ideal country. At first, since relations with Duff had gone well, Katsujiro wanted to appoint some trading company as Iwai's agent, but since this did not work out, Iwai set up its own office in New York. In 1917, to step up imports from the United States, Iwai established another office in San Francisco, but this had to be closed in 1920 as part of the contraction policy to cope with the depression which began early that year. Before this, the New York office had been promoted to a branch, and it remained as the major office in the United States until late 1941.

Katsujiro's second initiative was in industrial investment. Since this was often necessary in order to establish a firm footing in trade channels, Iwai's industrial investment was, of course, related to its trading activities; whether that was the only reason or not is somewhat ambiguous. When Iwai was established as a limited company in 1912, manufacturing was listed in the articles of association as one of the objectives. During the second decade, especially during the First World War, Iwai set up many import substitution companies. Having dealt in imported goods for many years, Katsujiro knew what goods would be demanded and what their trade channel was in Japan, so that he must have seen a great opportunity to earn profits in establishing import substitution companies. In the 1910s, Japanese industry was slowly shifting its emphasis to the heavy-chemical industry (Iwai had been importing mostly heavy-chemical goods) and, during the First World War, when the supply route from Europe was cut, a great push was given to the growth of this industry. Faced with such opportunity, it seems that he undertook industrial investments on their own merits, though this had important repercussions on Iwai's trading activities. Katsujiro probably had his sights set on converting the trading company to an industrial—commercial combine.

Industrial investments forced Iwai to get involved in domestic transactions. At the time when it was a pure importer, its basic role was to obtain goods from abroad directly or indirectly and supply them to Japanese wholesalers and retailers. The goods it handled were mostly chemicals and heavy industrial products which were not manufactured in Japan. But as industrialization progressed in the heavy-chemical field, and Iwai itself became involved, it became necessary to handle the products of Japanese companies. Otherwise, because import substitution was progressing, the import business was bound to taper off.

Establishment of affiliates and subsidiaries was a means of

securing supply sources for its domestic transactions, although they were not the only sources. Yahata Steel became one important supply source in the late 1910s. Then, in the mid-1920s, since Yahata was suffering from excess capacity, it decided to step up sales to the private sector and appointed Iwai, along with several others, as an authorized agent. Since Yahata was the dominant steel manufacturer, this gave Iwai a firm footing in the marketing of steel products. Besides Yahata, Iwai became an agent for a number of other manufacturers. For example, it handled cotton fabric made by manufacturers in the Nagoya area and the woollen fabric made by a company called Tokyo Seiju-sho (later, Tokyo Keori).

It was around 1905 that Iwai started undertaking exports. This was desirable from two viewpoints. For one, if Iwai was to send its employees abroad and establish offices, overhead cost per transaction would become smaller by increasing transactions handling both export and import. Furthermore, if export proceeds could be used for import, the amount of money to be sent abroad would become smaller, and the costs of foreign exchange would decline to that extent. For another, in order to expand the sales of Japanese manufacturers, which is one important service a trading company can offer when establishing agency rights, or other close relations, it is valuable to have a sales network abroad.

The offices in London, New York, and Australia were set up primarily for import, the first two for importing heavy-chemical industrial products, and the last for importing wool. Exports handled by these offices resulted from the desire to reduce overhead cost per transaction. In contrast, it seems that the offices in China and South-East Asia were established primarily for export. In 1905, two employees were sent to China on an observation mission, and four years later, Katsu-jiro himself went there. In 1907, one employee was sent to India for six months to promote exports. In 1908, another employee was sent to the Philippines, and in 1909, to Indonesia also for export promotion. In the mid-1920s, Iwai was actively marketing galvanized iron sheets in China, the Philippines, Indonesia and other Asian countries. In the late 1930s, the Dairen office was marketing the steel products of Nippon Seitetsu and the galvanized iron sheets of Iwai's subsidiary.

Imports from China and South-East Asia began as the network expanded in these regions. From the Philippines, the import of tobacco leaves and abacca (the raw material for Manila rope) began in the mid-1920s, and that of wood and iron ore in the mid-1930s. Iwai bought a timber company in Mindoro and used it as the supply source of wood. For iron ore, a company called Philippine Iron Mines was the supply source. Other major imports from South-East Asia were coal (Vietnam) and rice (Burma and Thailand). In Dairen, besides the marketing of steel products, the office was engaged in buying billet and wool for manufacturers in Japan.

5. NISSHO[67]

SUZUKI SHOTEN

Like many of the other trading companies, Nissho's history goes back further than its actual date of founding, February 1928, and it is to the history of its direct ancestor, Suzuki Shoten, that one must turn first for the story.

Suzuki Shoten was founded by a man named Suzuki Iwajiro. Like Iwai Bunsuke, the founder of Iwai, he was born of a poor family, and was apprenticed to a merchant. He later opened his own store and became a successful importer. Iwajiro, who was apprenticed to a confectionery shop, first became good at judging the quality of sugar, and because of this and other skills, when he joined the Kobe branch of an Osaka sugar merchant, he moved up quickly to the top post. When the owner of the store died, Iwajiro bought the Kobe office and became independent in 1877 (the founding year of Suzuki Shoten). In the next seventeen years until his death in 1894, his store grew by marketing sugar bought from foreign merchants in Kobe and undertaking money exchange for Japanese merchants who came to Kobe to do business with them.

In the mid-1890s, when Iwajiro passed away, Suzuki Shoten was a prosperous store and well-known in the Kobe area, but it was an inconspicuous company in terms of the Japanese economy as a whole. This situation, however, changed greatly in the next twenty to twenty-five years. By the end of the First World War, Suzuki had become comparable to Mitsui Bussan in size and had established a world-wide reputation. Its name became so widely known that the *New York Times* wrote about John D. Rockefeller and Suzuki Yone (Iwajiro's wife) in an article entitled 'The Richest Man and Woman in the World'.[68]

The man who built up Suzuki to these great heights was Kaneko Naokichi. He entered the store in 1886, and by the time Iwajiro died, he had risen to become one of the two most important employees of the store. Leaving the sugar trade to the other, he took responsibility for camphor imports. In this connection, he developed close relations with Taiwan, which supplied 80 to 90 per cent of camphor at that time, and became close to Goto Shinpei, who as Governor of Taiwan played an important role in developing the island's sugar and camphor industries and establishing the Bank of Taiwan, one of Japan's 'national policy' banks.[69] Kaneko's first success was that he obtained agency rights for camphor, which was the monopoly good of the colonial government. Because of this success, camphor became another major product of Suzuki Shoten.

As late as 1902, when Suzuki was reorganized to become an unlimited partnership (capitalized at ¥500,000), its main transactions were still with foreign merchant houses in Kobe and the major products it dealt in were natural products such as sugar and camphor. It appeared, as yet, that no basic changes had taken place, but changes were beginning. For one, Suzuki appointed agents in London, Hamburg and New York to export natural products. For another, it began to move into manufacturing. A mint processing plant was established in 1900, and a camphor processing plant and a sugar refinery in 1903. In the following several years, two more camphor processing plants, a fish oil manufacturing plant, and a steel manufacturing plant were either bought or newly established.[70]

An important turning point came in the period 1909–14. In order to step up diversification in transactions, a new trading company called Nippon Shogyo (Nippon Trading Society Ltd.) was set up in 1909. To secure a base in the shipping industry, a company called Minami Manshu Kisen (South Manchurian Steamships) was set up in Dairen. Then, branch or representative offices were set up in the United States, Europe, Australia and China. The primary purpose of these offices was to promote exports from and imports to Japan, but it also gave rise to offshore trade (trade between foreign offices). For example, the storage space of the ships which had brought steel from London to Japan began to be used to ship rice from Saigon to France.

When the First World War broke out, Suzuki had a basic infrastructure for trade expansion. It had offices in major cities in the West and China and had a shipping company to meet basic transportation needs. This does not mean, however, that Suzuki was bound to increase its transactions and earn profits as large as it did during the war. The great expansion was possible because the infrastructure was combined with Kaneko's acumen. The shock of the first several months after the beginning of the war forced prices down, and it appeared as if the economy would plunge into a depression; but based on the information he collected from both within and without the country, Kaneko judged that prices would rise sharply and saw this as a heaven-sent opportunity for his company.

Three to four months later, prices began to skyrocket, and Suzuki earned over 100 million yen at this time.[71] This made it possible for Kaneko to hire a large number of new workers, expand the office network within Japan and abroad, and step up diversification in transactions. At the same time, he continued aggressive buying, and in 1917, the volume of sales exceeded 1,500 million yen (exports and imports amounted to 1,200 million yen and offshore trade 340 million yen).[72]

Since the sales of the hitherto largest trading company, Mitsui Bussan, were roughly 1,000 million yen in this year, it is clear that Suzuki had become the largest trader.

The war came to an end in late 1918, but the boom continued in Japan until early 1920. In Europe, because of the devastation and dislocation during the war, there was an acute shortage of food, and it was necessary to import it from abroad. By exporting wheat and flour from the United States, sugar from Java and soybeans from Manchuria, Suzuki earned large profits. At this time, the British trading companies, incapacitated during the war, had not made a comeback, and so Japanese trading companies like Suzuki could play a much larger role in European imports.[73]

The period after March 1920 when prices began to plummet is the beginning of Suzuki's decline. The price decline is probably to be blamed for the fatal blow to Suzuki which had been engaged in speculative buying, and in 1921, it got into financial trouble. In order to rescue the company, Kaneko demonstrated his clout as a privileged merchant by obtaining large loans from the Bank of Taiwan. Its loans, which stood at 80 million yen at the end of 1920, increased steadily in the following years and rose to about 380 million yen in March 1927. Since Suzuki's capital was only 130 million yen at this time (Suzuki Shoten Ltd. was capitalized at 80 million yen and Suzuki Gomei Kaisha at 50 million yen), the 380 million yen was an enormous figure. Despite such large assistance from the Bank of Taiwan, however, Suzuki could not solve its financial troubles. Towards the end of March 1927, in order to get out of the quagmire, the Bank of Taiwan suspended its transactions with Suzuki, and several days later, Suzuki suspended all of its payments. In reality this was bankruptcy, though legally it was not, since Suzuki remained for another several years as a liquidation company.

NISSHO

From the ashes of Suzuki a new company was born. Originally, it was planned that a trading subsidiary, Nippon Shogyo, which had been engaged mainly in cotton, cotton yarn and wool trading, would take over Suzuki's profitable businesses and Takahata and some others would move there, but, for some reason, this plan was abandoned. Instead, Nissho was set up by about forty former employees of Nippon Shogyo and Suzuki Shoten, with Takahata Seiichi and Nagai Kotaro as chief executive officers. It may appear that since Nissho was legally a separate company, it did not inherit any complications from Suzuki's failure, but in reality, the story was not that simple. For one thing, Nissho wanted to take over some profitable agency rights from Suzuki, but this had to be done delicately, for, if they were worth anything, the creditors probably would demand that they be sold. For another thing, since Suzuki caused large losses to many people (it was trying to settle the claims by paying 5 per cent), even to raise 1 million yen as the capital of a new company was difficult for Takahata and Nagai. Fortunately, the Bank of Taiwan and a few other financiers placed confidence in this small group of competent young men under Takahata and Nagai (mostly in their 30s) and backed their efforts to make a new start in foreign trade.

The economic climate in the first several years of Nissho's history was not favourable, and reflecting this, its sales fluctuated between 20 and 40 million yen. Then, the turning point came in 1933 when Suzuki Shoten (which remained as a liquidation office) had settled all claims of its creditors, and was dissolved. Now cleared of debt problems, the Suzuki family threw behind Nissho whatever influence it still had and helped it establish close relations with some of the former Suzuki companies such as Teikoku Jinken, Kobe Steel, and Harima Shipbuilding. Also, in 1933, the gloomy period which had started with the crash of March 1920 came to an end, and the Japanese economy entered a new phase of expansion.

There were two important developments for Nissho in the mid-1930s. One was the beginning of transactions with Nippon Seitetsu (the dominant steel company set up in 1934 by merging Yahata Steel with several private steel makers). At first,

Nissho had agency rights for the wire rods of Kobe Steel. In view of the limitation of capital and personnel which could be allocated to the steel trade, Nissho could not handle as many steel products as it wished, and so concentrated its resources on wire rods. Then, in 1934, Kobe Steel formed with Nippon Seitetsu a syndicate to regulate the production and marketing of wire rods. At this time, Nissho, together with Mitsubishi Shoji, Mitsui Bussan, Iwai, and Ataka, was appointed as its agent. The other major development of the period was a tie-up with Union Oil. Earlier, Nissho had taken over Suzuki's negotiations with Richfield (an American oil company) and consummated the deal, but since Richfield got into trouble through mismanagement, Nissho switched to Union Oil. Since this was a much bigger company, this tie-up strengthened Nissho's position in oil trade.

Its growth in the mid-1930s is reflected in the increase of both sales and capital. The amount of sales (40 million yen in 1932) increased to 70 million yen in 1933, 98 million yen in 1936 and 162 million yen in 1937. Capital, which was originally 1 million yen, was raised to 3 million yen in 1934 and then 5 million yen in 1937. As the amount of capital increased, the overseas network was extended. The company started with three offices abroad (Fort Worth, Bombay and London). Then, in 1934, an office was set up in Dairen, in 1935 in New York, in 1937 in Calcutta, and in 1938 in Shanghai. The records also show that in 1938 Nissho had an office in Los Angeles.

Towards the end of the 1930s, Nissho experienced another expansion. Sales increased from about 160 million yen in 1938 to 206 million in 1940. After Japan had plunged into war in China, it became increasingly important to secure strategic materials, and, in order to facilitate the import of pig-iron and steel, import cartels were formed. A cartel to facilitate import of pig-iron from India was formed by nine trading companies. Nissho was an important member because of its close relations with Tata, India's largest iron and steel producer; it also joined the six-member cartel for iron and steel imports from the United States with the backing of Kobe Steel. As a result, its New York office became busy with buying scrap iron and steel from American manufacturers and dealers. Oil was, of course, another strategic material, and by using the tie-up with Union Oil, Nissho contributed to Japan's import of oil for stockpile.

In March 1941, capital was increased to 7.5 million yen from the previous 5 million yen. By this time, because of the unstable political climate, offices in Bombay, Calcutta, Surabaya, London, New York and Los Angeles had been closed. Most foreign offices were now in East Asia: 1 in Korea, 1 in Taiwan, and 15 in China. The only other offices were those in Saigon and the Palau Islands. By this time, Nissho had acquired 8 manufacturing subsidiaries: 4 in Japan and the rest in China. In addition, there was a number of related companies (Kobe Steel, etc.) for which Nissho was a large shareholder.

6. OTHER TRADING COMPANIES

KANEMATSU

F. Kanematsu & Co. was a pioneer in the trade between Japan and Australia.[74] In the mid-1880s, Kanematsu Fusajiro, founder of the company, foresaw an increase in the demand for wool and planned to import it directly from Australia. At this time the cotton industry was developing in Japan, but the wool industry was almost non-existent. Fusajiro was convinced that the wool industry was bound to develop, so in 1887, he went to Australia to investigate the situation there and to make the necessary contacts. After he returned to Japan, he opened a store in Kobe, and in the following year (1890), a branch office in Sydney.

As Fusajiro expected, the demand for wool increased in subsequent years. First, wool began to be used as material for kimono cloth, which had traditionally been either cotton or silk. Later, wool became an important material for making Western clothes, especially uniforms for the armed forces. As a pioneer in wool import, Fusajiro reaped great profits from the increased demand, but, he could not continue to dominate the trade. As wool became more and more profitable, other trading companies (Mitsui Bussan, Okura Shoji, Takashimaya Iida, etc.) entered the field and encroached upon Kanematsu's market. In 1910, Kanematsu managed to control about 60 per cent of the market. In the following years, however, competition became tougher, and Kanematsu's share dwindled to from a quarter to a third. Nevertheless, it managed to occupy the top position in wool import throughout the pre-war period.

Fusajiro's career and world-view were quite different from those of the other founders of trading companies discussed thus far. Although he was born a commoner in the late Tokugawa period, through hard work and ingenuity he became a lower samurai, and received formal education; and then, when Westerners came to Japan, he learnt English from a missionary. After the Meiji Restoration, he decided to become a merchant and had a hand in various ventures, but since he was not very successful in any of these, he decided to join the Mitsui Bank. He did not stay with the bank for long, however. After leaving the bank, he participated in the formation of a shipping company called Osaka Shosen. He then proceeded to take over the management of a newspaper in Osaka (Osaka Mainichi). It was after these ventures that he began the Australian trade. Even after this, he was involved in many public activities.

The development of Kanematsu took place in the 1910s. Early in the decade, the amount of capital was raised from ¥30,000 to ¥300,000 by converting retained earnings to capital. Then in 1916, it was raised to ¥600,000, and in 1922, to 5 million yen. These increases were made possible by the large profits the company made during the boom years of the First World War.

Fusajiro died in 1913, about twenty years after he founded the business and before the war boom began. After his death, there were no prominent figures in the company. In the case of C.Itoh, the leading figure was the second Chubei; in the case of Iwai, Katsujiro. The set-up in Kanematsu was not like that at Mitsui either, where the Mitsui family retained ownership and let prominent managers such as Masuda Takashi run the company, for the Kanematsu family relinquished ownership. In 1907, Fusajiro had made the company a joint venture between himself and his subordinates, so that at the time of his death, the family owned only half of the shares. In the following several years, even those shares were transferred; thus, it was his subordinates who owned and managed the company after his death.

During Fusajiro's time, Kanematsu's trade had been almost exclusively with Australia, but during the First World War, the company began to trade with other countries. The first impetus to this regional diversification came in 1916 when Australia restricted the export of its products as a wartime measure. Because of this, Kanematsu looked to Latin America and South Africa which were alternative sources of wool at that time. Alternative sources of wheat and other products which Kanematsu had been importing from Australia had also to be found. The United States became the supplier for wheat.

After the First World War ended, the Australian trade became the most important again, but trade with other countries continued. For a while, Kanematsu traded largely with non-Asian countries, but in the 1930s, especially after the Sino-Japanese War began in 1936, it became imperative to emphasize trade with China; Kanematsu had established offices in about fifteen Chinese cities by the end of the decade.

The 1930s was also a decade when Kanematsu experienced fundamental changes in the pattern of trade. By the end of the 1920s, its main business was import, export was of secondary importance, and domestic trade was minuscule. In the next decade, however, import declined, while export and domestic trade registered substantial gains. The export increase was made possible by expansion into China. The trade with Australia—the import of wool in particular—declined in importance as restrictions on import of non-essential goods became more severe in the late 1930s.

ATAKA

Ataka Yakichi, founder of Ataka and Co., was the most educated among the founders of trading companies discussed in this chapter.[75] Unlike the others, he received a college education. In 1889, he entered Tokyo Commercial College (the present Hitotsubashi University) which was, at that time, the only school offering courses in business and management. Upon graduation several years later, he joined an Osaka-based trading company called Kusakabe Shoten, which had pioneered the Hong Kong trade. An important factor in his decision to join the company was his desire to follow in the path of a famous merchant named Jeniya Gohei who had undertaken foreign trade in the late Tokugawa period despite a law prohibiting it. Jeniya Gohei was a hero at Yakichi's birthplace.

Soon after he joined Kusakabe Shoten, he was sent to Hong Kong, at that time the most important trading centre in Asia. One significant activity he undertook there was to import sugar from Java. Until then, the sugar trade had been dominated by Mitsui Bussan and a few Western trading companies. In order to enter into this trade, Yakichi made a trip to Java in 1901 and succeeded in persuading a large sugar merchant (Chinese) to deal with his company. Since sugar passed through many intermediaries before it reached refineries in Japan, its direct import from a producing centre was immensely profitable.

Despite Yakichi's efforts, Kusakabe Shoten went bankrupt soon after the Russo–Japanese War broke out (the war caused a panic in Osaka). When this happened, Yakichi decided to start his own business. In 1904, he set up Ataka and Co. in Osaka, and soon after established a branch office in Hong Kong. He took over the sugar trade from Kusakabe Shoten.

Sugar thus played an important role in Ataka's early history, but the company is actually known as a steel trader. Apparently, at some point Ataka switched from sugar to steel. It seems that the turning point came around 1910, when the largest sugar refinery in Japan at that time suspended all payments to its creditors. Since this refinery was Ataka's most important customer, this suspension of payments hit Ataka hard. The refinery was eventually rehabilitated, and Ataka got the entire amount of its credits paid by the mid-1910s. In the meantime, however, the suspension seems to have caused financial troubles and triggered the change in Ataka's business strategy.

Ataka had been handling steel import even earlier but it was after 1910 that steel became relatively important. At this time, a large quantity of steel had to be imported from the West because domestic production could not meet the demand. Ataka increased its participation in steel import. Fortunately, the sales network the company developed in this connection also proved useful later on in marketing the products of Yahata Steel, the dominant steel producer in pre-war Japan. In the mid-1920s Ataka became one of the five trading companies which Yahata appointed to be its authorized agents. At the time, Ataka's share was about 9 per cent, but when another agent, Suzuki, went bankrupt in 1927, a large part of its share was given to Ataka, since it was also, like Suzuki, an Osaka-based company and thus in a better position than other firms to substitute for the bankrupt firm. Ataka's share rose to 19 per cent. This figure can be interpreted to mean that since Yahata was the dominant steel producer and steel import dwindled in the late 1920s, a substantial amount of steel consumed in the private sector in Japan passed through Ataka.

Though steel was its major commodity, Ataka was not a specialized steel dealer. In addition to steel, it handled machinery, textiles, fertilizer, wood, pulp, paper, chemicals, etc. Among these, machinery and pulp were relatively the most important. In machinery, Ataka obtained agency rights from numerous machinery producers in the West (the most famous was Gleason Works, a well-known machine tool maker in the United States). It also invested in several machinery producers and marketed their products (one of these produces Olympus cameras today). In the field of pulp, the most important development was that Ataka became the exclusive agent of Oji Paper, the largest paper manufacturer in pre-war Japan. Prior to this, Ataka had been importing pulp from abroad.

Ataka's expansion abroad is somewhat unusual. In the early 1910s, it had offices in Hong Kong and Dairen, but sold them to Suzuki in 1913. The reason for this is not clear, but it may be related to the financial difficulties Ataka faced in connection with the suspension of payments at the sugar refinery discussed earlier. Anyway, from 1913 until 1923 when the London office was set up, Ataka did not have any offices abroad. From 1923 to 1932, the London office was the sole overseas branch. Then, in the second half of the 1930s, Ataka established many foreign offices. This should not be interpreted as a global expansion, however, for Ataka's offices were located mostly in China and South-East Asia. The only exception was the New York office, established in 1938.

This pattern of overseas expansion suggests the following scenario. In the 1910s and 1920s, Ataka turned inward, and for import, it depended mostly on its agents abroad. The only exception was in the case of the London office set up in 1923 to purchase steel, woollen yarn, fertilizer, chemicals, machinery, etc. Export from Japan to the London office was not important. Then in the second half of the 1930s, since the various companies Ataka dealt with in Japan had become ready for export, it became necessary to go abroad to seek a market for their products. Ataka concentrated its efforts in China and South-East Asia, for given the level of industrial development at that time, this region appeared most promising.

ASANO BUSSAN AND OKURA SHOJI

Both Asano Bussan and Okura Shoji were zaibatsu trading companies, though much smaller than, for example, Mitsubishi Shoji or Mitsui Bussan. For one thing, they did not have banks, so they had to depend on the Daiichi Bank and the Yasuda Bank (the present Fuji Bank) for finance. Also, the industrial companies they controlled were not as large as Mitsui's and Mitsubishi's. In fact, Okura did not have any large manufacturing companies under its umbrella. The main pillars of the Okura zaibatsu were, besides Okura Shoji, a construction company (the present Taisei) and a mining company operating mainly in China. In the case of Asano, the stake in the manufacturing industry was larger. Asano was involved in production of cement, steel, and ships. The cement company (Asano Cement) was especially important; it accounted for more than half the cement production in pre-war Japan. Still, Asano's companies were no match for Mitsui's, let alone Mitsubishi's.

Okura Shoji was a pioneer in foreign trade.[76] Okura Kihachiro, founder of the company, made a large fortune in dealing in guns in the turbulent years of the late Tokugawa period. He bought guns from Western merchants in Japan and sold them to the Tokugawa shogunate and provincial governments. But he was not satisfied with this inward oriented trade. He wanted to deal directly with manufacturers in the West. Thus, in 1872 he went abroad to make observations and to establish contacts. Soon after he returned to Japan, he set up Okura Gumi Shokai (the predecessor of Okura Shoji) and in the following year (1874), opened a branch in London. This was the first foreign office established by a Japanese trading company.

Weapons continued to occupy a large share of Okura's business. As official purveyor to the Army, it made large profits in the Taiwan expedition (1874), Sino–Japanese War (1894–5), and Russo–Japanese War (1904–5). As new weapons (machine guns, tanks, etc.) were developed in the West, they were imported by Okura for the Army. Because of this relationship with the Army, Okura was stigmatized as 'the merchant of death'. But over a period of time, the machinery and equipment it handled diversified, and it established itself as an expert machinery importer. For example, it imported steel-making machinery for Japanese steel producers; locomotives for the Japan National Railway and South Manchurian Railroad; generators for power companies; Caterpillar construction machinery; Marconi electronic equipment; and Lockheed aircraft. Okura obtained agency rights from a number of machinery producers in the West.

Despite brilliant records in its early years, Okura Shoji eventually slipped behind other trading companies. One reason for this was that it remained essentially an importer. There were a large number of products Japan needed to import, and Okura made large profits by importing them earlier than others. But as Mitsui Bussan and other trading companies began direct import and as the import needs changed with the development of Japanese industry, Okura could not maintain its former position. The only area where it had a considerable advantage over others was in machinery; here, through past transactions, Okura had acquired a certain degree of expert knowledge as well as agency rights from a number of Western manufacturers.

Asano Bussan was born much later than Okura Shoji.[77] In 1918, the year when the Japanese economy was enjoying the prosperity brought about by the war in Europe, Asano set up a trading company with an American trading firm, called W. R. Grace and Co. This venture turned out to be a fiasco. In the spring of 1920 when the post-war crash occurred, the company's Osaka branch lost about 6 million yen in cotton speculation (the paid-up capital was 1 million yen at this time). Grace proposed liquidation of the company, but since Asano had to honour the debts of its affiliated companies in order to preserve its credibility, it insisted on carrying on the business. Grace did not go along with this, and transferred all its holdings and withdrew from Asano Bussan. Despite these troubles in its early years, however, Asano Bussan became a prosperous company after the mid-1920s.

Asano Bussan was the most dynamic company in the pre-war oil trade. The earliest oil trade was the import from Mexico in 1921. Soon afterwards, Asano Bussan switched to California as the source of its oil supply, which brought it into contact with Standard Oil of California, and it obtained Standard's agency rights in Japan in 1931. After Standard Oil of California went to the Persian Gulf, Asano Bussan began oil import from the Middle East. In the mid-1930s, it constructed oil tanks at Shinagawa, Tokyo, and bought two oil tankers to meet its transportation needs. In 1940, it handled about 65 per cent of Japan's oil import.

In steel also, Asano Bussan had become a major trader by the mid-1920s. As was true for other trading companies as well, import was the major source of supply in the early years. Asano imported steel from the United States and Belgium, and later from Germany. In the 1930s when Japanese steel production increased and replaced import, steel manufacturers organized under the Asano zaibatsu became important product sources. Asano Bussan's steel plant at Kokura, Kyushu, supplied steel wires and rods; the steel factory of Asano Shipbuilding supplied steel plates; and Nippon Kokan, Asano's affiliated company, supplied steel pipes. In 1937, Asano Bussan became one of the seven authorized agents for Nippon Seitetsu (a company created in the early 1930s with the merging of Yahata Steel and smaller steel manufacturers). Around the same time, it joined the seven-member cartel to import scrap iron from the United States, the major source of supply at that time.

Because import substitution progressed in Japan and imports were linked to exports, the 1930s was not a happy period for Okura Shoji; but for Asano Bussan, it was the golden decade. Oil was required for wartime preparation and as a source of energy, and steel was in great demand as a result of stepped-up industrialization. Asano's past investment in steel production boosted the position of Asano Bussan in the 1930s.

THREE COTTON TRADERS

Toyo Menka, Nippon Menka, and Gosho were known as the 'Japanese Three' in the raw cotton markets of the world. They supplied about two-thirds of the raw cotton used by the Japanese cotton textile industry, which had become the largest in the world by the 1920s.[78] Besides raw cotton, they handled cotton textile products such as yarn and fabric. Because they were an all-round dealer for the Japanese cotton textile industry, they grew in size as the industry grew. In 1920s and early 1930s, since the textile industry was still the leading sector of the Japanese economy, the cotton traders were the vanguard of Japanese exporters.

Toyo Menka was established in 1920, when the cotton division was separated from Mitsui Bussan.[79] One reason for this move in Mitsui was to give more freedom and independence to the cotton division, whose position had been threatened by the rise of late starters such as Nippon Menka and Gosho. Since these later companies were independent entities, when large profits were made, they were able to keep a large portion of the profits as reserves for future use. In contrast, the cotton division of Mitsui Bussan had most of its profits taken away by the headquarters, from which it would then have to borrow working capital with interest. This put the cotton division in a disadvantageous position *vis-à-vis* its competitors. Further, the cotton division was not given enough freedom in speculation (though it had more freedom in this than other divisions), since speculation was against the basic policy of the company of sticking to agency business. In the cotton business, however, speculation played an important role, and other cotton traders used it to expand.

When Toyo Menka was separated from Mitsui Bussan, it took over all cotton businesses, and thus the commodities it handled consisted of raw cotton, yarn, fabric, and finished products. Mitsui Bussan retained silk and after establishing Toyo Rayon, handled rayon. Since Toyo Menka agreed not to handle these products in exchange for the promise of Mitsui Bussan not to handle cotton products, it could not become an all-round textile trader.

Nippon Menka was established in 1892 by spinners and cotton merchants in order to import raw cotton directly from abroad.[80] Earlier, spinners established a cotton trading company called Naigai Wata, but as demand grew, it could not handle their needs alone, so Nippon Menka was set up. The close relationship with spinners in the company's early years is indicated by the fact that its headquarters were in the same building as a spinning company which was one of its major investors. As the company grew, however, under the presidency of Kita Matazo (who took over management of the company in 1903), it became independent of spinning companies and became a genuine trading company.

Gosho's establishment was slightly different from that of Nippon Menka.[81] There was a man named Kitagawa Yohei from Goshu (another name for Omi province) who was engaged in the cotton business. He was not solely a merchant, since he operated a small spinning mill, but he had a strong commercial mentality. In dealing with foreign merchants in Japan who supplied him with raw cotton, he became convinced that if cotton could be imported directly from abroad, he could make a lot of profits. Since he did not have enough capital of his own, he asked other men from his province to invest in his venture. Merchants from Goshu were known for being individualistic, and, in general, were not attracted by such joint ventures. Yet, in this rare case, a union was effected. Tazuke Masajiro, who founded Tazuke Shoten (one of the Senba Eight), and Abe Fusajiro, who later headed Toyo Boseki, were among the investors at this time. The company was established in 1905 and, at first, was engaged in spinning as well—the company took over Kitagawa Yohei's spinning mill—but this was separated out several years later.

The growth of Nippon Menka and Gosho in subsequent years was phenomenal. When Nippon Menka was set up in 1892, the amount of its paid-up capital was about ¥100,000. Over the next ten years, this increased fivefold. Then, under Kita Matazo, it increased from ¥500,000 in 1903 to 26 million yen in 1925. The large increase took place during the First World War. In Gosho's case, growth was less spectacular, but it was nevertheless large. When the company was established in 1905, the amount of capital was ¥400,000, but this increased to 20 million yen in 1920. Again, the increase was due largely to enormous profits made during the First World War.

Around 1930, the tide turned against Nippon Menka and Gosho. This is reflected in the large deficits they incurred at this time. Nichimen lost 39 million yen in 1929, 2.5 million yen in 1930, and 1.2 million yen in 1931, about 43 million yen altogether. As a consequence of such large losses, the company faced a crisis. It managed to survive by rescheduling the loans of its main bank (the Bank of Tokyo) and reducing its capital by three-quarters. Gosho's losses were not as large as Nichimen's, but they were substantial. At first, losses were met by reducing capital by a quarter, but losses in the mid-1930s caused Gosho's investors to feel desperate. Toyo Boseki, then Japan's largest spinner, was asked to take over the company, and in 1936, Gosho became a subsidiary of Toyo Boseki.

Why such a dramatic turn of fortune? There were two basic reasons for this. One was that competition reduced trade margins and forced both Nippon Menka and Gosho to rely on speculation for profits.[82] At first, they received comfortable margins by pioneering the import of raw cotton from distant places. In India, for example, a major source of supply throughout the pre-war period, the unbearable heat, contagious diseases, and inconvenient transportation acted as a barrier which pioneers had been able to exploit for profits. As the trade route became established, however, and business became more widely known, a number of companies made entry into this trade and challenged established traders.

The uncomfortable positions Nichimen and Gosho fell into are reflected in the fact that in order to obtain orders from spinners, they frequently had to offer raw cotton at prices less than replacement costs in the countries of origin.[83] They were able to do this by buying raw cotton when its price was considered to be low (stock purchase) and postponing purchase for an order when prices were high (short sales). Sometimes, cotton traders could make profits in this way, but not always and consequently a number of companies came to grief.

The other reason for the dramatic turn around 1930 was the shift in bargaining power in favour of spinners. In the early years, spinning companies were small and did not have a high credit standing with banks, so they had to depend on cotton traders for working capital. This meant that part of the margins cotton traders obtained were returns to the financial service they rendered. As spinning companies became large, the situation changed: they no longer had to depend on trading companies for capital. At first, the spinning sector of the textile industry was fragmented, but by the 1920s a number of mergers had taken place, and several large spinning companies were born. Also, the fact that they had a production cartel (Japan Spinners' Association) made it possible to regulate production to earn 'normal' profits when business was bad and to continue to grow. Unfortunately there was no such adjusting mechanism for trading companies.

Although Nippon Menka and Gosho began to incur losses around 1930, their troubles actually seem to have begun much earlier, possibly with the panic of 1920.[84] They did not record losses at this time; indeed, they seem to have hidden their losses and continued aggressive business policy as in the past. They even paid dividends to stockholders, hoping that things would get better soon, but the basic troubles undermining their position did not go away. Probably, they had to report large losses around 1930, because they could no longer hide their financial problems.

In contrast, Toyo Menka continued to grow in the 1920s and 1930s.[85] Since it was established after the panic of 1920, unlike Nippon Menka and Gosho, it did not have to carry hidden losses in the 1920s. This was one very important factor in Toyo Menka's healthy growth, but there were, of course, many others. For example, since Toyo Menka was not involved in the silk trade, because of its agreement with Mitsui Bussan, it was not affected by the dramatic decline of silk prices which began in 1929 in the United States, then the major export market. Since fabric was much more important for Toyo Menka in the 1920s than for Nippon Menka and Gosho (while it was still part of Mitsui Bussan, the cotton department had emphasized all-round service to the cotton textile industry), it was able to earn stable profits from its exports. For Nippon Menka and Gosho, however, raw cotton was the main activity. Furthermore, the fact that Toyo Menka was a subsidiary of Mitsui Bussan and thus a member of the Mitsui zaibatsu pos-. sibly gave it numerous advantages, including the favourable treatment it probably received from the Mitsui Bank.

The troubles Nippon Menka and Gosho faced in raw cotton pushed them to diversify their business.[86] Fabric exports, for example, were given a new impetus. The two companies organized the production of printed cloth, and marketed it actively in China and South-East Asia. When production of rayon increased, they entered into this business and pioneered its exports. Also, they expanded the silk business they had started at Yokohama during the First World War. As a consequence of these diversification efforts, the relative importance of raw cotton declined in the 1920s. Around 1930, at Gosho the share of raw cotton was down to 50 per cent, the remaining 50 per cent being accounted for by silk, fabric, etc. During the 1930s, as rayon and cotton fabric increased in importance, the share of raw cotton probably declined further. As a result, by the mid-1930s, both Nippon Menka and Gosho were not simply importers of raw cotton; they were integrated textile traders.

OTHER TRADING COMPANIES

In the mid-1930s numerous companies were engaged in the export of cotton fabric from Japan. They can be classified into the following four groups according to the commodities in which they specialized in their early years. The first group consists of Nippon Menka, Gosho and several others which began as importers of raw cotton, while the second group is made up of companies which started as dealers of cotton yarn. The most notable among the latter were Maruei, Tazuke, Takemura, Mataichi, Takenaka, Yagi, Toyoshima and Iwata, the so-called Senba Eight (Senba is an area in Osaka where wholesalers are concentrated). The third group consists of Yamaguchi, Tamurakoma, and Itoman, which started as importers of Western fabric, and the textile merchants which had handled traditional (silk and cotton) cloth make up the fourth.[87] Among the largest in the fourth group were Inanishi and Ichida.

Despite the differences in the way in which they started business, all four groups were engaged in fabric exports by the mid-1930s. In the case of the cotton importers, the handling of textile products began as a complementary activity to cotton sales; later when raw cotton became too speculative a business, greater efforts were directed toward fabric sales as a more stable source of profits. The situation was similar for the yarn dealers. Since the yarn price was linked to the cotton price, it fluctuated widely, and as competition became tougher and spinners larger, yarn ceased to be a profitable commodity. The fabric importers, on the other hand, switched to domestic transactions as import substitution began, and as fabric became competitive in the international market, they started exports. Traditional cloth merchants became involved in exports for the same reason. The difference between the third and fourth groups became obscure over time, as the progress of import substitution made the difference between traditional and Western cloth less significant.

The overseas expansion of these smaller trading companies was largely restricted to China and the two Japanese colonies (Taiwan and Korea). Some companies went into South-East Asia, but most left this area to their travelling salesmen, rather than setting up permanent offices. Nearly all offices of Japanese trading companies belonged to large trading companies such as Nippon Menka, Gosho and Toyo Menka. One notable exception was Daido Boeki, the company set up as part of the reorganization of C.Itoh.[88]

There were a number of traders in other textile fields. In silk, such trading companies as Mogi Gomei, Ono Shoten, and Yokohama Kiito had become substantial in size by the late 1910s. In wool, Takashimaya Iida became an important trader. Takashimaya Iida was originally the export department of Takashimaya, a store dealing in kimono cloth. It was later separated out as a trading company (the retail department became the present Takashimaya Department Store).[89] In rayon, the largest trader was Chori, originally a silk trading company which began to handle rayon in the early 1920s, soon after production of that commodity began.[90]

In steel, there were numerous wholesalers.[91] Relatively important ones included Takashimaya Iida, Irimaru Sangyo, Okaya, Morioka, and Kishimoto. Originally, Kishimoto had been an authorized agent of Yahata Steel; it later opted out to market the products of Nippon Kokan. All the other companies had close ties with Yahata Steel, and in 1948 when Yahata appointed eleven companies as primary agents, they were included. Irimaru Sangyo, Okaya, and Morioka were specialized steel dealers, whereas Takashimaya Iida handled many other commodities besides steel (for example, wool). The latter's relationship with Yahata began in the mid-1920s when Yahata succeeded in producing silicon steel with Takashimaya Iida's financial help.

Besides textiles and steel, there were a number of other fields in which trading companies developed. In the field of chemicals, for example, Nagase acted as agent for Union Carbide, Eastman Kodak, and Chemical Industry of Basle (the present Ciba-Geigy). Nagase originated as a dyestuff trader in Kyoto. Involvement with dyestuffs later became the pivot for diversification into chemicals. In the field of paper, Nakai Shoten, which had handled traditional Japanese paper (*washi*) in the late Tokugawa period, began to deal in machine-made paper in the mid-1870s. This company grew as a sales agent for Oji Paper, the largest paper manufacturer in pre-war Japan.[92]

A number of relatively large trading companies disappeared in the 1920s. Mogi Gomei, which was probably the largest among specialized silk traders, went bankrupt soon after the crash of 1920. Takada Shokai, the largest machinery importer, disappeared in 1925. A couple of years later, Suzuki Shoten, which once rivalled Mitsui Bussan in scale, went bankrupt. Furukawa and Kuhara made the trading divisions of their non-ferrous mining companies independent and started foreign trade during the war boom in the second half of the 1910s—by following the move of Mitsubishi which also had non-ferrous mines—but they faced financial disaster several years later.[93] Masuda Boeki, which made a fortune in sugar, grain, and shipping during the war boom, faced a similar fate.

The bankruptcy of small trading companies was not news-worthy and did not receive public attention: nor did the companies which phased out wholesale activities voluntarily receive much attention. There were a number of yarn merchants in Osaka who changed businesses in the 1920s.[94] One company, Naigai Wata, switched from cotton import to textile production in China. This proved to be a wise move for the company, for by pioneering Japanese investment in China, it became an immensely successful textile company.[95] Maruzen, originally a general importer, tried to survive as a specialized importer by concentrating on books and medicine. When even this strategy failed, the company excluded medicine, and became a successful importer and retailer of Western books.[96]

7. COMPARISION

Since the discussion so far has focused on individual companies, it is not clear at this point how they stood in relation to each other. Comparative analysis is not a simple task, since data are inadequate. Usually, sales are taken as the standard for comparison, but, unfortunately, the data on sales are very unsatisfactory. What is available is assembled in Table 3.3.

TABLE 3.3
Sales in the Pre-war Period
(Unit: million yen)

	1904–6	1914–16	1924–6	1934–6	1940
Mitsui Bussan	169	537	1,119	1,689	3,446
Mitsubishi Shoji	–	–	321	863	2,278
Marubeni	*	*	46	137	218
Iwai	10	*	*	200	310
Nissho	–	–	–	85	207

Source: Mitsui Bussan, *Mitsui Bussan Shoshi*, 1951, pp. 143–7; Mitsubishi Shoji, *Ritsugyo Boeki-roku*, 1958, p. 947; Marubeni, *Marubeni Zenshi*, 1977, pp. 212–13; Iwai Sangyo, *Iwai Hyakunen Shi*, 1964, pp. 170 and 362; and Nissho, *Nissho Shiju-nen no Ayumi*, 1968, p. 609.

Note: *indicates that the data is not available.

–indicates that the company did not exist at this point in time.

TABLE 3.4
The Share of Major Trading Companies
in Total Exports and Imports in 1937—1942

Company	Semi-annual Exports and Imports (million yen)	Percentage of Total
Mitsui Bussan	504.9	18.3
Mitsubishi Shoji	283.9	10.3
Toyo Menka	178.8	6.5
Nippon Menka	136.3	4.9
Gosho	109.4	4.0
Iwai	59.0	2.1
Kanematsu	53.1	1.9
Ataka	36.4	1.3
Nissho	32.6	1.2
Naigai Tsusho (Okura Shoji)	32.6	1.2
Asano Bussan	20.7	0.8
Subtotal	1,447.7	52.5
Total Exports and Imports	2,754.3	

Source: Mochikabu Kaisha Seiri Iinkai, Nihon no Zaibatsu to Sono Kaitai, reprint, Hara Shobo, 1973, p. 539.

If one is satisfied with foreign trade figures, a more comprehensive range of data is available for the late 1930s and early 1940s (see Table 3.4). But there are a few problems even with this data. For one thing, it excludes trading companies whose sales were made primarily within Japan (thus, Marubeni does not appear). It also excludes C.Itoh, even though that company's exports and imports were probably only slightly smaller than several of the companies listed in the Table. Furthermore, the period is biased against textile trading companies, since their activities were constrained in various ways by wartime measures.

The availability of data on paid-up capital is most satisfactory, as can be seen from Table 3.5. The major trouble with using paid-up capital as an index for comparison is that its

TABLE 3.5

Paid-up Capital in the Pre-war Period

(Unit: ¥1,000)

	1904–6	1914–16	1924–6	1934–6	1940
Mitsui Bussan	1,000	20,000	100,000	100,000	300,000
Mitsubishi Shoji	—	—	15,000	15,000	100,000
C.Itoh	*	2,000	7,000	7,066	12,500
Marubeni			5,000	8,166	10,000
Iwai	*	2,000	10,000	12,000	15,000
Nissho	—	—	—	3,000	5,000
Okura Shoji	*	4,000	8,000	8,000	10,000
Kanematsu	100	400	5,000	7,000	7,000
Ataka	*	*	3,000	3,850	8,500
Asano Bussan	*	*	1,000	2,500	10,000
Nippon Menka	842	2,000	23,000	6,882	10,575
Toyo Menka	—	—	15,000	18,333	35,000
Gosho	400	958	20,000	15,500	15,500

Source: Mitsui Bussan, *Mitsui Bussan Shoshi*, 1951, pp. 115–22; Mitsubishi Shoji, *Ritsugyo Boeki-roku*, 1958, pp. 3–11; Marubeni, *Marubeni Zenshi*, 1977, pp. 208–11; Itohchu Shoji, *Itohchu Shoji Hyakunen*, 1969, pp. 562–3; Iwai Sangyo, *Iwai Hyakunen Shi*, 1964, pp. 170 and 362; Nissho, *Nissho Shiju-nen no Ayumi*, 1968, p. 609; Watanabe Wataru and Kaneko Fumio, 'Okura Zaibatsu no Kenkyu, No. 6', *Tokyo Keidai Gakkaishi*, July 1978, pp. 28–9; Kanematsu, *Kanematsu Kaiko Rokuju-nen*, 1950, pp. 56, 62, 73, 90, and 136; Ataka Sangyo, *Ataka Sangyo Rokuju-nen Shi*, 1968, pp. 976–9; Asano Bussan, *Eigyo Hokokusho*, various years; Nichimen Jitsugyo, *Nichimen Shichiju-nen Shi*, 1962, pp. 477–83; Toyo Menka, *Tomen Shiju-nen Shi*, 1960, pp. 77, 138, 495, and 499; and Gosho, *Gosho Rokuju-nen Shi*, 1967, pp. 23–5.

Note: *indicates that the data is not available.

—indicates that the company did not exist at this point in time.

significance varied from one company to another. For joint stock companies, paid-up capital was perhaps a significant indicator of the total capital the firm could command, but for family enterprises (and most companies were of this type), it may not have meant much. How much capital such companies could raise often depended more on the backing their owners could give (for example, by giving guarantees).

Despite these problems inherent in deducing from data, by supplementing statistical data with the discussion in the preceding sections, it is possible to draw a rough picture. It is clear, for example, that Mitsui Bussan was the largest trading company in most of the pre-war years. In its first two decades, it faced challenges from other trading companies such as Okura Shoji, but by 1900 it had established supremacy in foreign trade. In the late 1910s, the possibility developed that Nippon Menka, a cotton trader which expanded rapidly during the war boom, might overtake Mitsui Bussan some day, but after the panic of 1920, it dissipated.

During the war boom years in the 1910s, Mitsubishi, Kuhara, and Furukawa made the trading divisions of their mining companies independent and these entered into foreign trade. Kuhara's and Furukawa's trading companies went bankrupt soon after, but Mitsubishi Shoji became a successful company. Despite problems in the 1920s, it developed rapidly in the 1930s with the growth of other Mitsubishi companies in heavy industry, and by the end of that decade, ran a close second to Mitsui Bussan. In 1944, it almost equalled Mitsui Bussan in volume of trade.[97]

Nippon Menka and Gosho were still comparable to Mitsubishi Shoji in size in the mid-1920s, but because the latter grew rapidly in the 1930s while they suffered from financial troubles, they fell well behind. On the other hand, other trading companies grew, and some of them became almost comparable to Nippon Menka and Gosho in size. Toyo Menka fared better than either Nichimen or Gosho, though it also lagged behind Mitsubishi Shoji.

Was there a sogo shosha in the pre-war period? Put another way, was there any company worthy of being called a sogo shosha? Mitsui Bussan and Mitsubishi Shoji could be considered such in the late 1930s. They handled a wide variety of commodities; their networks covered the entire globe; they handled both exports and imports; and their power was large. As shown in Table 3.4, when Toyo Menka's share is included, Mitsui Bussan controlled about a quarter of Japan's foreign trade. Mitsubishi Shoji's share was smaller, yet substantial.

Other trading companies were either too specialized in area

and commodities or too small to be considered sogo shosha. Marubeni was essentially a domestic wholesaler. C.Itoh, Kanematsu, Nippon Menka, Toyo Menka, and Gosho were textile traders. Iwai, Nissho, Okura Shoji, Ataka, and Asano Bussan did not concentrate on any particular commodity, but their size was not large enough to qualify them as general trading companies. In foreign trade, Iwai, largest among the five, accounted for only 2.1 per cent of the total in the period 1937–42.

It is possible to conclude, therefore, that toward the end of the pre-war period, there were two giant trading companies: Mitsui Bussan and Mitsubishi Shoji. The other trading companies in Table 3.4 were noticeable, i.e., not small by pre-war standards, but they were no match for these two. Moreover, Mitsui Bussan and Mitsubishi Shoji were not merely giants within Japan. They had outgrown Jardine Matheson and all other Western trading companies which had dominated Japan's foreign trade in the early Meiji years, and even threatened Western companies' positions in other Asian countries. Thus, by the late 1930s, Mitsubishi Shoji and Mitsui Bussan had become Asia's giants as well.

1. In the early 1940s, Mitsui Bussan compiled a multi-volume history of the company, but it has not been made public. The reason for not publishing it is said to be that since it was prepared to prove to the military how the company had cooperated to promote national interests, it contains passages and data which are embarrassing today.

Mitsui Bunko, a depository of Mitsui documents, which has one set of the multi-volume history, seems to have made it available to a small number of scholars. References cited in the following notes on Mitsui Bussan use it as the major source of information.

Mitsui Bussan published in Japanese *Mitsui Bussan Shoshi* (1951) and *Chosen to Sozo* (1977), but they are too short to cover its one century history. Since the company's history provides various lessons for people interested in trading companies, the company should publish a much more detailed history (which is, at least, comparable with the history of other sogo shosha). In this connection, it is interesting to watch what will result from Mitsubishi Shoji's preparation for its company history which began in early 1980. If it wants to claim social responsibility—a word sogo shosha frequently use nowadays—Mitsubishi Shoji should make serious efforts to make its history comprehensive as well as informative.

2. Iwasaki Hiroyuki, 'Seisho Hogo Seisaku no Seiritsu', *Mitsui Bunko Ronso*, 1967, p. 221.

3. Ibid., p. 219.

4. Ibid., p. 238.

5. Nagai Minoru, *Jijo Masuda Takashi-o Den*, 1939, p. 169.

6. Minomura Seiichiro, *Minomura Rizaemon Den*, 1969, p. 168.

7. Unless specified otherwise, statistical data in this section come from Mitsui Bussan (1951).

8. Matsumoto Hiroshi, 'Nihon Shihon Shugi Kakuritsu-ki ni okeru Mitsui Bussan Kaisha no Hatten', *Mitsui Bunko Ronso*, 1973, p. 123.

9. Mitsui Bussan (1977), p. 115.

10. Yamaguchi Kazuo (ed.), *Nihon Sangyo Kin'yu-shi Kenkyu: Boseki Kin'yu-hen*, Tokyo Daigaku Shuppan-kai, 1970, p. 162.

11. Matsumoto, p. 113.

12. Ibid., p. 173.

13. Matsumoto Hiroshi, 'Sekitan Hanbai Puru-sei no Seiritsu to sono Keika', *Mitsui Bunko Ronso*, 1977, p. 378.

14. Nagai, p. 190.

15. Ibid., p. 134.

16. Ibid., p. 181.

17. Matsumoto (1973), p. 191.

18. Yamaguchi (ed.), p. 223.

19. Osaka Boseki had previously obtained the bulk of its supply from the Kochi area near Osaka. See Takamura Naosuke, *Nihon Boseki-shi Josetsu*, Hanawa Shobo, 1971, Vol. 1, p. 93.

20. The three companies were Kanegafuchi Boseki, Miike Boseki, and Mie Boseki. Yamaguchi (ed.), p. 161.

21. Yamamoto Jotaro-o Denki Hensan-kai, *Yamamoto Jotoro-o Denki*, 1942, p. 131. Hereafter referred to as *Yamamoto Jotaro*.

22. Yamaguchi (ed.), p. 168.

23. Matsumoto (1973), p. 159.

24. Togai Yoshio, *Mitsui Bussan Kaisha no Keiei-shi teki Kenkyu*, Toyo Keizai Shinpo-sha, 1974, p. 81.

25. *Yamamoto Jotaro*, p. 116.

26. Yamaguchi (ed.), p. 162.

27. Togai, p. 95.

28. Matsumoto (1973), p. 114.

29. Ibid., p. 114; and Matsumoto (1977), p. 378.

30. Togai, p. 95.

31. Matsumoto (1977), p. 378.

32. Togai, p. 95.

33. Yamaguchi (ed.), p. 223.

34. Ibid., p. 162.

35. Matsumoto (1977), p. 378.

36. Matsumoto (1973), p. 172.

37. For the history of Siber, Wolff & Co., see Togai Yoshio, 'Kiito Shoken o Meguru Naigaisho no Kakuchiku', *Senshu Daigaku Shakai Kagaku Kenkyusho Geppo*, No. 66 (1969).

38. The Mitsui family's major interests in the early Meiji era lay in the Mitsui Bank, and it took precautions to prevent the failure of Mitsui Bussan from affecting the bank. For example, the bank gave a ¥50,000 line of credit, but was not held responsible for any indebtedness in the case of Mitsui Bussan's failure. The line of credit, together with the small assets held by two sons of the Mitsui family, which did not amount to much (since they were not first sons) was the extent of the wealth the Mitsui family pledged to Mitsui Bussan.

39. Mitsui Ginko, *Mitsui Ginko Hyakunen no Ayumi*, 1976, various pages.

40. Nagai, p. 287.

41. Tamaki Hajime, *Nihon Zaibatsu-shi*, Shakai Shiso-sha, 1976, p. 130.

42. Chucho-kai Nakamigawa Sensei Denki Hensan-Iin, *Nakamigawa Sensei Den*, 1939, p. 196.

43. Tamaki, p. 129.

44. The basic source of data in this section on Mitsubishi Shoji is Mitsubishi Shoji, *Ritsugyo Boeki-roku*, 1958. One major problem with using this source is that although it is not confidential, it is difficult to obtain. The public relations office of the Tokyo headquarters has a copy. Mishima Yasuo used this source in 'Sekitan Yushutsu Shosha kara Sogo Shosha e: Mitsubishi Shoji' in Miyamoto Mataji *et al.* (eds.), *Sogo Shosha no Keiei-shi*, Toyo Keizai Shinpo-sha, 1976.

In this section, references are given only for sources other than *Ritsugyo Boeki-roku*.

45. The chronological table in Mitsubishi Sogyo Hyakunen Kinen Jigyo Iinkai, *Mitsubishi no Hyakunen*, 1970, takes the year 1870 as the founding year of Mitsubishi. This source is hereafter cited as *Mitsubishi Hyakunen*.

46. Iwasaki Koyata Den Hensan Iinkai, *Iwasaki Koyata Den*, 1957, pp. 23—7: hereafter, cited as *Koyata Den*.

47. The Iwasaki family remained as a major shareholder and received dividends (large dividends during war boom years), but lost direct con-

trol over its management. Therefore, it was no longer a Mitsubishi company. Influence was, however, sometimes exerted for the purpose of Mitsubishi's new businesses (for example, obtaining orders for shipbuilding).

48. Ibid., pp. 174—5.

49. Yamada Kiyoshi, *Mitsubishi no Hito to Keiei*, Kigyo Bunka-sha, 1974, p. 114.

50. *Mitsubishi Hyakunen*, p. 20.

51. Ibid., p. 116.

52. *Koyata Den*, pp. 214—17.

53. Ibid., p. 240.

54. Ibid., pp. 26—70.

55. Ibid., p. 180.

56. Ibid., p. 255.

57. Ibid., p. 254.

58. Ibid., p. 259.

59. For example, Mitsubishi Shoji became the exclusive agent of Nisshin Flour Mill, Iwaki Cement, Nichiro Gyogyo, Taihei Gyogyo, and Daito Shokuhin. For a list of companies for which Mitsubishi Shoji held exclusive agency rights, see Mishima, p. 138.

60. This company, Nippon Kiito Kaisha, became one of Mitsubishi Shoji's many subsidiaries. It is difficult to make a comprehensive list of subsidiaries and affiliated companies from *Ritsugyo Boeki-roku*, for it is not often stated whether or not close relations (such as agency rights) with companies were established through equity holding, or in the event that equity was acquired, how long it was held (or when it was disposed of). Mishima identifies some of the companies in which Mitsubishi Shoji held equity, but the list is far from complete. See Mishima, pp. 139—40.

61. The basic sources of data in this section are Itohchu Shoji, *Itohchu Shoji Hyakunen*, 1969 and Marubeni, *Marubeni Zenshi*, 1977. References are given only for other sources.

62. In the early 1910s, 'C.Itoh' became the official English name of the company. The normal spelling of the family name is 'Ito', but the company decided to adopt 'Itoh' to emphasize the long 'o'. See Itohchu Shoji, *Itoh Chubei-o Kaiso-roku*, 1974, p. 337.

63. Ibid., pp. 14—18.

64. The English name of Marubeni remained as Itohchu Shoten until 1929.

65. Itohchu Shoji (1974), p. 208.

66. This section is based on Iwai Sangyo, *Iwai Hyakunen Shi*, 1964.

67. The basic source of data in this section is Nissho, *Nissho Shijunen no Ayumi*, 1968. References are given only for other sources.

68. Quoted in Nissho, p. 283.

69. Katsura Yoshio, 'Sangyo Kigyo Ikusei to Shosha—Suzuki Shoten', in Miyamoto Mataji *et al.* (eds.), pp. 197—200.

70. Ibid., pp. 202—10.

71. Ibid., p. 214.

72. Ibid., p. 217.

73. Ibid., p. 221.

74. The following discussion on Kanematsu is based on Kanematsu, *Kanematsu Kaiko Rokuju-nen*, 1950.

75. The following discussion on Ataka is based on Ataka Sangyo, *Ataka Sangyo Rokuju-nen Shi*, 1968.

76. The basic source of information on the Okura zaibatsu and Okura Shoji is Watanabe Wataru *et al.*, 'Okura Zaibatsu no Kenkyu', *Tokyo Keidai Gakkaishi*, 6 parts, 1976—8.

77. The following discussion on Asano Bussan is based on the handwritten memoirs of Oda Mitsuji, one-time managing director of Asano Bussan, available at the archives section of Marubeni.

78. The raw cotton trade in the pre-war period is discussed in detail in Nihon Menka Kyokai, *Menka Hyakunen*, 2 vols., 1967.

79. Toyo Menka, *Tomen Shiju-nen Shi*, 1960, and Ogino Chuzaburo (ed.), *Kodama Ichizo Den*, 1934, are the two major sources of data on Toyo Menka in the pre-war period.

80. Nippon Menka, *Nippon Menka Kabushiki Kaisha Goju-nen Shi*, 1937, and *Kita Matazo-kun Den*, 1933 are the two major sources of data on Nippon Menka in the pre-war period.

81. Gosho, *Gosho Rokuju-nen Shi*, 1967, is the major source of data on Gosho in the pre-war period.

82. There are numerous sources describing the difficulties cotton traders faced in the 1920s. For example, see Matsui Kiyoshi, *Kindai Nippon Boeki-shi*, Yuhikaku, 1959, Vol. 3, p. 295.

83. This phenomenon is pointed out also by a foreign observer. See British Economic Mission to the Far East, *Report of the Cotton Mission*, 1931, p. 17.

84. Suzuki Shigemitsu, a former president of Toyo Menka, recalls this in Nihon Menka Kyokai, p. 680.

85. This paragraph is based on an interview with Yajima Saburo, a former managing director of Toyo Menka. The interview took place in June 1980.

86. This paragraph is based on interviews with Yajima Saburo of Toyo Menka; Kanbara Takeo, a former president of Gosho; and Fukui Keizo, a former president of Nichimen. The interview with Kanbara took place in April 1980 and that with Fukui in February 1980.

87. Out of the Senba Eight, Yagi Shoten is the only company

which has published a company history. See Yagi Shoten, *Sogyo Hachiju-nen Shi*, 1972. For the evolution of companies in the third category, see Itoman, *Itoman Goju-nen Shi*, 1933; and Yamaguchi Gen, *Yamaguchi Gen Hachiju-nen Shi*, 1965. Tamurakoma is preparing a company history at present. Its pre-war history is available in handwritten form. For the evolution of Ichida and Inanishi, companies in the fourth category, see Ichida, *Kurieito Hyakunen*, 1974; and Inanishi, *Kaikoroku*, 1927.

88. The overseas activities of smaller trading companies are described in Nihon Menshifu Yushutsu Kumiai, *Nihon Mengyo Boeki Shoshi*, 1957. For Daido, see Marubeni, *Marubeni Zenshi*, pp. 108–33.

89. For the pre-war history of Takashimaya Iida, see Takashimaya Iida, *20-shunen Kinen Takashimaya Iida*, 1936.

90. Chori's pre-war history is briefly described by Ohashi Riichiro, a former president of the company, in *Senba Konjaku Monogatari*, 1967, pp. 96–105.

91. Sato Noboru, *Nihon Tekko Hanbai-shi*, Osaka, Kyodo Shinbun-sha, 1978, is, at present, the only major source of data on steel trading companies in the pre-war period.

92. For the pre-war history of Nakai Shoten, see Nihon Kami Parupu Shoji, *Hyakusanju-nen Shi*, 1975.

93. For Furukawa Shoji, see Furukawa Kogyo, *Kogyo Hyakunen Shi*, 1976; and Furukawa Toranosuke-kun Denki Hensan-kai, *Furukawa Toranosuke-kun Den*, 1953; and for Kuhara Shoji, Kuhara Fusanosuke-o Denki Hensan-kai, *Kuhara Fusanosuke*, 1970.

94. Taniguchi Kaichiro, *Ito Hitosuji*, 1960, p. 95.

95. Naigai Wata, *Naigai Wata Kabushiki Kaisha Goju-nen Shi*, 1937, various pages.

96. Maruzen, *Maruzen Shashi*, 1951, various pages.

97. Mitsui Bussan, *The 100 Year History of Mitsui & Co., Ltd., 1876–1976*, 1977, p. 88.

4

Historical Evolution: The Post-war Period

1. THE ORDEAL

REGULATIONS

THE period from the mid-1930s to the early 1950s covers what may be termed the 'abnormal' years of Japan's modern history. In the early 1930s, Japan stepped up preparation for war and started imposing regulations on the economy. After 1937 when the China Incident occurred, regulations became so pervasive that the economy became virtually a command economy. This remained the basic economic system of Japan during the Pacific War (December 1941–August 1945) and the first half of the Occupation period (September 1945–March 1952).

The China Incident dragged on, contrary to the expectation of the Japanese military, and led to the Pacific War in December 1941. In the first several months of the war, Japan did well and brought all South-East Asia under its control, but from the time of the Midway naval battle in mid-1942, the tide turned against Japan. The war continued for another few years, but in August 1945, Japan finally surrendered. This defeat brought about fundamental changes in Japan's politics, economy and society, implemented by the Allied Powers which occupied the country for several years.

The political events outlined above had various adverse effects on trading companies. Commerce thrives when market forces are given free play, but when price and output are regulated, it languishes. For about ten years from the late 1930s, the prices of most manufactured goods were regulated; the only function left in Japan for trading companies was to collect and distribute goods according to the instructions of the government. In the area of foreign trade, there was more freedom of operation, even though trade was restricted to China and South-East Asia, the region Japan controlled. Still, however, the requirements of the military weighed heavily on trading companies. With Japan's defeat in the war, even their slight freedom in foreign trade was lost and the activities of trading companies were confined to the home market.

This does not mean, however, that there was no foreign trade in early post-war Japan. Export and import continued, though the volume was substantially lower than in the pre-war period; and now these activities were undertaken by the General Headquarters (GHQ) of the Supreme Commander of the Allied Powers. The GHQ decided what was to be imported and exported, and used a Japanese government agency (Foreign Trade Agency) as its administrative body. Japanese trading companies acted as subcontractors for this agency.[1]

Government regulations were gradually lifted during the Occupation period. First, in August 1947 it became possible to sell some goods to foreign buyers in Japan or importers abroad by correspondence. At this time, the number of foreign buyers and the length of their stay in Japan was regulated, but in the next two years, virtually all restrictions were removed. Then in early 1949, regulations on the export prices of textile goods, the major export in the early post-war years, were removed. At this time, however, it was still not permissible for Japanese traders to go abroad. After this became possible in mid-1949, traders went first to the United States, Pakistan, South America, Africa, and Thailand, where no strong anti-Japanese feeling remained.[2]

Price regulations on domestic trade were also removed as Japanese industrial production recovered, but this came later than the removal of regulations on export. Even around March 1949, prices in the black market were about three times as high as official prices. In the next one-year period, however, industrial production made a quick recovery, and the ratio of black market to official prices declined. Around March 1950, the official prices of some goods became higher than their black market prices, and for many goods, price regulations became unnecessary. The last commodity left was cotton yarn, the regulation on which was lifted in July 1951.[3]

By mid-1950, most price regulations had been lifted and domestic trade had become free, but regulations on import remained because of the shortage of foreign exchange. In 1950, only 10 to 20 per cent of import was free. In the following several years, import became easier for manufacturers who contributed to export directly or indirectly, but even as of 1959, 70 per cent of imports required government approval.[4] It was not until the early 1960s that import liberalization made substantial progress. By the mid-1960s, government regulations on import had been virtually lifted, but this was fifteen years later than the decontrol of export and domestic trade.

THE WEAKENED POSITION OF TRADING COMPANIES

Japan's defeat in the Pacific War had one particularly adverse effect on trading companies. Large companies were heavily involved in foreign trade (in China and South-East Asia during the war), and were hit hard when with the defeat, Japan's assets abroad were confiscated. For example, Nichimen (Nippon Menka) lost assets abroad valued at 36 million yen (its paid-up capital at this time was 30 million yen).[5] Of course, trading companies were not alone in suffering from confiscation of overseas assets. Naigai Wata, which began as an importer of raw cotton in the middle of the Meiji era and later switched to textile production, had almost all of its assets in China. The loss of its overseas assets was too great for it to make a comeback in the post-war period. Similarly, Okura was heavily involved in China before and during the war, and its post-war recovery was greatly affected by loss of assets there. There were many other manufacturers and investors who were affected by the loss of overseas assets. In general, however, losses were heaviest for major trading companies.

The position of trading companies *vis-à-vis* manufacturing companies became weak in the post-war years. This was a result of the fact that the government emphasized production of heavy industry and left hardly any freedom for trading companies during the war, and then in the early post-war period, made the recovery of industrial production its foremost objective and channelled its investment funds to industrial enterprises. Trading companies were left in the cold. At the same time, the scarcity of goods made the position of trading companies weak, whereas manufacturers did not face any marketing problems under such circumstances. Anything produced could be sold, so no great skill was required in finding customers, the major role of trading companies. With their function thus reduced, trading companies often had to resort to obsequious behaviour in order to obtain the goods they wanted to handle.

THE TWO GIANTS GO

The dissolution of the zaibatsu was a major post-war institutional reform. The zaibatsu had wielded too much economic power in the pre-war period, so they had to be crushed as part of economic democratization. The zaibatsu had collaborated with the military before and during the war, for which they had to be punished. The zaibatsu had had too strong an influence on politics before the war; for political democracy to be established, they had to be destroyed. Such seems to have been the reasoning of the GHQ which ordered the dissolution of the zaibatsu. The holding companies of the Yasuda, Mitsubishi, and Mitsui zaibatsu were dissolved in 1946.

The dissolution of Mitsubishi Shoji and Mitsui Bussan is related to, but somewhat different from, the dissolution of the zaibatsu. What the zaibatsu dissolution accomplished was to abolish the non-operating holding companies of the zaibatsu.

Operating companies under them, such as Mitsubishi Shoji and Mitsui Bussan, became independent as a consequence. Yet, one problem remained: that is, these independent companies were holding companies in their own right, and were so designated in December 1946. Still, if the fact that they were holding companies were the only reason for their dissolution, they need not have been dissolved; it would have been enough to divest them of their industrial holdings.

Another possible reason for their dissolution is that they were dominant in foreign trade. Several months after these two giant companies were dissolved, the Elimination of Excessive Concentration of Economic Power Law was passed, and about a dozen large manufacturing companies were ordered to split. Yet, the divisions required by law were nowhere near as drastic as in the case of Mitsubishi Shoji and Mitsui Bussan. The manufacturing companies were split into at most several companies. Mitsubishi Shoji and Mitsui Bussan, on the other hand, were shattered: Mitsui Bussan was split into 180—250 companies, Mitsubishi Shoji into around 140 companies.[6]

The order of July 1947 to Mitsubishi Shoji and Mitsui Bussan came, according to Tabe Bunichiro, a former president of Mitsubishi Shoji, 'like a bolt out of the blue'.[7] They were discussing with the GHQ a plan to split their companies (not nearly as drastically as was ordered), but had not received any indication that a dissolution order would be forthcoming. In fact, just before the order was issued, Mitsui Bussan had proposed a plan to split the company into about ten smaller companies, and had received a favourable response.[8] Then, for reasons it did not explain at the time, the GHQ chose to destroy the two companies.

The timing for the GHQ order can be explained. A month later, private foreign trade began on a limited basis. The dissolution of these two dominant foreign trading companies had to be implemented before private trade began, if confusion was to be avoided.[9] Still, it is not clear why the order had to be so drastic. Mizukami Tatsuzo, a former president of Mitsui Bussan, suggests the following two reasons.[10] First, the Allied

Powers wanted to have revenge on Mitsubishi Shoji and Mitsui Bussan because they saw them as collaborators of the military in Japan and abroad. Second, Western trading companies, British in particular, which had had humiliating experiences in the pre-war period, wanted to destroy their competitors.

The dissolution of the zaibatsu had effects on other trading companies. Besides the four major zaibatsu (Mitsui, Mitsubishi, Sumitomo, and Yasuda), there were many other less important zaibatsu which were also ordered to dissolve. Their trading companies became independent, but they had to carry on business without the great support of the former zaibatsu companies in the manufacturing industry. For example, Asano Bussan could not expect much support from former Asano companies. For companies such as Iwai, which were trading as well as holding companies, the dissolution of the zaibatsu meant the loss of manufacturing companies.

THE KOREAN WAR BOOM AND ITS AFTERMATH

The Korean War brought temporary prosperity to trading companies. For example, Kanematsu's annual sales increased from about 15 billion yen before the war boom, to about 60 billion.[11] At the same time, Kanematsu made enormous profits and raised its capital from 50 million yen to 80 million yen in January 1951, and to 300 million yen several months later. Many other trading companies had similar experiences.

The boom period seemed identical to that during the First World War. After having weathered many difficult years, traders became intoxicated with the boom and went wild in speculation. They seemed to have forgotten the lessons of the panic which followed the First World War boom. The crash came soon after the armistice was signed in mid-1951.

With Mitsubishi Shoji and Mitsui Bussan gone, C.Itoh, Marubeni, Gosho, Toyo Menka, and Nichimen formed the top strata. Behind them were other Osaka-based companies strong in textiles, such as Kanematsu, Maruei, Tazuke, and Tamurakoma. Takashimaya Iida, a Tokyo-based company strong in steel and wool in the pre-war period, made large profits by handling the so called 'three new products': soybeans, rubber, and leather. These companies made enormous profits by undertaking stock purchase and short sales during the boom, but when the panic came, they were hit.

Although losses were large for these companies, exact amounts are not known. According to one estimate, Toyo Menka, Tamurakoma, Takashimaya Iida, and Daiichi Tsusho (an offspring of Mitsui Bussan) lost somewhere between 2 and 3 billion yen, whereas Marubeni, Gosho, Maruei, Tazuke, and Kanematsu lost between 1 and 2 billion yen. (The losses of C.Itoh are not estimated.[12]) These losses were incurred at a time when the largest paid-up capital was 300 million yen. Thus, for many companies, losses were several times the amount of paid-up capital.

Not all trading companies suffered large losses. Iwai, Nissho, Ataka, and other trading companies whose main business was in steel, machinery, or chemicals—commodities which were not subject to speculation and did not exhibit wide fluctuations in price—experienced neither extremely large profits during the boom, nor large losses after the panic. They adhered primarily to commission business.

2. TOWARDS GREATER CONCENTRATION

THE AGE OF ATOMISTIC COMPETITION

The dissolution of Mitsui Bussan and Mitsubishi Shoji fragmented the trading sector of the Japanese economy. How various trading companies stood in relation to each other in the next few years is not known. Since this was a period when much money was made on the black market, it is likely that small, aggressive companies (either non-existent or relatively unknown today) made large profits, whereas the large prewar companies worried about government reprisal were unable to take advantage of the situation fully. In fact, a few Mitsubishi and Mitsui offsprings, companies which would later play an important role in re-grouping, had to borrow money from black marketeers in this early post-war period.[13]

The chaotic situation had come to an end by early 1950, but even then nearly two dozen companies were competing for supremacy. For a time, the so-called 'Five Cotton Traders of the Kansai Area' (C.Itoh, Marubeni, Gosho, Toyo Menka, and Nichimen) formed the top group. Closely following them were Kanematsu, Mataichi, Maruei, Itoman, Nissho, Ataka, Iwai, and Nippon Kensetsu (the predecessor of Sumitomo Shoji). Among major Mitsui offsprings challenging the 'Five Cotton Traders', were Daiichi Bussan, Nippon Kikai Boeki, Muromachi Bussan, and Daiichi Tsusho, and among Mitsubishi offsprings, Miyako Shoji, Santo Shoji, Kyowa Koeki, Taihei Shoko, Meiko Shoji, and Marunouchi Shoji.

At this time, C.Itoh was Japan's leading company. After the Korean War boom, former Mitsui and Mitsubishi companies rose rapidly, but C.Itoh managed to occupy the leading position until 1955. This was quite a change from the pre-war period, when the top trader was consistently Mitsui Bussan. Closely following C.Itoh was its sister company, Marubeni. In foreign trade, Marubeni's share was smaller than Kanematsu, Nichimen, and Tomen's (see Table 4.1), but the mere fact that it had become one of the leading traders in the post-war period was surprising because the company had been basically a domestic trader in the pre-war period. The rise of Kanematsu was also somewhat surprising—it had played an important role in the trade with Australia in the pre-war period but had never been a leading trader.

In the early post-war years, Osaka-based textile traders had two advantages. One was that since they were dealing with soft goods (textiles, food, etc.), their relations with the military before the war had been limited. Therefore, they did not have to face retribution meted out by the Allied Powers after the war. They were even promoted as substitutes to fill the vacuum created by the disappearance of the two 'obnoxious' companies, Mitsubishi Shoji and Mitsui Bussan. Also important in their rise was the fact that the products in which they specialized, namely textiles, spearheaded industrialization in the early post-war years. Abroad, textiles were the only major

TABLE 4.1

The Share of the Top Ten Trading
Companies in Foreign Trade in the 1950s

1951 Financial Year		1952 Financial Year		1958 Financial Year	
Company Name	Percentage of Total	Company Name	Percentage of Total	Company Name	Percentage of Total
C.Itoh	4.7	C.Itoh	4.6	Mitsubishi Shoji	9.9
Nichimen (Nippon Menka)	4.3	Kanematsu	4.4	Mitsui Bussan	8.1
Toyo Menka	4.0	Nichimen (Nippon Menka)	4.3	Marubeni	6.9
Marubeni	4.0	Toyo Menka	3.7	Nichimen (Nippon Menka)	6.0
Kanematsu	3.1	Marubeni	3.6	C.Itoh	5.4
Gosho	3.0	Fuji Shoji	3.3	Toyo Menka	3.9
Daiichi Bussan	2.2	Daiichi Bussan	3.3	Nissho	3.0
Iwai	2.0	Daiichi Tsusho	2.7	Kanematsu	2.9
Nissho	1.9	Gosho	2.5	Gosho	2.5
Takashimaya Iida	1.3	Tokyo Boeki	2.4	Kinoshita Shoten	2.0
Subtotal	30.5		34.8		50.6

Source: Fair Trade Commission.

product the Japanese economy could supply at competitive prices. In Japan, there was a large pent-up demand for textiles because production had been neglected during the war.

The effect of the dissolution of Mitsubishi Shoji and Mitsui Bussan is reflected in the decline in the share of the top ten companies in foreign trade (see Table 4.1). In the late 1930s, their share was slightly over 50 per cent, but after Mitsui Bussan and Mitsubishi Shoji were eliminated, the share declined substantially. In 1951, it was as low as 30 per cent and in 1952, 35 per cent. During the Korean War boom (from mid-1950 to mid-1951), the share seems to have been even smaller, reflecting the fact that textile and other soft goods traders (who do not appear in Table 4.1) were very active. After the panic, the trade volume of these traders declined because they faced serious financial problems.

GOVERNMENT POLICY

In the immediate post-war period, because the increase of industrial production was its most urgent task, the Japanese government neglected trading companies. When goods were scarce, it could not afford to pay much attention to marketing problems. As industrial production recovered and basic consumer needs were satisfied, different problems emerged. One problem was how to increase export. Although industrial production recovered to the pre-war level in the early 1950s, export did not, for the Chinese market, which had been the most important in the pre-war period, was lost because of the Communist revolution. Also, silk, a major export before the war, was in no great demand because nylon had appeared as a substitute. It was an urgent problem for the Japanese government to increase export, not so much for employment as for the import of resources and technology—the two basic ingredients of post-war Japanese growth.

Belatedly, the government began to pay attention to the problems of trading companies.[14] After Mitsui Bussan and Mitsubishi Shoji were shattered, too many small companies remained. This may have seemed an ideal situation from the point of view of the democratically minded GHQ authorities, but for the Japanese government, which preferred order, the situation was not desirable. The government felt that something had to be done to bring order to the trading community, but was constrained by the institution of political democracy. In short, the government was not free to intervene at will in economic matters.

Ichimada Naoto, at various times Governor of the Bank of Japan, Finance Minister, and Minister of International Trade and Industry, was an ideologue of the government's reorganization plan. He thought that the ideal trade set-up would include one Mitsubishi company, one Mitsui company, and one or two Osaka-based companies.[15] As he saw it, three to four companies were enough to handle most of Japan's foreign trade requirements, and he was willing to use all the power he could command to effect such a plan.

Ichimada's chance to act came after the Korean War boom. Many Osaka-based textile traders lost heavily in the panic, and were not able to survive without external aid. The 'Five Cotton Traders of the Kansai Area', the Senba Eight, and other textile traders hoped that the Bank of Japan would make special relief loans. The government, of course, could not allow all those trading companies to disappear (since it would cause a crisis in the Kansai economy), but at the same time, it did not want to help all of them. Ichimada apparently decided to give aid to large textile trading companies and let the others fade away.[16]

The Bank of Japan rarely surfaced in the affairs of trading companies, but below the surface seems to have played an important role in their reorganization. Companies selected to remain were given help, and the others left with little or no support. When financial problems became the bottle-neck in mergers, the Bank of Japan seems to have promised certain aid to banks which would assume losses and facilitate mergers. This was apparently the case when Marubeni received the aid of the Fuji Bank in its merger with Takashimaya Iida, a company severely hit by the panic.

The Ministry of International Trade and Industry (MITI) played a different role. In the case of import, for which it acted as a window, MITI chose its agents from among the large trading companies (for example, in the trade with Turkey, the import of raw cotton from Mexico, and the import of rice from Korea).[17] The effect of MITI's policy was felt more directly when trading companies applied for foreign exchanges to establish offices abroad. MITI acted on the principle that too many overseas offices had been established in some countries and that this had been harmful to national interests. Around 1954, there were 60 to 70 Japanese traders in Argentina, and over 20 offices in Calcutta and Bombay.[18] These numbers were considerably higher than in the pre-war period, while the volume of trade was down to about half. MITI did not want this situation to be repeated in other countries, and therefore restricted the number of foreign offices. As might be expected, it favoured large companies in granting permissions.[19]

As general measures to promote trading companies, the government took several actions.[20] For instance, from the mid-1950s, foreign exchange, which had previously been allocated exclusively to manufacturers, was also allocated to trading companies, which enabled them to take initiatives in import. Also, those which exported and earned foreign exchange were allowed to use part of it for import and foreign offices. As a measure to promote export, tax laws were changed so that trading companies could also benefit from incentives (this measure had been restricted to manufacturers before). Furthermore, the government eased import finance by lengthening usance.

It should be pointed out at this point that these measures undoubtedly promoted trading companies, but were not designed to put trading companies in an advantageous position *vis-à-vis* manufacturing companies. They simply rectified the situation in which manufacturers alone benefited, and made it possible for trading companies to receive some of the benefits which had been formerly denied them. The government still gave more assistance to industry than to trade, but it deserves some credit for recognizing the need to create strong trading companies to facilitate Japan's industrial growth.

THEY RETURNED LIKE A PHOENIX

The disappearance of Mitsui Bussan and Mitsubishi Shoji from the trading scene was only temporary. The present Mitsubishi Shoji was born in 1954, and the present Mitsui Bussan in 1959. In a way, they are the phoenix of post-war Japan—once destroyed by the cursing fire of the GHQ, they re-emerged from its ashes with renewed youth, and are now living another cycle of years.

The rebirth of Mitsubishi Shoji went fairly smoothly. After all business activities of the former Mitsubishi Shoji were suspended in July 1947, it remained as a liquidation company (in order to take care of the assets and liabilities of the former Mitsubishi Shoji) and retained several former employees. Since it did not have any revenue, in 1950, after obtaining approval from the government (to be more precise, the Holding Company Liquidation Commission), it set up a company called Kowa Jitsugyo to engage in warehousing and real estate. In the meantime, the company name and its 'three diamond' trade mark were protected by the liquidation company.[21] Then in 1952, after the San Francisco Peace Treaty was signed and Japan regained sovereignty, the government lifted the ban on the use of former zaibatsu names, so Kowa Jitsugyo changed its name to Mitsubishi Shoji (see Figure 4.1). At this time, it was not engaged in trading.

By 1950, about a dozen companies had emerged as major Mitsubishi offsprings. Some grew on their own, others by merger. In 1952, three important mergers took place: Kyowa Koeki took the initiative to create Tozai Koeki; Taihei Shoko to create Tokyo Boeki; and Kyokuto Shoji to create Fuji Shoji. Among the three, Fuji Shoji was the largest (closely following the top five Osaka-based textile traders), but there was no great difference in size among the three. Furthermore, since these companies were not greatly affected by the crash

FIGURE 4.1
The Rebirth of Mitsubishi Shoji

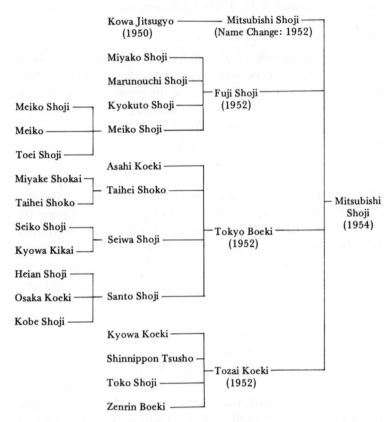

Source: Mitsubishi Shoji, *Mitsubishi Shoji, Sono Ayumi: 20-shunen Kinen-go*, 1974, p. 22.

after the Korean War boom, none of them suffered major financial losses, one difficult problem, for example, for Mitsui Bussan.

By the end of 1952, a blueprint had been made by former Mitsubishi companies (including former Mitsubishi manufacturers and the Mitsubishi Bank) to restore Mitsubishi Shoji.[22] The plan was to merge the three trading companies with

Kowa Jitsugyo, which had assumed the name of Mitsubishi Shoji but was willing to relinquish it at an opportune time. The similarity of the three companies in size and financial condition, the strong backing of former Mitsubishi manufacturers and the Mitsubishi Bank, the *esprit de corps* which had been nurtured at Mitsubishi Shoji before the war—all these augured well for the grand merger.

Still, it took a little over a year for the merger to take place.[23] The three companies had common roots, but for several years had been separate and pursued different objectives. Also, their top executives were concerned about protecting the interests of their stockholders and employees as well as their vested interests. These differences were smoothed out during 1953, and in January 1954, the decision to merge was finalized. Several months later, the present Mitsubishi Shoji was born, and it soon became Japan's leading trading company.

The rebirth of Mitsui Bussan occurred after prolonged throes and was marred by some desertions.[24] As in the case of Mitsubishi Shoji, the company name and trade mark were protected by the liquidation company and later handed over to a warehousing and real estate company (Nitto Soko Tatemono), with the understanding that they would be protected until a possible grand merger in the future. But *esprit de corps* was weak in Mitsui Bussan, where before the war individual initiative had been encouraged and rivalries among its traders created. Muromachi Bussan, born from the metals department of Mitsui Bussan, merged the warehousing and real estate company and changed its name to Mitsui Bussan. This complicated the situation, for some other major Mitsui offsprings, such as Daiichi Tsusho and Daiichi Bussan, were bigger and more diversified than the new Mitsui Bussan, and had no intention of being merged.

The driving force of the grand merger was Daiichi Bussan. This company was set up by people in the construction material section of the general merchandise department in Mitsui Bussan, soon after its dissolution. Mizukami Tatsuzo was asked to head the company, but he brought in Niizeki Yasutaro as president, and the company grew rapidly in subsequent years by the team-work of these two men. Daiichi Bussan was innovative particularly in the field of finance. For example, it went public at an early stage and raised capital in the stock market. It also succeeded in introducing foreign capital. By 1950, its paid-up capital had reached 200 million yen, one of the highest at the time.

Daiichi Bussan's major business was construction materials at first, but around the time of the Korean War boom, non-ferrous metals had emerged as its most important product. The crash after the boom affected the company somewhat, but benefiting from experience gained before the war, it sensed a danger in the boom, and rid itself of all stocks before the crash came. Thus, the company was in good financial position after the crash, and merged other Mitsui offsprings which were affected by the crash. In 1953, it merged Goyo Boeki, in 1954, Mitsui Mokuzai, and in 1955, Nippon Kikai Boeki and Daiichi Tsusho (see Figure 4.2). The mergers of 1955 were particularly important, since at that time, the major Mitsui offspring were Daiichi Tsusho, Nippon Kikai Boeki, Daiichi Bussan and Muromachi Bussan (which had changed its name to Mitsui Bussan). By merging Nippon Kikai Boeki and Daiichi Tsusho, Daiichi Bussan lacked only Muromachi Bussan to complete a grand merger. However, Muromachi Bussan, essentially a steel trader, was in a sound financial position, and had no intention of being merged. Rather, it wanted to be the successor of the former Mitsui Bussan by merging Daiichi Bussan. So, Daiichi Bussan, which was considerably larger than Muromachi Bussan and widely considered to be the successor of the former Mitsui Bussan, decided to consolidate its position by merging other Mitsui offsprings. In 1957, it merged Kokusai Bussan, and in 1958, Taiyo and Toho Bussan. In the meantime, Muromachi Bussan merged Nagoya Koeki, but this did not change the fact that it was still the much smaller company.

The grand merger finally took place in 1959. Muromachi Bussan was affected by the 1958 recession, and began to face

FIGURE 4.2
The Dissolution and Rebirth of Mitsui Bussan

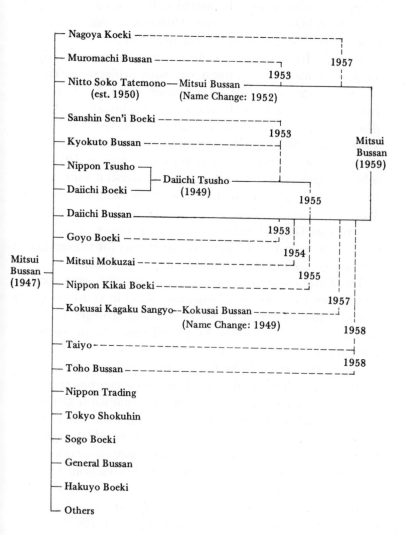

some financial problems. Added to this was the pressure from other Mitsui companies which began to feel the need for re-grouping in the face of Mitsubishi's carefully orchestrated group activities in new industrial fields. Faced with such financial problems and pressure, Muromachi Bussan could no longer resist the merger with Daiichi Bussan.

Several Mitsui offsprings did not join the merger. Nippon Trading, whose main business was with Bridgestone Tire, remained independent for several more years. Hakuyo Boeki (which was headed by Miyazaki Kiyoshi, president of Mitsui Bussan at the time of dissolution) was absorbed by Nissho in 1956, while Sogo Boeki, strong in the trade with socialist countries, was absorbed by Sumitomo Shoji in 1970. Two other offsprings, Tokyo Shokuhin and General Bussan, grew to be major trading companies. Tokyo Shokuhin, now called Toshoku, is a major trader of foodstuffs, while General Bussan, the present General Sekiyu, is a major trader of oil. These defections from the merger account in part for the weakened position of the new Mitsui Bussan in post-war trade.

There are a number of reasons why Mitsui Bussan encountered more troubles than Mitsubishi Shoji in re-grouping. As pointed out earlier, personal rivalry was stronger in Mitsui Bussan than in Mitsubishi Shoji, reflecting the difference in their training programmes before the war. Mitsui Bussan encouraged its traders to be independent and gave them a large degree of freedom, while Mitsubishi Shoji emphasized group spirit and team-work. Another reason is that while Mitsubishi Shoji was supported by other Mitsubishi companies, Mitsui Bussan was one of the major pillars of the Mitsui zaibatsu. When the zaibatsu and the holding company were destroyed, former Mitsui companies lost considerable cohesion. To make the situation worse, two other pillars were adversely affected. Mitsui Mining was weakened by labour disputes and the decline in the demand for its major product (coal), while the Mitsui Bank was weakened when it let the Daiichi Bank (which it had merged during the war) become independent once more, and lost its pre-war eminence.

TOWARDS GREATER CONCENTRATION

There were a number of mergers in the first half of the 1950s. As mentioned earlier, Mitsubishi offsprings regrouped themselves into three companies in 1952 and finally into one large company in 1954, and by 1955, most major Mitsui offsprings had been absorbed by Daiichi Bussan. In addition, Takashimaya Iida, which had been hit by the crash after the Korean War boom, was absorbed by Marubeni; also, Maruei, the largest of the Senba Eight, was absorbed by Nichimen.

These mergers, plus the government policy of favouring large trading companies, increased the degree of concentration in trade. The share of the top ten trading companies in foreign trade was as low as 30 per cent in 1951, but it increased gradually in the next several years, and in the middle of the decade, returned to the pre-war level of 50 per cent. At the same time, Mitsubishi's share reached its pre-war level.

Needless to say, however, not everything was the same as in the period before the war. Mitsui Bussan's share was down to 8 per cent in the 1958 financial year. In the next few years, it increased somewhat, but remained around 10 per cent, about half its pre-war share. To the extent that Mitsui Bussan's share declined, the shares of other trading companies (excluding Mitsubishi Shoji) increased. The prolonged throes of rebirth had weakened the position of the new Mitsui Bussan.

3. THE GROWTH OF MITSUBISHI SHOJI AND MITSUI BUSSAN

Through mergers, Daiichi Bussan had become a fairly large company by the middle of the 1950s, so even after the new Mitsubishi Shoji was born, it was a close competitor. In 1954, it surpassed Marubeni in size, and then in the following year, became larger than C.Itoh. In 1956, Marubeni, which had merged Takashimaya Iida, temporarily overtook Daiichi Bussan, but in the following few years, the latter regained the number two position, behind Mitsubishi Shoji. When the new

TABLE 4.2
Sales in the Post-war Period
(Unit: billion yen)

Financial Year	Kanematsu	Gosho	Marubeni	C.Itoh	Mitsui Bussan	Mitsubishi Shoji	Sumitomo Shoji	Nissho	Iwai	Nichimen	Toyo Menka	Ataka
1949										12		
1950	14	10	51	69	27		14	45	33	45	47	
1951	62	36	96	133	53		28	45	51	82	85	41
1952	53	67	89	120	70		36	46	40	74	74	38
1953	66	57	134	158	118		47	53	49	106	92	50
1954	69	88	127	152	133	150	42	60	44	105	96	46
1955	65	78	211	200	220	270	53	92	57	123	113	58
1956	76	79	323	293	318	377	88	142	81	181	150	77
1957	95	106	346	310	360	415	107	120	78	178	165	88
1958	92	106	328	290	361	382	102	130	73	174	174	75
1959	100	99	462	409	517	499	153	190	105	230	208	101
1960	126	113	612	543	639	643	196	246	121	304	277	138
1961	195	140	738	690	789	799	263	237	163	384	358	182
1962	209	164	763	739	817	886	272	364	162	409	372	188
1963	251	161	976	951	1,043	1,129	369	451	227	493	487	243
1964	286	184	1,134	1,105	1,206	1,318	451	487	282	588	591	283
1965	311	204	1,153	1,184	1,525	1,463	496	595	324	581	639	295
1966	344	215	1,379	1,245	1,775	1,728	628	704	402	591	738	343
1967	542	(113)	1,593	1,455	2,079	2,147	785	(382)	458	650	853	443

TABLE 4.2 (continued)

Year										
1968	608	1,779	1,622	2,414	2,517	996	(626)	715	1,002	518
1969	715	2,163	2,056	3,089	3,241	1,307	1,507	777	1,184	657
1970	843	2,698	2,547	3,747	4,069	1,695	1,860	889	1,377	842
1971	970	2,909	2,773	4,134	4,529	1,976	1,924	925	1,392	943
1972	1,193	3,399	3,169	4,954	5,176	2,416	2,400	1,163	1,550	1,164
1973	1,911	4,648	4,228	6,957	7,484	4,018	3,382	1,755	1,830	1,615
1974	2,320	5,548	5,229	8,610	9,407	5,117	4,003	2,094	2,440	2,093
1975	2,308	5,762	5,630	7,885	9,140	5,509	3,958	1,694	2,394	1,998
1976	2,335	6,438	6,332	9,024	9,609	5,825	4,525	1,810	2,521	1,490
1977	2,160	6,350	6,355	8,649	9,324	5,883	4,282	1,752	2,247	
1978	2,039	6,271	6,560	8,360	8,836	5,849	4,176	1,789	2,136	

Source: Yuka Shoken Hokokusho, various years.

1. The financial year is usually from 1 April to 31 March, but there are a few exceptions. For Kanematsu in the period 1950–60 and Nissho in the period 1951–9, it was from 1 October to 30 September, and for Iwai until its merger with Nissho, it was from 1 June to 31 May.

2. The figures for Mitsui Bussan are Daiichi Bussan's until 1959.
3. The figures in parenthesis are half-year sales.
4. There are no sales figures for Ataka in 1977 and 1978, because it merged with C.Itoh in October 1977.

Mitsui Bussan completed its grand merger, it became the top trading company. Throughout most of the following years, however, it lost this position to Mitsubishi Shoji, though it remained a close runner-up (see Table 4.2).

In retrospect, Mitsubishi Shoji may be seen to have had better growth potential. It was only when merger took place that Mitsui Bussan surpassed Mitsubishi Shoji.[25] The catch-up of 1959 was the result of the grand merger, and that of 1965 was the result of its merger with Kinoshita Sansho. This company grew rapidly at first as a specialized steel trader, and around 1960, diversified into textile and various other fields to become a general trading company. The diversification brought difficulties, and by the middle of the 1960s, it was no longer possible for the company to survive. At first, it approached Gosho about a merger because the latter wanted to merge a trading company in a heavy goods field to complement its textile trade.[26] Unfortunately, however, a merger did not materialize. Worried about the troubles of their customer, Yahata Steel, Fuji Steel and the Fuji Bank took the problem to Mitsui Bussan, which decided on a merger quickly, to avoid the likelihood that Mitsubishi Shoji might merge Kinoshita and widen the difference between the two.[27]

A slight lead established by merger usually cannot be maintained, for the business of the two companies involved in the merger overlaps in a number of fields. Since this overlap is not eliminated right away, the trade volume immediately after a merger is usually inflated, but as the elimination of overlap proceeds, the trade volume declines. In this way, the slight leads Mitsui Bussan had both in 1959 and 1965 were wiped out relatively quickly. This was also the case in other mergers, as will be discussed later.

Around 1960, Marubeni was close behind Mitsui Bussan and Mitsubishi Shoji, and together they constituted the top group, but the so called 'three M period' was short. From the early 1960s, the difference between Marubeni on the one hand and Mitsui Bussan and Mitsubishi Shoji on the other, widened, gradually at first and then rapidly. In 1974, the difference between Mitsubishi Shoji and Marubeni was over 60 per cent. In the following few years, it narrowed somewhat, but still remained substantial. In the meantime, C.Itoh and Sumitomo Shoji grew quickly; together with Marubeni, they form the second strata today.

As the structure of the Japanese economy changed in favour of the heavy-chemical industry in the 1960s, Marubeni was handicapped in competition with Mitsubishi Shoji and Mitsui Bussan, because it did not receive strong backing from the Fuyo group to which it belonged. On the other hand, Mitsubishi Shoji belonged to a very cohesive group strong in the heavy-chemical industry, and greatly benefited from its backing. In the field of heavy industry, Mitsubishi Heavy Industries, Mitsubishi Electric, and Mitsubishi Steel Manufacturing belonged to the Mitsubishi group; in the chemical industry, Mitsubishi Chemical Industries, Mitsubishi Petrochemicals, Mitsubishi Plastics Industries, Mitsubishi Monsanto Chemical, and Asahi Glass were members (see Appendix 1). As a sales and purchasing agent for these companies, Mitsubishi Shoji grew as their production increased.

The close relations between Mitsubishi Shoji and Mitsubishi Heavy Industries are particularly noteworthy.[28] The latter is one of the top manufacturers of ships and general machinery. It is difficult for other trading companies to sell to this company, for it prefers to buy its raw materials and machinery from Mitsubishi Shoji. For example, 80 to 90 per cent of the steel used by the company is handled by Mitsubishi Shoji. Mitsubishi Heavy Industries also prefers that Mitsubishi Shoji handle the sales of its products. Mitsubishi Shoji was its exclusive agent for ships, a major export in the 1960s and early 1970s. In plant export, which recently accounted for about 10 per cent of total exports and has become the single most important component of exports, Mitsubishi Heavy Industries closely cooperates with Mitsubishi Shoji.

The Mitsui group is larger than the Mitsubishi, but is much less cohesive and much weaker in heavy industry. Its weakness in heavy industry dates back to the pre-war period, but there was no problem in group solidarity then. In the early post-war years, when the holding company was dissolved and Mitsui Bussan smashed, the group was weakened considerably. To make the situation worse, the Mitsui Bank was weakened by its separation from the Daiichi Bank and it became a second class bank. Because of these problems, some former Mitsui companies (Toyota, Toshiba, Ishikawajima Zosensho, Onoda Cement, etc.) drifted away from the group. Even among those which remained, group solidarity was weaker than in the Mitsubishi group, possibly because the Mitsui Bank could not play a unifying role due to the shortage of funds.

Nevertheless, the Mitsui group is more unified than most others, and it has as its members large companies in the heavy-chemical industry. It is still somewhat weak in heavy industry, but Japan Steel Works and Mitsui Shipbuilding and Engineering are important assets, and Toshiba (Tokyo Shibaura Electric) and Toyota, which rejoined the group recently, can be counted upon from time to time. In the chemical industry, the Mitsui group is as strong as the Mitsubishi. Mitsui Toatsu Chemicals and Mitsui Petrochemical Industries are two leading companies in this field.

The defection of General Bussan was important in the decline of Mitsui Bussan's relative importance in post-war trade. Since General Bussan had taken over the oil trade of the former Mitsui Bussan, the new Mitsui Bussan had to establish new contacts and build up from scratch. It set up a number of service stations and participated in the establishment of an oil refinery in order to expand its oil business, but these actions were taken after it became clear that General Bussan would remain independent. In the meantime, it lagged behind Mitsubishi Shoji, which had moved into the field aggressively. Machinery and fuel were for a long while the two major commodities responsible for the supremacy of Mitsubishi Shoji over Mitsui Bussan, but the difference in machinery sales has narrowed considerably in recent years. In oil and liquefied natural gas (LNG), Mitsui Bussan is well behind Mitsubishi Shoji.

Mitsubishi Shoji's oil business began soon after the grand merger. The Japanese government (MITI) was reluctant to let trading companies handle the import of oil (it preferred that refineries import directly), but Mitsubishi Shoji managed to obtain permission by undertaking a number of combination deals (e.g., the import of oil for the export of Japanese products such as tankers and industrial plants). As it became active in oil deals, the company became involved in the LNG project at Alaska in 1960 and a few years later, at Brunei. The import of LNG from Alaska began in 1969, and that from Brunei in 1977. In the early 1970s, when oil producing countries began direct sales (bypassing the major), Mitsubishi Shoji's oil trade made a sudden jump. In 1978, the year for which the most recent data are available, oil and LNG accounted for 40 per cent of Mitsubishi Shoji's imports and about 20 per cent of its total sales.[29]

In the meantime, Mitsui Bussan did not remain idle. It increased its oil trade after the oil shock by participating in direct sales from oil producing countries, and also began importing LNG. Nevertheless, its oil and LNG trade is much smaller than Mitsubishi Shoji's. For example, Mitsubishi Shoji's share in the oil import by trading companies in 1976–7 was about 45 per cent, while Mitsui Bussan's share was about 5 per cent.[30] In LNG import, Mitsui Bussan's import from Abu Dhabi is about 2 million tons a year, whereas Mitsubishi Shoji's import from Alaska is 1 million tons and that from Brunei is about 5 million tons.

Mitsui Bussan's petrochemical project in Iran was undertaken to boost its position in oil. It agreed to undertake a petrochemical project with other Mitsui companies in exchange for the oil concession right in the Lorestan area, southwest of Teheran.[31] Unfortunately for Mitsui Bussan, not only was it impossible to find oil in the area, its petrochemical project also ran into difficulties. The risk in oil drilling was probably calculated in advance, so the failure was not a serious blow, but the difficulties of the petrochemical project, especially those related to the political turmoil which occurred from late 1978, were unexpected, and as a result, Mitsui Bussan today faces serious financial problems.

4. THE SIAMESE TWINS: MARUBENI AND C.ITOH

DAIKEN SANGYO

After regulations became pervasive as a consequence of the China Incident of 1937, it became difficult for trading companies to maintain a *raison d'être* unless they diversified into production. To accomplish this, it was necessary to merge and pool resources. Sanko was created in 1941 by the merger of Marubeni, C.Itoh and Kishimoto Shoten. The former two were the Itoh family business, but the third was owned by the Kishimoto family. The close relations between the heads of the two families made the merger possible.

As the Pacific War progressed, it became imperative for the Itoh family to gather all of its businesses under one umbrella, for otherwise there was the likelihood that under the exigencies of war, a company which was primarily a trader might be ordered to dissolve by the military. Thus, the Itoh family merged its spinning company with Sanko and another trading company, Daido Boeki, and established Daiken Sangyo in 1944 (see Figure 4.3). Prior to this time, the spinning company had diversified into the heavy-chemical industry and had established several subsidiaries in this field, while the two trading companies had set up a number of manufacturing subsidiaries. From the beginning, in other words, Daiken Sangyo was a manufacturing, trading, and holding company.

After the war, the GHQ became interested in this company. After the major zaibatsu were dissolved, Daiken Sangyo was designated a holding company and later ordered to divest its holdings. Then in early 1948, the Elimination of Excessive Concentration of Economic Power Law was directed toward Daiken Sangyo, and it was told to separate its manufacturing and trading divisions. In compliance with this order, Daiken

FIGURE 4.3
The Formation and Dissolution of Daiken Sangyo

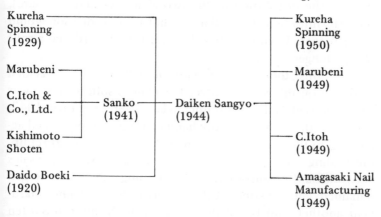

Sangyo was dissolved and four independent manufacturing and trading companies were established in late 1949 and early 1950.

In 1947, Daiken Sangyo's greatest concern was what would become of its trading division.[32] Around that time, Mitsui and Mitsubishi's semi-annual sales were about 2,000 million yen, whereas Daiken Sangyo's were 700 million yen. It was much smaller than the two, in other words, but it remained a strong third, outdistancing Iwai and Toyo Menka, whose sales were around 400 million yen. In early 1947, since Mitsui Bussan and Mitsubishi Shoji were preparing reorganization plans, Daiken Sangyo was compelled to prepare a contingency reorganization plan of its own. Initially, it hoped that the GHQ would be satisfied with dividing the company into two, but after the dissolution of Mitsui Bussan and Mitsubishi Shoji was carried out in the middle of the year, it seemed likely that Daiken Sangyo would face a similar fate. In order to avoid this, the company proposed a plan to split into eight to twelve smaller entities.

The GHQ policy towards Daiken Sangyo seems to have wavered. At first, it seemed inclined toward a three-way split, but soon after the dissolution of Mitsui Bussan and Mitsubishi Shoji, apparently decided to issue a dissolution order for Daiken Sangyo also. A few months later, for some reason (maybe the dissolution of the two giants seemed adequate), the GHQ informed Daiken Sangyo that a simple division would be sufficient. Finally, in late 1947, it issued word that a split was no longer a necessity.

After this, the trading division of Daiken Sangyo decided to divide on its own initiative. The plan to split into two was first proposed to the GHQ either in late 1946 or in early 1947, and since then, the company had been slowly reorganized according to the plan. In 1944 when Daiken Sangyo was set up, the trading division had a general headquarters, but the sales networks and organizations of the trading companies merged remained fairly distinct. C.Itoh constituted one line, Marubeni another, and Daido Boeki the third (Kishimoto Shoten became independent early in the post-war years). Since Daido Boeki was small, if the trading division were to be split into two, it would be divided along the C.Itoh and Marubeni lines. The question was what to do with Daido Boeki. This was fairly easily solved, however, since Marubeni was somewhat smaller than C.Itoh and was weaker in foreign trade, it was best for Daido to join Marubeni so that the two new companies could start on an approximately equal basis (the GHQ was insisting on equal size, whatever the number of splits).

Even after it became clear that there was no longer any necessity to split, the Marubeni side wanted the plan to be executed, for its men had a number of grievances against C.Itoh. Ever since Marubeni and C.Itoh had merged in 1941, former Marubeni staff had been discriminated against. The top position in Sanko and later the trading division of Daiken Sangyo were occupied by people from C. Itoh, and some Marubeni zealots were transferred to subsidiaries. After Daiken Sangyo's two top executives, Itoh Chubei and Itoh Takenosuke, resigned, anticipating a forthcoming purge, Ichikawa Shinobu, a Marubeni man who had been sent off to a subsidiary, was brought back as an executive managing director, and he was insistent about the reorganization plan.

In mid-1948, Daiken Sangyo decided to split the trading division into two companies and sent out a notice to this effect to its customers. On 1 December of that year, the day when regulations on export were lifted, two trading companies were born: Marubeni and C.Itoh. The Siamese twins were finally separated. If the trading division had not been split, it would not have been able to ride out the turbulent 1950s and 1960s, for the company lacked solidarity. The separation gave rise to two unified companies and contributed to the dynamics of post-war trade.

MARUBENI

In a way, the post-war history of Marubeni is a history of mergers.[33] As shown in Figure 4.4, there were four mergers worth noting. Among them, the merger with Takashimaya Iida in 1955 and that with Totsu in 1966 were the major ones. The other two were of less significance, though important in the post-war evolution of the company. Daiichi Kozai, which was merged in 1960, was an authorized agent of Nippon Kokan, a major steel manufacturer, and this merger brought Marubeni into close contact with the steel manufacturer. This led to the merger with Totsu in 1966. Nanyo Bussan was an

FIGURE 4.4
The Evolution of Marubeni

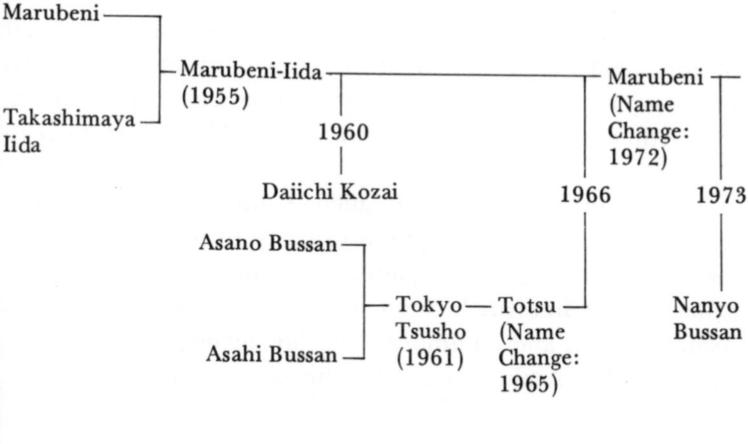

importer of non-ferrous metals from the Philippines, copper in particular, and accounted for a fairly large share of non-ferrous imports. Because the scale of investment required to obtain marketing rights for mineral products had been increasing, Nanyo Bussan saw its future as a specialized importer as dim. It therefore approached Marubeni, whose position in the trade with the Philippines was strong. Marubeni was interested in this merger to strengthen its non-ferrous metal department.

Takashimaya Iida was a large trader in the years around 1950. Activity in the steel business in the pre-war period helped it become an authorized agent for Yahata Steel and Fuji Steel in 1948. In the pre-war period, it handled only special steel, but in the early post-war period, it managed to break into the trade of ordinary steel. In this Takashimaya Iida benefited by the disappearance of Mitsui Bussan and Mitsubishi Shoji. Steel was not, however, its dominant business. Its main business was in soft goods. It was strong particularly in wool, but handled also most textile goods and their raw materials. In addition, it handled food and the 'three new products' (rubber, leather and soybeans). In the early 1950s, it was one of the most diversified traders.

Perhaps Takashimaya Iida diversified too quickly. The company was hit hard by the crash after the Korean War boom. At this time, it lost about 600 million yen (its paid-up capital was 200 million yen). If it had done well in subsequent years, it could have survived with relief loans, but in the second half of the 1954 financial year, it lost heavily again. This forced the company to the point of either going bankrupt or merging with another company. It was merged by Marubeni in 1955.

Totsu had formerly been called Asano Bussan. After the war, Asano Bussan faced the possibility of being ordered to dissolve, so in August 1947, it set up another trading company called Asahi Bussan.[34] Soon after, infighting began within Asano Bussan, and a number of leading members of the company left for Asahi Bussan. The history of Asano Bussan in the subsequent years is somewhat obscure, but the steel trade with Nippon Kokan seems to have provided the basis for its growth. Asahi Bussan's subsequent evolution is better known: it became an authorized agent of Nippon Kokan, and grew rather rapidly. By 1961 when it merged Asano Bussan, Asahi Bussan had become much the larger company. After the merger the company name was changed to Tokyo Tsusho. The name was changed again in 1965, to Totsu.

Totsu's troubles began in 1962 when a slump hit the steel market. Then in 1965, one of its important customers, Sanyo Special Steel, went bankrupt, and it incurred bad debts amounting to almost 2 billion yen (an amount equal to its paid-up capital). To make the situation worse, Totsu lost about the same amount in a sewage construction project in Saudi Arabia. Nippon Kokan attempted to rescue Totsu by itself at first, but was busy constructing a large steel plant at the time. The Fuji Bank (its main bank) urged it to concentrate on the plant and not get deeply involved in Totsu's affairs, so Nippon Kokan took the problem to Marubeni.

Marubeni was interested in these mergers for a number of reasons. For one thing, Marubeni, basically a textile trader in the beginning, saw the mergers as a means of strengthening its non-textile fields, especially steel. Also, in the mid-1950s, although Marubeni had acquired the former employees of Daido, the number of traders experienced in foreign trade was too small to expand as rapidly as management desired. The merger of Takashimaya Iida, a foreign trader since before the war, could solve this bottle-neck. Furthermore, the merger of Takashimaya Iida would strengthen Marubeni's network in eastern Japan. As an Osaka-based company, Marubeni's network in Tokyo was weak, whereas Takashimaya Iida was Tokyo-based and had been successful in selling goods to the government.

Without the mergers, it would have been extremely difficult (if not impossible) for Marubeni to get into the steel trade, for major manufacturers use only a limited number of traders as their primary wholesalers. Marubeni wanted to merge Takashimaya Iida because it was a primary wholesaler for Yahata Steel and Fuji Steel. This merger made it possible to initiate a large-scale steel business with the two steel manufacturers. The merger of Totsu made Marubeni the top trading company for Nippon Kokan, which also adopted a distribution system similar to that of Yahata and Fuji.

Diversification into machinery was simpler than that into steel for two reasons. One was that Marubeni could act as agent for machinery manufacturers abroad. In fact, this was a role played by trading companies such as Mitsui Bussan and Okura Shoji in the Meiji era. Machinery required knowledge different from that required for textiles, but a determined trading company could acquire it through retraining and the hiring of engineers. Once this problem was solved, as long as a trading company succeeded in finding customers, it could find foreign manufacturers willing to grant agency rights. Obtaining agency rights for General Electric's industrial equipment was Marubeni's major accomplishment in the early 1950s. In the late 1950s, Marubeni became the exclusive agent for Lockheed Aircraft and won a number of large contracts from the Defense Agency and Japanese airlines.

The other reason why diversification into machinery was simpler than diversification into steel was that the Japanese machinery industry had historically been more fragmented than the steel industry, so there was more room for manoeuvring by Marubeni. In the case of steel, products are fairly well standardized and the industry is an oligopoly. The manufacturers can to a large extent dictate the terms of distribution. But in the case of machinery, products are varied, and the industry fragmented. As a result, Marubeni had greater control over distribution. It brought small manufacturers under its control and acted as their agent. It helped manufacturers introduce technology from abroad and in return, became an agent for the products made by that technology. Finally, because machinery was less standardized, Marubeni was able to play a role in its sales promotion.

When Marubeni was formed in December 1949, about 90

per cent of its business was textiles. Today, the share of textiles is about 10 per cent, and Marubeni has become a sogo shosha. The company stands out as an exception among textile traders making this transformation. What accounts for Marubeni's success? Among a number of factors involved, the most important was perhaps the strategy of Ichikawa Shinobu, president of the company in its first fifteen years. One of his contributions was a vision of the future. He wanted to convert Marubeni from a predominantly domestic textile trader to a diversified company for which export, import, and domestic trade were of roughly equal importance. In retrospect, it is apparent that there was no other viable strategy for the company if it were to grow, but in the early 1950s, there was considerable uncertainty as to what strategy textile traders should adopt. Uncertainty was heightened especially after the crash, when many textile traders lost heavily on the 'three new products'. Many trading companies, as well as their banks, felt that they should stick to the trade with which they had been most familiar, but Ichikawa believed that although textiles would remain an important industry, its relative importance would decline, and that if the company were to grow, it had to diversify into non-textiles, especially steel and machinery. Along this line, he implemented various policies (including the merger with Takashimaya Iida).[35]

His other major contribution was securing a tie-up for Marubeni with the Fuji Bank. In the early 1950s, the Fuji Bank had hoped that Daiichi Bussan would become its major trading company, but because Daiichi Bussan opted for the Mitsui group, it was compelled to look for another trading company. Ichikawa seized this opportunity, recognizing that the Fuji Bank could finance Marubeni's rapidly expanding requirements for working capital and investment funds and, at the same time, help establish close contacts with a number of manufacturers who were its customers.[36]

The tie-up with the Fuji Bank was of great benefit to Marubeni. Its merger with Takashimaya Iida was arranged by the Fuji Bank. Also the Fuji Bank persuaded Nippon Kokan to take the problem of Totsu to Marubeni and helped establish close contacts for Marubeni with this steel manufacturer. Furthermore, the Fuji Bank formed the Fuyo group (Fuyo is another name for Mt. Fuji) and made Marubeni its major trading company. The Fuyo group is not as large or as tightly knit as the Mitsubishi and Mitsui groups, but it is more cohesive than other bank-centred groups, and Marubeni benefited from group affiliation with it.

C.ITOH

C.Itoh was equally aware of the need to diversify in order to maintain the leading position in trade, and took various measures to accomplish this objective. As a result, the share of textiles in its total sales declined from 90 to 60 per cent in the first decade and from 60 to 40 per cent in the second decade. Still, this decline was much slower than in the case of Marubeni. In the first decade, Marubeni's textile share declined to 49 per cent and in the second decade, to 22 per cent.

One reason for C.Itoh's relatively slow decline in textiles was that it diversified by its own power, i.e., without numerous mergers. In the 1950s and 1960s, C.Itoh merged a few companies—Taiyo Bussan in 1955, Morioka Kogyo in 1961, and Aoki Shoji in 1964—but they were minor companies compared with those merged by Marubeni (Takashimaya Iida and Totsu). Taiyo Bussan was a small trading company set up by people who had returned from the Shanghai branch of C.Itoh, during the time when Daiken Sangyo's future was uncertain; the company later became strong in the textile trade with South-East Asia. Aoki Shoji was also a textile trader, with strength in Oceania and Africa. Morioka Kogyo was the only company which specialized in a non-textile commodity. As a well-known steel trader whose founding dated back to the mid-Tokugawa period, it was an authorized agent of Yahata Steel.[37] Merger of this company enabled C.Itoh to strengthen its steel trade, but not as much as Marubeni's two major mergers augmented its trade in steel.

The fact that C.Itoh did not have a group affiliation hampered its efforts to diversify. At first, its main bank was the Sumitomo Bank, and because of this connection, to some extent, C.Itoh acted as a marketing and purchasing agent for the Sumitomo group, since Sumitomo Shoji's overseas network was weak. From the viewpoint of the Sumitomo Bank, it would have been ideal if the two trading companies had merged, but C.Itoh was not interested in such a proposal. Therefore, the Sumitomo Bank decided to support Sumitomo Shoji as the main trading company for the group, and as Sumitomo Shoji grew, C.Itoh's relations with the Sumitomo group weakened.

The only other groups it could approach in the 1950s were the Kawasaki and Furukawa groups. A drawback in the case of the Furukawa group was that since Nissho had already established contacts with this group, C.Itoh would have to compete with Nissho for what was in reality a relatively small business (small compared with other major groups). The Kawasaki group, on the other hand, was still isolated and looking for a large trading company which could help export its products and import the technology it needed from abroad. C.Itoh took this opportunity to establish close contacts with the Kawasaki group. This tie-up helped C.Itoh in its diversification, but the help received was not as significant as the benefits Marubeni received from its group affiliation. After all, the Kawasaki group consisted of only a few companies, and, besides, it was a subgroup within the Daiichi Bank group (the Daiichi Bank was the main bank of the Kawasaki group). Marubeni's situation was different—it was the major trading company for the Fuyo group to which a number of large manufacturers belonged.

In order to overcome these problems, C.Itoh aggressively used loans and investment. For example, it helped manufacturers who did not have enough money to set up a distribution sytem by either extending them loans or setting up sales companies. It also gave financial help to manufacturers short of money for large-scale investments. Abroad, it tied up with mining companies for resource development and imported raw materials (iron ore, oil, etc.) for Japanese manufacturers. In addition, it created its own group by either setting up new companies or taking over those in financial trouble. All major trading companies have their own groups of companies, so C.Itoh is no exception, but it should be noted that the degree of its involvement is much greater than is ordinarily the case. In 1971, for example, C.Itoh's investment in subsidiaries was 22 billion yen, whereas Marubeni's was 13 billion yen, and the ratio of investment to total sales was 1.58 per cent for C.Itoh and only 0.80 per cent for Marubeni.[38] That is, C.Itoh had to make about twice as much effort in investment as Marubeni in order to generate the same amount of business. This was largely because C.Itoh did not have a strong group backing.

C.Itoh had one advantage over Marubeni: when the two were separated, C.Itoh had inherited a much larger number of traders experienced in foreign trade. Accordingly, it made foreign trade its strong point, and utilized the market gap between Japan and foreign countries in order to break into the non-textile trade. For example, in the 1950s, C.Itoh became a successful trader of aircraft and aircraft parts by becoming an agent for Douglas, Beech Aircraft, Bendix International, Rolls Royce, Goodyear, etc. In steel, C.Itoh brought foreign orders for ships to shipbuilding companies and in return persuaded them to buy the steel it handled. It also secured major foreign customers in places where its offices were located, and passed their orders to Japanese steel makers. These efforts helped C.Itoh establish close contacts with the steel makers, which eventually resulted in the company obtaining agency rights for domestic wholesaling.

Diversification by means of investment and the utilization of the market gap did not proceed smoothly initially. C.Itoh inevitably undertook a number of investments which produced no or only minor results. Diversification by utilizing the market gap was costly as well, because money had to be invested in manpower training and also because there was a long gestation period until newly-established businesses became profitable. In the meantime, additional funds had to be secured to finance diversification efforts.

Textiles were C.Itoh's major source of profits in the 1950s and 1960s. Although it had no obvious advantages over other traders, C.Itoh did better than the others. Why this was so is not entirely clear. One can argue, as *ex post facto* rationalizations, that C.Itoh had a more dedicated group of people, that a greater degree of freedom was given to people who had good ideas, or that the company was more innovative in changing the composition of textile goods to correspond to changes in the market situation. Such suppositions cannot be verified, but it is certain that C.Itoh had as the heads of its textile departments, people who were skilled at reading the price trends of what they handled. Echigo Masakazu was such a person. He made large profits through speculation twice in the first half of the 1950s. The profits of his second speculation exceeded 1,000 million yen at a time when the paid-up capital was 600 million yen, and made it possible for the company to finance various diversification measures in the next several years.[39]

In the early 1970s, the Daiichi Bank and the Kangyo Bank merged to become the Daiichi Kangyo Bank. This merger made C.Itoh the major trading company for the Daiichi Kangin group. From that point onwards, C.Itoh had a major group affiliation. The Daiichi Kangin group, however, is not a very cohesive group, as seen, for example, in the fact that it has today three sogo shosha within the group (see Appendix 1). Besides C.Itoh, these are Nissho-Iwai and Kanematsu-Gosho.

Two major subgroups in the Daiichi group were the Kawasaki and Furukawa groups. C.Itoh had been the major trading company for the former, while Nissho-Iwai represented the latter. The Kangyo Bank had a group called Jugosha Kai, for which Kanematsu-Gosho was the main trading company. When the two banks merged, it was presumed that Nissho-Iwai would withdraw its commitments from the Furukawa group and make the Sanwa group its only affiliation, but it did not do so. Kanematsu-Gosho's main bank, the Bank of Tokyo, did not have a group to speak of, so this company also did not withdraw in favour of other commitments. It was not possible for the Daiichi Kangyo Bank to sever the various relationships it had cultivated in the past, so it retained all three trading companies in the group. As a result, the benefits of the group did not accrue to C.Itoh alone, although it has been the main trading company for the group and benefited most from the organizing role of the bank.

In 1977, C.Itoh belatedly merged a major trading company, Ataka, and attained the third position in trading, surpassing Marubeni for the first time in twenty years. Ataka had got into financial trouble after the oil shock, and by the end of 1975, its main banks (the Sumitomo Bank and the Kyowa Bank) decided that the company could possibly not rehabilitate itself alone. They approached C.Itoh with the problem because they figured that it might be interested in the fact that Ataka was strong in heavy goods. At this time, C.Itoh was still weak in steel. Merger negotiations did not go smoothly for Ataka was a sogo shosha, involved in a number of fields which overlapped with C.Itoh's. To facilitate the merger, Ataka's business was divided into several components, and C.Itoh absorbed the steel, chemical, machinery and foodstuffs divisions. The volume of these goods amounted to about 600 billion yen, equal to nearly 10 per cent of C.Itoh's sales before the merger.

The major component of the business which C.Itoh absorbed from Ataka was steel. Ataka had been one of the major wholesalers for Nippon Steel, and after the merger, C.Itoh became not only the third largest trader of Nippon Steel's products (after Mitsui and Mitsubishi), but also the fifth largest trader of steel (after Mitsui, Mitsubishi, Sumitomo, and Marubeni). The share of steel in C.Itoh's sales rose from 14.3 per cent to 18.7 per cent.

In short, the merger with Ataka conferred two benefits: that is, it boosted the trade of steel and other heavy-chemical goods, and it made C.Itoh the third ranking trading company. On the cost side, C.Itoh assumed part of Ataka's liabilities. While the Japanese economy was expanding rapidly, it was not difficult to write off liabilities in view of future earnings (this is the main reason why most of the major mergers in the 1950s and 1960s went well). Now that the rate of growth has slowed down, however, costs present a more difficult problem. At present, there are certain indications that the benefits have outweighed the costs, but it is still too early to tell what will be the final judgement.

5. THE THREE COTTON TRADERS: TOYO MENKA, NICHIMEN (NIPPON MENKA), AND GOSHO

At the end of the pre-war period, Toyo Menka was by far the largest among textile traders, but in the early post-war period, this was not the case. It remained one of the so-called 'Five Cotton Traders of the Kansai Area', but occupied the middle position among them. The reason for the decline of its relative position was that its ties with the Mitsui zaibatsu became a negative factor after the war.[40] It was placed on the 'black list' of the GHQ as a Mitsui member, and though it was not dissolved like Mitsui Bussan, it had to watch every move it made. Toyo Menka was especially careful not to engage in black market operation lest this should give the GHQ an excuse to take drastic measures against it. Consequently, it fell behind other trading companies which were able to make money on the black market—the degree of involvement varied by size—and use it for expansion.

Toyo Menka's pre-war ties proved to have a couple of other drawbacks. In comparison with other large textile traders, Toyo Menka was much less diversified as a result of its agreements with Mitsui Bussan. It was essentially a trader of raw cotton and cotton products, and did not handle other textile goods, let alone non-textile goods. When it was separated from Mitsui Bussan, it became free to engage in any trade, but it had to build its foundations almost from scratch. In cotton textiles, Toyo Menka's major supplier before the war was Kanebo, and this relationship continued also after the war. Now,

however, Toyo Menka was faced with competition for Kanebo's business from Mitsui Bussan's offsprings. For example, the
silk business of Mitsui Bussan was taken over by Sanshin Sen'i,
which establisehd close relations with Kanebo because it produced silk textiles. Since Sanshin Sen'i was free to handle cotton goods, it handled Kanebo's cotton as well as silk textiles,
and took away part of Toyo Menka's traditional business.

Around 1950, Toyo Menka and Nichimen (Nippon Menka
changed its name to Nichimen Jitsugyo in 1943) had sales of
roughly equal size. Of the so-called 'Five Cotton Traders of
the Kansai Area', C.Itoh was the largest, Marubeni the second.
Toyo Menka and Nichimen were third and fourth, while Gosho was the smallest (see Table 4.2). In the 1950s, C.Itoh's
leading position was obvious, but there was not much difference between Marubeni and Toyo Menka or Nichimen. In the
following years, however, the difference between C.Itoh and
Marubeni on the one hand and Toyo Menka and Nichimen on
the other grew increasingly wide. In 1977 and 1978, the last
two years listed in Table 4.2, Toyo Menka and Nichimen's
sales were about one-third of C.Itoh's or Marubeni's, and
with Kanematsu-Gosho, they constituted the bottom strata
of sogo shosha.[41]

One reason for the slower growth of these companies is that
as a result of having been foreign trade specialists before the
war, their network for domestic trade (which has accounted
for about half of the total sales of sogo shosha in the post-war
period) was weak. C.Itoh and Marubeni had much better
domestic networks: C.Itoh had been engaged in both foreign
trade and domestic trade before the war, and Marubeni had
been basically a domestic trader, so there was no question
about its strength within Japan. Aware of this problem, Nichimen absorbed Maruei in 1954 and Tazuke in 1960 (both
among the Senba Eight), to augment its network to some extent. Toyo Menka was more conservative regarding merger, so
it attempted to solve the problem largely on its own.

Because both Toyo Menka and Nichimen had distinguished
traditions in the field of raw cotton and cotton goods, it was

probably more difficult for them than for other companies to sacrifice textiles for diversification into non-textile goods, especially heavy goods. This does not mean, however, that they were not aware of the need to diversify. In fact, they were not far behind C.Itoh and Marubeni in degree of awareness, but they seemed to have lacked the will to carry out diversification. C.Itoh was willing to use large amounts of money made in textiles for diversification despite initial setbacks, whereas Marubeni carried out major mergers for this purpose. In contrast, neither Toyo Menka nor Nichimen carried out major mergers or made all-out efforts to diversify.

In the case of Toyo Menka, there have been three mergers in the post-war period. In 1955, it absorbed Kanegabuchi Shoji, a subsidiary of Kanebo; in 1961, Taiyo Bussan, a subsidiary of a sugar refinery; in 1963, Nankai Kogyo, a steel trader, whose main business was with Nippon Kokan. Nichimen also made three mergers: besides those with Maruei and Tazuke already mentioned, there was one in 1963 with Takada Shokai, a machinery trader.

Diversification into foodstuffs, wood, and pulp went fairly well. In these fields, Toyo Menka and Nichimen made the best use of their overseas networks and their skills in foreign trade to find sources of supply. In machinery, also, their long experience in foreign trade was of great help. They obtained agency rights from a number of foreign suppliers and made inroads into this business. Their main obstacle was their relationships with Japanese steel manufacturers. In the post-war period, steel was not an imported product, so it was imperative for them to establish close contacts with Japanese steel manufacturers if they wished to increase their steel business. The steel manufacturers, however, had already chosen their primary wholesale agents in the early post-war years. It was very difficult for companies not chosen at that time to break into the trade.

One obvious solution was to merge with a steel trader. This was the road Marubeni took. Toyo Menka decided to merge with a steel trader in 1963, but this merger did not produce a

significant change, for the company merged was not a large
steel trader and the timing was slightly late for a merger of
that size to make a great difference. Nichimen attempted the
same solution as C.Itoh, that is, it used its overseas network
and loans and investment; but this was a long, tedious way
to increase steel trade.

The fact that Toyo Menka and Nichimen had weak support
from their main banks also handicapped their growth. The
Bank of Tokyo had been Nichimen's main bank since before
the war. As long as foreign trade was the company's main
business, this relationship served Nichimen well, but when in
the post-war period, domestic trade became an important
source of growth, it became imperative for Nichimen to find
a bank which could give large yen loans. Around 1955, the
Bank of Tokyo arranged for the Sanwa Bank to finance Nichimen's domestic operations, which greatly aided its growth in
the subsequent years.[42] However, the support which Nichimen received from the Sanwa Bank was limited; it could not
become the bank's major trading company because Iwai and
later Nissho-Iwai (after the two merged) fulfilled the role.
Less than full support from its main bank surely limited Nichimen's potential growth.

Toyo Menka's main bank was the Mitsui Bank, a tie made
before the war which had unfortunate consequences for Toyo
Menka in the post-war period.[43] As pointed out earlier, the
Mitsui Bank became a second class bank, in no position to be
the major financier of both Toyo Menka and Mitsui Bussan
(Daiichi Bussan before 1959). Choosing between the two,
the bank gave greater support to Mitsui Bussan. Toyo Menka
felt that it had been discriminated against, and wanted to
switch to the Fuji Bank since that bank was looking for a
substitute for Daiichi Bussan which it had promoted. The Mitsui Bank jealously blocked this move, however. Faced with a
bleak future in its relationship with the Mitsui Bank, Toyo
Menka determined to find another main bank, even if it meant
a confrontation with the Mitsui Bank.

Toyo Menka began to favour the Tokai Bank in the late

1950s, and by the middle of the 1960s, had made it its main bank. This move is generally interpreted as signifying that Toyo Menka became a member of the Tokai group, and this is not mistaken, but the benefits from group affiliation seem rather small in this case. The main reason for Toyo Menka's tie-up with the Tokai Bank was to secure funds, not group affiliation. Even today, this seems to be the underlying factor in the relations between the two. As a group, the Tokai Bank group is still loosely organized and not functioning effectively.

Gosho's post-war history is unique.[44] When the zaibatsu were dissolved, Gosho was separated from Toyo Boseki and became an independent company again. During the Korean War boom, it was generally thought that Gosho, as one of the 'Five Cotton Traders of the Kansai Area', would become a leading trader. But the company was hit hard by the crash after the Korean War, and its history in the subsequent years is one of decline. In 1952, it was surpassed by Daiichi Bussan, in 1957 by Sumitomo Shoji and Ataka, in 1962 by Iwai. After that, it became the smallest of the sogo shosha, and in 1967, ceased to be independent. Kanematsu merged Gosho, and changed the name to Kanematsu-Gosho.

Gosho had several weaknesses. As was seen to be a weak point in the case of Toyo Menka and Nichimen also, the fact that Gosho had been a foreign trade specialist before the war had left it without a good network for domestic trade in the post-war period. Another by far more important weakness was that Gosho lagged behind other companies in diversification. Toyo Menka and Nichimen had also faced problems in diversification, and although they did not solve them as effectively as did C.Itoh and Marubeni, they did considerably better than Gosho. Toyo Menka and Nichimen succeeded in breaking into the machinery business and making it a profitable venture, whereas Gosho failed. Steel was the weak point of both Toyo Menka and Nichimen, yet Gosho's performance was even worse. Gosho's diversification was successful only in soft goods (foodstuffs, wood, pulp, etc.).

When comparing Gosho with Nichimen, one clear difference

emerges in the field of finance. For both, the Bank of Tokyo had been the main bank since before the war (as foreign trade specialists, they had established close relations with the foreign exchange bank, Yokohama Specie Bank, the present Bank of Tokyo). This relationship proved to be unsatisfactory in the post-war period when domestic trade became an important source of growth, for the Bank of Tokyo did not have enough money to finance it. As explained earlier, Nichimen succeeded in securing the Sanwa Bank as its major source of finance for domestic trade, but Gosho did not make significant efforts to look for another bank. It retained the Bank of Tokyo as its main bank, receiving only slight assistance in domestic trade. This seems to have been an unfortunate decision on Gosho's part, for there were several independent city banks that it could have approached for greater support in the mid-1950s.

There is one peculiar feature in Gosho's post-war history: most of its presidents came from outside the company. The first president had been an employee of Toyo Menka at first, then president of a cotton trading company (Showa Menka), and was brought to Gosho after that by Toyo Boseki. The second president had also been with another cotton trading company before being brought to Gosho by the Bank of Tokyo. The third president came from the Bank of Tokyo. The fourth was a Gosho man proper, but it seems that the Bank of Tokyo made him president to execute the *coup de grâce*—the merger with Kanematsu.

Gosho's major troubles began when Komamura Sukemasa was brought in as first president by Toyo Boseki. His background was in textiles, and for a textile man, he was unusual in approaching politicians and trying to link politics to business. To a certain extent, he was successful. He excelled, for example, at getting foreign exchange allocations from MITI. However, he seems to have lacked a sense of balance. He spent too much money for the benefits he extracted. Towards the middle of the 1950s, his political activity became a liability rather than an asset. To make the situation worse, he used people from his former company (Showa Menka) as close advisers, and antagonized many Gosho people. As virtual ruler of the company in its first ten years, to a large degree he set the course for Gosho's post-war history.

Efforts to solve Gosho's problems through merger began relatively early. When Komamura was president, he was approached by the president of the Sumitomo Bank about the possibility of merging Gosho with Sumitomo Shoji, a company weak in textiles and lacking traders experienced in foreign trade. These discussions remained informal, and were never brought up in Gosho's board meetings. The next set of discussions was with Kinoshita Sansho. This time, it was Gosho that explored the possibility of a merger, since Kinoshita Sansho was in the weaker position. This merger presented an excellent opportunity to Gosho to strengthen its weakness in steel, but the deal did not materialize, mainly because the Bank of Tokyo was not willing to get deeply involved in the financial troubles of Kinoshita.

Gosho's problems became serious in the mid-1960s. In the early 1950s, when the crash occurred, Gosho had suffered heavy losses, but after the mid-1950s, it managed to earn profits though it often did not pay dividends. In 1965, profits declined to an abnormally low level, and in the first half of the following year, losses amounted to one-third of the paid-up capital. Around this time, the Ministry of Finance apparently advised the Bank of Tokyo to merge Gosho with another company before the situation worsened. Despite the protests of Gosho people, the Bank of Tokyo opted for a merger. By absorbing a large part of Gosho's liabilities, it arranged the merger with Kanematsu, another company for which it was the main bank.

6. STEEL CENTRED TRADING COMPANIES: IWAI, ATAKA, AND NISSHO

Ataka, Iwai, and Nissho are often described as having been steel traders in the early 1950s. If this means that they specialized in steel in the way that C.Itoh, Marubeni, etc. did in textiles, the description is not entirely accurate, for in the latter case, textiles accounted for about 90 per cent of sales, whereas the importance of steel was much lower for Ataka, Iwai, and Nissho, accounting for only about 30 to 40 per cent of their total sales. As discussed in the previous chapter, steel became their most important commodity in the 1920s and 1930s, but they dealt in many other commodities as well. This situation remained true also in the early post-war years.

Ataka and Iwai's steel business was with Nippon Seitetsu (Nippon Steel) as it had been also in the pre-war period. Their special relationships with this dominant steel manufacturer were re-established when they were appointed, together with nine other trading companies, as its authorized agents in 1948. Even after Nippon Seitetsu was split into Yahata Steel and Fuji Steel, Ataka and Iwai acted as the primary distributors for the two companies. For Nissho, the situation was different. As in the pre-war period, it imported scrap-iron and pig-iron for Kobe Steel, and at the same time, marketed its products. The tie with Kobe Steel became particularly important when it constructed a blast furnace and became a major integrated steel maker. Nissho also developed close ties with Fuji Steel by using its position as a supplier to small-scale open hearth processors in the Kansai area. Nissho bought pig-iron from Fuji Steel and sold it to processors as a raw material.

IWAI

One notable feature of Iwai's early post-war history is that its relative position declined. In the mid-1930s it had been a much larger company than either Ataka or Nissho. It had become an industrial and commercial combine by virtue of numerous investments since the early 1910s, but the other two companies had remained simple traders. During the zaibatsu dissolution in the early post-war years, Iwai had to divest itself of industrial holdings and thereby lost control of a number of industrial companies. In the early 1950s, a group called Saisho-kai was formed by former Iwai companies (Daicel,

Toa Wool Spinning and Weaving, Nisshin Steel, Tokuyama Soda, Japan Bridge, and Fuji Photo Film), which contributed to Iwai's growth. Now, however, these companies were much less dependent on Iwai for purchasing raw materials and machineries and marketing their products than they had been in the pre-war period.

Steel was unquestionably Iwai's main business.[45] It was also fairly strong in wool textiles, sugar, wood, and industrial soda. In the case of wool textiles, a wool spinning company it established in 1921, called Chuo Keito Boseki (Central Wool Spinning, which later changed its name to Toa Wool Spinning and Weaving), provided the basis for trade. In 1965, Iwai merged a trading company specializing in woollen yarn, and further strengthened its position in this field.

In the 1950s, Iwai did not move aggressively into new fields as did many other major trading companies.[46] It did not accept the challenge of taking great risks, remaining content instead with the way things were presently moving. In the early 1960s, however, after Iwai Hideo took over presidency from his uncle, Yujiro, the company became more aggressive. In the fields in which it lacked experience, it recruited traders with the necessary skill, and also brought in an executive of the main bank, the Sanwa Bank, as its executive vice-president. This was the first time a member of the top management had been recruited from outside. The merger of the trading company specializing in woollen yarn was also part of this aggressive business strategy.

Unfortunately, this aggressive policy caused financial troubles later. From the mid-1960s, a number of Iwai's customers went bankrupt, and it ended up with a large amount of bad debts. How serious its troubles were is difficult to tell from its financial reports, since whether or not a particular credit is uncollectable is often an arbitrary judgement. It is generally believed that Iwai was in financial trouble at the time but that it could have survived if real efforts had been made.[47] Its main bank, the Sanwa Bank, apparently wanted to merge Iwai with Nissho (a company with which the bank had become intimate since the establishment of a leasing firm, Orient Lease, in the mid-1960s) to create a large trading company which could act as the main trading company of the bank's group. On Iwai's side, the president apparently felt that the future for a trading company of Iwai's size was not propitious and that it would be better to merge with another company before it was too late.

One basic problem of Iwai's was that it was a sort of family company, though in a much different sense than in the pre-war period. At the time of the zaibatsu dissolution, the family had to relinquish a large part of its holdings, retaining only about 20 per cent of the outstanding shares in 1950. Since then, the family share had declined as the total capital increased, and thus, control of the company by the family was far from complete. In other words, it was not a family company in the typical sense; but it was not a completely public company either, for the family remained an important shareholder and the post of president was reserved for family members.

Among Iwai's executives in the post-war period, the only family members who appear are Iwai Yujiro who headed the company from the early 1930s for about thirty years and Iwai Hideo who took over the presidency from Yujiro and retained the post until the merger with Nissho. As far as family presidents are concerned, Yujiro and Hideo seem to have been quite competent. Yet, they are often held responsible for the troubles Iwai encountered from the mid-1960s. The problem was not so much their competence as with the negative effects of family control on open discussion of business strategies: Iwai had become a paternalistic organization where the wisest policy for subordinates was silent conformity.[48] The only choice open for people who had different ideas or who wanted to pursue different policies was to leave the company, and, in fact, many did.

ATAKA

Prior to the mid-1960s, Ataka's growth was similar to Iwai's in many ways. The only noticeable difference was that Ataka was a bit more successful outside the steel trade.[49] In textiles, its dealings covered wool, cotton goods, synthetic textiles, and garments. It dealt in wool before the war, and in the mid-1960s, became one of the top ten wool importers. It was also active in exporting cotton fabric to South-East Asia, the Middle East, and Africa, and garments to the United States and Western Europe. When synthetics became important, it tied up with Asahi Chemical Industry, Toray, and Teijin, and marketed their acrylic yarn and polyester fabric. It was one of the first companies to set up a joint venture abroad in order to promote exports from Japan. For example, in the early 1960s, it set up a factory in Singapore to produce socks by using nylon yarn from Japan.

In wood, its main business at first was to sell logs imported by a foreign trading company from the Philippines. In the mid-1950s, Ataka sent its men to the Philippines and began importing directly. As the Philippine source began to dry up, Ataka tied up with Jardine Matheson and became active in North Borneo. From the United States, soon after the Korean War, it began importing red cedar, hemlock and Douglas fir.

In machinery, Ataka continued to be an agent for an American machine tool manufacturer, Gleason, and maintained its position in this field. It was also successful in selling steel-making machines to Yahata Steel and textile machines to its customers abroad.

Ataka was cautious in risk-taking, seemingly satisfied with slow growth up to the mid-1960s. As other trading companies expanded in size, however, Ataka faced the possibility that it would be outdistanced by others and become an obscure, medium-sized company. Around this time, Ataka apparently changed its policy from a conservative to an aggressive one. Without merger, by the mid-1970s, it had caught up with Tomen and Nichimen. Ten years earlier, sales of these companies had exceeded Ataka's by 50 per cent.

As in the case of Iwai, the new aggressive policy seems to have generated financial problems.[50] In 1972, Ataka began supplying BP's oil from the Middle East to a refinery in Canada called Newfoundland Oil Refinery. Ataka hoped this business would increase its sales so it could surpass its competitors, but the deal was a financial disaster. Ataka obtained the right to supply oil from the refinery by agreeing to extend credits, a normal function for a sogo shosha. What was unusual in this case was that the total amount of unsecured credits Ataka extended amounted to about eleven times its paid-up capital. Initially, Ataka had no intentions of allowing such huge credits, but as the troubles of the refinery worsened, Ataka extended additional credits in order to prevent the bankruptcy of the refinery. Because it had considered the oil trade an extremely important step for expansion, it had not investigated carefully the financial status of the refinery before hastily committing too many resources.

Ataka's banks began to notice problems in mid-1975. Soon after, a mission from Japanese banks was sent to New York, where the oil trade was coordinated. By the end of the year, it became clear that most of the credits would not be collectable in the foreseeable future, so it seemed impossible for Ataka to rehabilitate itself on its own. The Sumitomo and the Kyowa Banks asked C.Itoh to consider a merger of Ataka. After investigating the situation for approximately a year, C.Itoh decided to take over Ataka's steel business and several other areas in which it was relatively weak. The merger finally took place in 1977.

One of Ataka's major problems had been that it did not have the strong backing of any enterprise group. With the Sumitomo Bank as its main bank until the mid-1960s, in a certain sense it was a member of the Sumitomo group. But since the Sumitomo group included other major trading companies—namely, Sumitomo Shoji and C.Itoh—Ataka's role in the group was insignificant. Around 1966, the Sumitomo Bank almost succeeded in merging Ataka with Sumitomo Shoji, but at the last moment, Ataka decided to remain independent, and from that point, leaned towards the Kyowa Bank. The Kyowa Bank became an important source of finance, but it did not have an industrial group, so Ataka remained essentially an unaffiliated company.

Ataka was a peculiar sort of family enterprise, and as in the case of Iwai, family involvement may be said to have adversely affected company development. During the zaibatsu dissolution, the Ataka family disposed of most of its holdings, so its control over the company as stockholder was much weaker than in the case of Iwai. However, the Ataka family retained strong influence over the company. The family's control was more personal than financial, so to speak. Ataka Eiichi, son of the company's founder, was a charismatic leader and, although he was not interested in management, has worked strenuously to create a personal clique. For instance, there were a number of people from the birthplace of the founder who had received their education with financial assistance from Eiichi or his father, and had thereafter pledged allegiance to the family. Through his clique, Eiichi controlled most important personnel decisions.[51]

One indication of Ataka Eiichi's influence over the company is the so-called Ataka Collection. Eiichi was a great pottery collector. He not only had money but a sense of what to buy. His collection included a number of valuable Korean pots from the Koryo and Yi dynasties. Through his collection, Eiichi undoubtedly made an important contribution to fine arts in Japan, but in doing so, he weakened the company. The money used was company capital, and it was not a small sum. Even his assistants in art collection were on the company pay-roll.

In short, the influence of the Ataka family was a negative factor, as in the case of Iwai. But there was one major difference between the two. The Iwai family did its best to modernize the company. Both Yujiro and Hideo were fairly competent, and devoted themselves to the growth of the company; but unfortunately, the turbulence of the post-war period did not allow any remnants of family influence for a company which aspired to become a sogo shosha. Only those which pushed rational management to the utmost could survive. The influence of the Ataka family was nothing but a drawback. Eiichi devoted himself to the enlargement of a clique loyal to himself, and weakened the management structure of the company. The disastrous oil deal should be considered against this background.

NISSHO

Nissho fared much better than either Ataka or Iwai. In the early 1950s, the sales of the three companies were roughly equal. In the following fifteen years, Nissho grew faster than the other two, and in the mid-1960s, Nissho's sales exceeded Ataka and Iwai's by about 50 per cent.[52]

One reason for Nissho's faster rate of growth was that it received support from a few groups. One group consisted of former Suzuki companies such as Kobe Steel and Teijin. Kobe Steel provided the basis for Nissho's steel and non-ferrous metal businesses, whereas Teijin provided its entry into synthetics. Other groups which supported Nissho were the Furukawa group and the Kawasaki group. Since the Kawasaki group had close relations with C.Itoh, Nissho was not its major trading company, but after relations between Kawasaki and Suzuki were taken over by Nissho in the 1930s, Nissho sometimes acted on Kawasaki's behalf thereafter. When the First Atomic Power Industrial group was formed, Nissho brought together former Suzuki companies, the Kawasaki group, and the Furukawa group. It is not clear whether the atomic power project was profitable or not, but it certainly played a role in strengthening Nissho's ties with member companies.

Nissho was more successful in non-steel fields than were Ataka and Iwai. It was, for example, the largest exporter of ships for many years. Nissho began by selling whaling boats to Norway in 1948, then in the 1950s and 1960s, sold a number of ships and tankers to Greek and Scandinavian companies and to American oil companies. Nissho also became sole agent for Boeing in 1956, and in the 1960s and 1970s, it sold about ninety Boeing planes to Japan Air Lines and All Nippon Airways. In 1964, it became an agent for McDonnell Aircraft, and in 1968 succeeded in getting McDonnell's F4E Phanthom chosen as the Defense Agency's major fighter.

In textiles, Nissho's close relations with a former Suzuki company, Teijin, were valuable. The ties were strengthened when Nissho helped Teijin introduce polyester technology from ICI by making use of its long standing business relations.[53] Also important in textiles was the merger of Hakuyo Boeki, Mitsui Bussan's offspring headed by Miyazaki Kiyoshi, president of Mitsui Bussan at the time of its dissolution. Hakuyo Boeki was strong also in foodstuffs. In this field, it had many major customers in Japan as an agent for Bunge, an international grain dealer.

Nissho was also active in non-ferrous metals. In 1959, it became an agent for ALCAN to market aluminium, and in 1960, for ICI to market nickel. With Furukawa it participated in the development of copper mines in the United States, to import copper to Japan. Ties with the Furukawa group were particularly valuable because Furukawa had non-ferrous mines, and Furukawa Electric was the country's major producer of copper wire. Kobe Steel also produced non-ferrous metals and supported Nissho's foothold in this field.

In the first half of the 1960s Nissho outdistanced Ataka and Iwai, and in 1966, caught up with Nichimen. Despite its rapid growth, however, in 1967 it was still just the seventh ranking company, and therefore too small to play a leading role in Japanese trading. About this time, while groping for a new expansionist policy, Nissho became interested in suggestions by the Sanwa Bank concerning the merger of Iwai. Although the two companies were similar in many respects, the merger would at any rate increase the size of the company, and also enable it to become the major trading company for the Sanwa group.

The merger took place in 1968, and Nissho became Nissho-Iwai. In 1969, the newly-formed company moved into fifth position, surpassing Sumitomo Shoji and Toyo Menka. Marubeni and C.Itoh maintained their higher ranks as larger companies, but it appeared that if Nissho-Iwai planned well, catching up with these two seemed possible. However, as was the case in other mergers, it was necessary to eliminate a number of redundant businesses, so the merger in fact did not produce some of the expected results. Nissho-Iwai managed to maintain a lead over Toyo Menka, but Sumitomo Shoji caught up with it in 1971 and the gap between the two widened in the following years. Sumitomo Shoji's sales approached those of Marubeni and C.Itoh; in the past several years, the three have formed the middle group of sogo shosha. Although Nissho-Iwai has grown faster than Toyo Menka and managed to stay above the bottom group, the gap between Nissho-Iwai and the middle group has remained fairly wide.

While Sumitomo Shoji was growing rapidly, Nissho-Iwai did not remain idle. It initiated various projects and entered into many new fields. To a large extent, it was successful in these ventures. The most noteworthy achievement was Nissho-Iwai's organizing role in the import of LNG from Indonesia. By adjusting the differing interests of Japanese institutional buyers, the national oil company of Indonesia (Pertamina), and an American oil company which had drilling rights at a place where gas was found, Nissho-Iwai succeeded in getting all parties to sign agreements in 1973. The Japanese government was also successfully brought in as the financier of this project, which proved to be the biggest LNG project to date in which Japanese companies have participated. The projection is for 150 million tons of LNG to be imported over a twenty-year period, beginning in 1977 (7.5 million tons per year). The first ship carrying LNG arrived in Japan in the spring of 1977.

Despite this and other accomplishments, Nissho-Iwai could not narrow the gap between itself and Sumitomo Shoji. It had the backing of the Sanwa group, but could not take full advantage of the benefits of group affiliation because Nichimen was still a member of the same group and had strong ties with some member companies (especially in oil and chemicals). Furthermore, in comparison with the Sumitomo group, the

Sanwa group was weak in heavy-chemical industry, the engine of growth in the post-war period. On the other hand, the Sumitomo group was not only strong in heavy-chemical fields, but also close-knit. Such strong backing is what made it possible for Sumitomo Shoji to catch up with and outdistance Nissho-Iwai without much difficulty in the first half of the 1970s.

7. THE RISE OF SUMITOMO SHOJI

In the early Meiji era, Sumitomo established a store in Kobe and two stores in Korea to market its copper products (copper mining built the foundation of the Sumitomo House during the Tokugawa period).[54] The Korean stores dealt in cotton yarn, tea and camphor in addition to copper products. Policy was changed, however, and Sumitomo decided not to get involved in pure commerce. In the following years, it set up sales offices in major cities in Japan, China, and Korea, but the only goods with which they dealt were those produced by Sumitomo companies, such as copper products, steel products, and chemicals. Sumitomo depended on Mitsui Bussan, Mitsubishi Shoji and other trading companies for the purchase of a large part of the raw materials and machinery needed by its manufacturing and mining companies, and for the marketing of some of its products.

In the late 1910s, when the Japanese economy was enjoying a boom, Sumitomo reconsidered the business strategy it had pursued, and considered a plan to set up a trading company. The general manager of the Sumitomo zaibatsu strongly opposed the plan, however, so it was not translated into action. He argued that while profits in production were earned by hard work, profits could be earned easily in trading by speculation, so if trading became an important part of Sumitomo's business, it would have adverse effects on production. He further argued that the money Sumitomo would use to train people in trading and establish an international network, could be better spent in the expansion of production. Because of his opposition, at a time when Mitsubishi, Furukawa, and Kuhara—companies in the same line of business as Sumitomo (non-ferrous mining)—entered foreign trade, Sumitomo stuck to its traditional policy.

Immediately after Japan was defeated in the Pacific War, Sumitomo decided to change its anti-trading policy. The major reason for this decision was that it was necessary for Sumitomo to enter new fields in order to absorb people from the holding company and Sumitomo's subsidiaries. The holding company was being dissolved, and Sumitomo's manufacturing companies had too many people for the level of production (which was low because of the shortage of raw materials). Sumitomo did not want to lose the high quality people it had nurtured. Various alternatives other than trading were considered, but trading seemed the best solution since it did not require a large amount of capital, yet its capacity to absorb labour was high.

Sumitomo Shoji's roots, however, date back to 1919. In that year, Sumitomo established a firm to manage land it expected would become valuable with the expansion of the Osaka harbour. During the war, this company merged with another Sumitomo real estate company which managed the Sumitomo Building, home of the main branch of the Sumitomo Bank and the headquarters of various Sumitomo companies. A month later, an architectural firm was added. The new company, essentially a real estate and construction company, was named Sumitomo Tochi Komu. This company was interested in handling construction materials, so Sumitomo's new trading division was added to it in November 1945. Since the name, Sumitomo, was banned as part of the anti-zaibatsu policies of the Occupation period, Sumitomo Tochi Komu changed its name to Nippon Kensetsu Sangyo (Japan Construction Industrial). Several years later, in 1952, when the ban was lifted, the name of the trading company was changed to Sumitomo Shoji.

Sumitomo's decision to add trading to the real estate and construction company proved to be a wise move. Sumitomo was inexperienced in trading, so the initial period was rough going, but the real estate division provided steady income for the company to tide over the difficult first decade. It also contributed to the rapid growth after the mid-1950s.

Metals and machinery accounted for about 80 per cent of Sumitomo Shoji's sales in the early 1950s. This was because the strength of Sumitomo companies was concentrated in this field. In steel, Sumitomo Metal Industries was active; in non-ferrous metals, Sumitomo Metal Industries (copper products) and Sumitomo Chemical (aluminium); in electric wire and machinery, Sumitomo Electric Industrial and Nippon Electric; and in general machinery, Sumitomo Machinery Manufacturing (which later became Sumitomo Shipbuilding and Machinery after it merged with a shipbuilding company). Some of these companies provided important sources of demand, and Sumitomo Shoji used this as a bargaining weapon to establish close ties with non-Sumitomo companies making metals and machinery.

Although Sumitomo Shoji had become a formidable member of the trading community by the early 1950s, it was relatively weak in foreign trade. The products of heavy industry, in which it was strong, were not exportable at this time. In addition, its contact with foreign manufacturers of machinery and industrial raw materials were not well established, since it was a new entrant into this field. Its overseas network was also noticeably weak: its first foreign office was not established until early 1952, and as late as 1955, it had offices in only several cities abroad. As a consequence of all these factors, foreign trade accounted for only about 20 per cent of sales, a share significantly lower than that of other major trading companies.

Sumitomo Shoji's spectacular rise began in the mid-1950s. In the early 1950s, it was the smallest among the top twelve companies (see Table 4.2). In 1956, however, it surpassed Kanematsu, Iwai, Ataka; in 1957, Gosho; in 1959, Nissho; in 1966, Nichimen; and in 1969, Toyo Menka. In the late 1960s, after Nissho and Iwai merged to become Nissho-Iwai, this company surpassed Sumitomo Shoji, but only temporarily. Sumitomo Shoji caught up with Nissho-Iwai in 1971, and widened the difference thereafter. In 1973, it almost caught up with C.Itoh, and seemed about to outdistance both C.Itoh and Marubeni and join the top group. Its growth declined somewhat after the oil shock, however; today Sumitomo Shoji occupies the middle echelon with C.Itoh and Marubeni.

The most important factor in the company's rapid growth in the 1950s was the backing it received from the Sumitomo group. In the early part of the decade, when textiles was a leading industry, the growth of Sumitomo Shoji was handicapped because the Sumitomo group did not have a textile company among its members. As heavy industry became a more important sector of the economy, however, and as products began to be exported, Sumitomo Shoji had a clear advantage over other Osaka-based companies as a result of ties with Sumitomo Metal Industries. From the late 1950s, Sumitomo Shoji acted as Sumitomo Metal Industries' major agent abroad. On this basis, it built its overseas network.

Clearly, the Sumitomo group provided the basis for Sumitomo Shoji's growth, but success was a result also of the initiatives and efforts the company made on its own behalf. In the late 1950s, the eight major Sumitomo companies marketed about 25 per cent of their products and made about 12 per cent of their purchases through Sumitomo Shoji. They marketed and purchased the remainder themselves or through other trading companies. Manufacturing companies in the Sumitomo group were normally interested in promoting Sumitomo Shoji, but business sense compelled them to opt for the best deals in marketing and purchasing and, hence, when other trading companies came with better offers, they used these companies. In order to grow, Sumitomo Shoji had to capture a larger share of the Sumitomo business by increasing the number of qualified traders and strengthening its networks both in Japan and abroad. At the same time, it could not ignore non-Sumitomo companies. Even if it succeeded in capturing a greater share, say 50 per cent, of the Sumitomo business, at least one-third of the trading company's total business had to be generated through non-Sumitomo companies. It was necessary, in other words, to strengthen its ties with these companies as well.

Sumitomo Shoji attempted to remedy its weaknesses in two ways. First, the company merged or brought under its control trading companies which had particular strength in areas in which it was weak. Accordingly, Sumitomo Shoji merged with a steel trading company in 1962, brought two textile trading companies under its control in the early 1960s, and in 1970, absorbed Mitsui Bussan's offspring, Sogo Boeki, a company which specialized in trade with the Socialist countries. The other approach it took to correct its deficiencies was to recruit experienced traders from outside, not a usual Japanese business practice. Serious recruitment efforts began as early as the beginning of the 1950s, when experienced traders of foodstuffs were recruited from Mitsui Bussan's offsprings. In the 1960s, textile traders were recruited. When Mataichi (one of the Senba Eight) merged with Kinsho, and Gosho with Kanematsu, a number of textile traders left these companies and joined Sumitomo Shoji. At the time of Gosho's merger, Sumitomo Shoji recruited a number of traders in other fields, such as pulp and paper. As a consequence of such an aggressive recruitment policy, in 1973 600 out of 3,800 male workers had been brought in from outside, a very high proportion for a Japanese company.[55]

In the early 1970s, when Sumitomo Shoji nearly caught up with C.Itoh and Marubeni, predictions based on its past growth suggested that the age of the 'Big Three' (Mitsubishi Shoji, Mitsui Bussan and Sumitomo Shoji) was approaching. The prediction proved inaccurate, however. In 1977 and 1978, the last two years recorded in Table 4.2, Sumitomo Shoji was the smallest of the middle group, about one-third behind Mitsubishi Shoji and Mitsui Bussan in sales.

When compared with Mitsubishi Shoji and Mitsui Bussan, Sumitomo Shoji seems weak in two areas. One deficiency is that the percentage of foreign trade is low. Foreign trade accounts for 40 per cent of Sumitomo Shoji's business, while for the other two companies, it is roughly 50 per cent. This 40 per cent represents a considerable improvement over the early 1950s when foreign trade was about 20 per cent, but the figure is still low. One explanation for this is that while Sumitomo Shoji has done fairly well in trade with the United States and other developed countries, its trade with South-East Asia and other developing regions has been weak.

A second basic weakness is simply the fact that the company's history is relatively short. The year 1919 is taken as its founding year, but trading really began in late 1945; Sumitomo Shoji's history as a trading company is thus just slightly longer than thirty years. This has been too short a period to build manpower, trust, and networks comparable to those of Mitsubishi Shoji and Mitsui Bussan.

8. OTHER TRADING COMPANIES

KANEMATSU

Since Kanematsu had neither numerous industrial holdings nor strong ties with the military, it was not greatly affected by the zaibatsu dissolution; in fact, its relative position improved in the early post-war years. In 1950, it was the largest company in terms of paid-up capital, and while it was somewhat smaller in terms of sales than the 'Five Cotton Traders of the Kansai Area', it had a good chance of catching up with them and becoming a leader of the trading community. In the following several years, however, although it did well in comparison with Gosho, Kanematsu was outdistanced by many other companies and became a somewhat obscure company.[56]

Kanematsu's relatively slow growth in the 1950s may be attributed to the crash after the Korean War boom. As a step towards diversification, the company had purchased large quantities of the 'three new products' at its own risk. When their prices plummeted after the boom, Kanematsu lost heavily and faced financial disaster. With the help of the Bank of Japan and the Bank of Tokyo, it managed to weather the crisis, but was forced to eliminate products in which it did not show strength and concentrate on wool, grain, and a few other products. Consequently, in the late 1950s it was well behind other trading companies in diversification, and imports accounted for too high a share for a sogo shosha.

Around this time, Kanematsu began to change its strategy. First, in order to strengthen its domestic trade, it approached the Kangyo, Hokkaido Takushoku, and Kobe Banks for yen loans, since its main bank, the Bank of Tokyo, essentially a foreign exchange bank, could not meet this demand.[57] In addition, in order to increase internal funds, Kanematsu elected to become a public company (previously, shareholding had been restricted to Kanematsu employees) and have its shares listed on stock exchanges. At the same time, Kanematsu made efforts to break into heavy goods by using ties with the three commercial banks mentioned above (eventually, the Kangyo Bank); absorbing a trading company (Sanko Bussan) which was strong in steel, cement and chemicals; and using the enhanced financial position these policies afforded to create affiliated companies.

The new strategy made Kanematsu a dynamic company again, but a little too late to narrow the gap with the major trading companies. Marubeni's and C.Itoh's performance far outstripped that of Kanematsu's; even Toyo Menka and Nichimen were twice as big as Kanematsu in the mid-1960s. What provided new impetus to Kanematsu was the merger with Gosho in 1967. As discussed earlier, Gosho lagged well behind other major trading companies, facing financial disaster in the mid-1960s. At this point, its main bank, the Bank of Tokyo decided to merge it with Kanematsu. Though this was a merger of two similar companies (both were strong in soft goods, particularly textiles), it went well.[58] The Bank of Tokyo assumed a large part of Gosho's liabilities, so the new company started out as a financially strong company. The merger was helped also by the fact that only those of Gosho's businesses which would complement but not compete with Kanematsu's (for example, cotton and wool, both textile materials but not competitive) were taken over; in large measure, other areas were not included in the deal.

In the late 1960s and early 1970s, Kanematsu-Gosho grew rapidly and caught up with Nichimen and Toyo Menka. Today, the three companies form the bottom-most strata of sogo shosha. As is true for the other two companies as well, Kanematsu-Gosho suffers from weak group affiliation. Its main bank, the Bank of Tokyo, does not have a group. By the late 1960s, the company had developed close ties with the Kangyo Bank, but when it merged with the Daiichi Bank to become the Daiichi Kangyo Bank, C.Itoh became its main trading company. Kanematsu-Gosho maintains a foothold in the Daiichi Kangyo group, but the role it plays in the group is small. For further growth, it needs a stronger group affiliation.

OKURA SHOJI

In some fields, Okura Shoji remains a well-known company, but in the eyes of the general public, because it is rarely mentioned in the mass media, the company has become obscure.[59] It is medium-sized, about one-fourth the size of Nichimen (the smallest of the sogo shosha), and it specializes in steel and machinery. Its situation now is quite changed from what it was in the Meiji era, when it attracted wide attention as a leading trading company.

The relative decline of Okura Shoji began in the 1920s when heavy industry made rapid progress and began to produce goods which had previously been imported. Until the late 1930s, however, the company retained considerable influence in the trading community because of the backing of the Okura zaibatsu. In the post-war period, it lost this support and had to grow on its own, for unlike other zaibatsu, Okura was not able to re-group and make a comeback. The zaibatsu's mining company, a major company, was operating in China, and its assets were confiscated at the end of the war. Loss of these assets plus the pressures added by regulations of the wartime and early post-war years, weakened Okura Shoji to the point where it could not pull together former Okura companies. Salvation might have been provided by a bank had it not been for the fact that the Okura zaibatsu had depended on the Yasuda Bank (the present Fuji Bank) and did not have a bank of its own.

Of course, Okura Shoji was not alone in having suffered the loss of overseas assets and separation from former affiliates. Judging from other examples then, it might be said that the company stood a chance of becoming a leading company in the early 1950s. It suffered no ill effects from the crash after the Korean War, for example. In 1954, however, the company encountered a serious financial problem.[60] In order to secure supply of coal for the Japan Procurement Agency, its Fukuoka office extended large credits to small and medium-sized coal mines. When these mines were stricken with a series of industrial strikes, the debts became uncollectable. Okura Shoji managed to weather the crisis, but in doing so was forced to stop dealing in many products which were not traditional lines of its business, and concentrate on the import of machinery. Consequently, it became a specialized trading company.

In 1964, Okura Shoji merged with Kishimoto Shoten, a steel trader. This company was a long-established trading company, whose founding dated back to the early nineteenth century. In the early Meiji era, when steel began to be imported from the West, the company began dealing in steel. Later, when Yahata Steel was established, Kishimoto Shoten became its agent. In the 1910s, however, Kishimoto participated in the formation of Nippon Kokan, and became its agent instead. This close relationship with Nippon Kokan continued until the merger with Okura Shoji.

In 1941, Kishimoto had merged with C.Itoh and Marubeni to form Sanko, but had separated out a few years later to become independent again.[61] In the first ten years or so, business was good, but it faced the same problems all steel traders faced, that is, the reduction of profit margins. As a solution, Kishimoto acquired metal processing companies, but because this was an unfamiliar field, it soon faced financial troubles. At this point, Nippon Kokan and the Fuji Bank (its main bank) arranged the merger of the company with Okura Shoji.

The merger was a good opportunity for Okura Shoji to diversify and expand. Having tied up with United States Steel and other machinery manufacturers abroad, it had been importing various machinery for Japanese steel manufacturers; it could strengthen its sales position if it could market their products. Furthermore, the merger made it possible for Okura Shoji to strengthen its network in Japan, one of its weak points.

After the merger, Okura Shoji's sales increased more rapidly than they had before. Obviously, the acquisition of the steel trade was an important factor, for this trade grew rapidly as a result of the high growth of the economy as a whole. At the same time, it should be noted that Okura Shoji had done fairly well in its traditional line of business, that is, the import of machinery. The company played an important role in the import not only of steel-making machinery but also of various industrial electronic equipment, a field in which Japanese manufacturers lagged behind (despite their success in consumer electronic equipment). Today, Okura Shoji is a medium-sized company in which metals account for about 50 per cent and machinery for another 25 per cent of total sales. It is too small and too specialized to be considered a sogo shosha.

STEEL TRADERS

The post-war period has been a tragic one for the large specialized steel trading companies.[62] In 1948 when Nippon Seitetsu appointed eleven companies to be primary distributors in Japan, six were specialized steel traders. Five of these have since disappeared. Nippon Tekko Kogyo was the first to face a crisis: it disappeared from the trading scene in the mid-1950s. Then in 1961, Morioka Kogyo was merged by C.Itoh.

In the mid-1960s, Kinoshita Sansho was merged by Mitsui Bussan, and Osaka Kozai became an affiliate of Mitsubishi Shoji. Osaka Kozai retained its identity for another ten years, but in 1977, was merged with Irimaru Sangyo to become Nittetsu Shoji, a sales subsidiary of Nippon Steel. After these five companies (Nippon Tekko Kogyo, Morioka Kogyo, Kinoshita Sansho, Osaka Kozai and Irimaru Sangyo) disappeared, Okaya became the sole steel trader left among Nippon Seitetsu's distributors.

The primary distributors of other steel manufacturers faced similar fates. Among Nippon Kokan's distributors, Nankai Kogyo merged with Toyo Menka in 1963; Kishimoto merged with Okura Shoji in 1964; and Totsu with Marubeni in 1966. In the case of Sumitomo Metal Industries, the two major distributors, Igeta Kokan and Yamamoto Kogyo merged to become Sumikin Bussan, in which the steel manufacturer owns a controlling share. Kawasaki Steel and Kobe Steel were much more active in taking initiatives in marketing than Sumitomo Metal Industries—they merged a number of steel traders.

In retrospect, three methods by which primary distributors might have been able to survive can be identified. They might have tried to become competitive with sogo shosha in financing; or, they could have exerted themselves to find new customers; thirdly, they might have shifted their activities into downstream services. In theory, each of these alternatives seem reasonable; in practice, however, none proved workable for steel distributors. Since their main method of business was to buy steel from manufacturers with cash and sell it on credit to large users and regional distributors, their most important function was financial, rather than marketing. However, when they competed with sogo shosha, they were in a disadvantageous position because as smaller companies, the conditions on which they obtained loans from banks were much less favourable than those granted sogo shosha. The steel distributors might have sought new customers abroad, but their backgrounds as domestic distributors hampered

them in this. Here again, their position was disadvantageous
vis-à-vis sogo shosha. Perhaps, steel distributors should have
begun to emphasize marketing and services to end-users in
Japan; in large measure, however, they stuck to established
methods of business.

Steel manufacturers were difficult for distributors to bar-
gain with; they were oligopolists, hence in the position almost to dictate the terms of marketing. Kansai-based manufacturers, for example, had sales subsidiaries against which
they judged the performance of steel traders. It was extremely difficult to extract better deals from them. Thus, lacking
high credit ratings and marketing ability abroad, the only
choice for distributors was to establish frequent contacts
with small end-users and to offer better services (e.g., delivery
of the correct amount of a particular kind of steel at the
specified time). That this course of business might lead to
success is well demonstrated in the case of Hanwa, a company
born in the early post-war period and one of the major steel
trading companies today. Most large steel traders, however,
did not choose this role—they were dependent on their
financial function in marketing and lost out in this to sogo
shosha.

TEXTILE TRADERS

As was true in the case of steel traders, the post-war history of the Senba Eight, textile traders, has been tragic.[63]
Around 1950, these companies were not as large as the 'Five
Cotton Traders of the Kansai Area', but they were able to
compete with the latter in many fields. After the crash following the Korean War boom, however, their growth was
stunted, and by the early 1960s, most had disappeared from
the trading scene. Maruei was the first to go: it was merged
by Nichimen in 1954. Then, Iwata went bankrupt. In the
late 1950s, Toyoshima was brought under the control of its
sister company in Nagoya. Then in the early 1960s, Tazuke
was merged by Nichimen; Mataichi by Kinsho; Takemura
by Teijin Shoji; and Takenaka became an affiliate of Sumi-

tomo Shoji (Takenaka later became Sumisho Sen'i). Since then, Yagi has been the sole survivor.

In many ways, the problems the Senba Eight faced were similar to those which beset steel traders. For instance, their suppliers (spinners in this case) were oligopolists and, thus, in the dominant bargaining position. Furthermore, they were dependent on their financing function as intermediaries between suppliers and users. Consequently, as in the case of steel traders, in the 1950s when sogo shosha with better credit ratings stepped up their trading in this field, interest payments cut into the profit margins of textile traders and their position was weakened. It might have been possible to find a way out of their crisis situation by going abroad to secure new markets or by going downstream and making designs for printing and garments, etc., but these companies also stuck to their established trade, and tried to make up for reduced margins by speculation.

One should add in their defence, of course, that they were handicapped in efforts to export. They lost heavily in the crash after the Korean War, and in the following years, because they did not get as much support from the Bank of Japan as the 'Five Cotton Traders of the Kansai Area', became much smaller companies. This made it difficult for them to establish foreign offices since the government (MITI) tended to favour larger companies in the allocation of foreign exchanges. Even if the smaller traders had been given a free hand, it would have been extremely difficult for them to make exports their major business, for, except for slight involvement in China in the 1930s, they were essentially domestic traders who lacked experience in foreign trade. In contrast, C.Itoh, originally a yarn store like all the Senba Eight, emerged successful because it was able to use foreign trade as an escape hatch after spinners improved their trading position on the domestic scene.

The growth of Chori in the post-war period provides another contrast with the Senba Eight.[64] Its main business, like that of the Senba Eight, was yarn and fabric, but unlike them,

Chori has continued to grow and has become a medium-sized company. The important difference in business tactics was that Chori handled new types of yarn and, thus, was able to play a greater marketing role. In the pre-war period, it began handling rayon yarn and became fairly successful in this field. In the post-war period, the company proceeded to handle nylon and polyester yarn, the demand for which rose sharply from the mid-1950s. The producers of nylon and polyester were much larger companies than the cotton spinners the Senba Eight dealt with, and in this regard, Chori was in a worse bargaining position, but because various experiments had to be made and greater sales efforts were needed for the new products, Chori was actually in a better position to reap large rewards for successful marketing. The company was not, of course, the sole trader in this field, but because it was the first to begin handling nylon and polyester successfully, it established an advantageous position early.

Itoman, Tamurakoma, and Yamaguchi all started as importers of Western cloth who later, when import substitution was completed, made printed cloth their specialities.[65] These companies continue to exist today. In Yamaguchi's case, heavy involvement in China and Korea during the war made reconstruction after the war difficult, so a small new company (Yamaguchi Gen) was established as a separate company. Itoman and Tamurakoma, on the other hand, retained their relative positions from the pre-war period, and were among the active textile traders around 1950. Both Itoman and Tamurakoma were hit by the crash after the Korean War, and in this regard they bear some resemblance to the Senba Eight, but they were in a better position to survive, because they had one skill which sogo shosha could not easily acquire even with better credit ratings: in short, they had designing skill. Their main business since the late Meiji era had been to create designs, get them printed on fabric at their own risk, and market the final product (printed cloth). They grew in size mainly because they surpassed other similar companies in designing and merchandising.

Among the three, Itoman is best known today. Based on its strength in printed cloth, it diversified into other textile fields, such as raw cotton, wool, synthetics, and garments, and became an integrated textile company. Later, it went into foodstuffs and other soft goods, and grew rapidly. Recently, Itoman took over Ataka's textile division when it was separated out, and further strengthened its position in the textile trade. Tamurakoma is in contrast a much smaller company which deals mainly in printed cloth and garments. It is one of the largest textile traders in the Senba district in Osaka, but it is not well-known to the general public. Yamaguchi Gen is much smaller still, and its visibility is even less.

9. CONCLUDING REMARKS

In the early 1950s, the position of trading companies *vis-à-vis* manufacturing companies was weakened considerably by the post-war confiscation of their overseas assets, the regulation of trade during and after the war, and the government's policy of giving top priority to manufacturing companies in its post-war reconstruction efforts. The dissolution of Mitsui Bussan and Mitsubishi Shoji further weakened the position of trading companies. In their place, the 'Five Cotton Traders of the Kansai Area' and other textile traders emerged as leading companies and competed for supremacy.

In the mid-1950s, the government recognized the need to strengthen trading companies. With this purpose in mind, it encouraged the merger of trading companies by offering the assistance of the Bank of Japan and, at the same time, favouring larger companies in the allocation of foreign exchanges. These measures did not bring about exactly what the government had hoped for, but they were useful in nurturing larger companies along the road to becoming sogo shosha. In the 1950s, a number of important mergers took place, and by the end of the decade, the number of companies in the top group was reduced to about fourteen. By that time, Mitsubishi Shoji and Mitsui Bussan had reappeared, and the degree of concentration of the top ten companies in foreign trade returned to the pre-war level.

In the next decade, further weeding took place. In the mid-1960s, Kinoshita Sansho was absorbed by Mitsui Bussan, and Totsu by Marubeni. Then a few years later, Iwai was absorbed by Nissho and Gosho by Kanematsu. Thus, by the end of the decade, ten companies formed the top group. All these were called sogo shosha. Then in the middle of the 1970s, Ataka ran into financial trouble and was merged by C.Itoh. Today, only nine companies remain as sogo shosha.

Although the degree of concentration in the post-war period has become equivalent to that of the pre-war period, a few important changes have taken place in the composition of the leading trading companies. For example, Mitsui Bussan, which dominated the pre-war trade, has become less important, though it is still the second ranking company. Another interesting change is that C.Itoh and Marubeni, textile trading companies in the pre-war period, have succeeded in diversifying to become major trading companies in the post-war period. The rise of Sumitomo Shoji has also been spectacular. Starting from scratch, it has become a leading trader in the span of about three decades. C.Itoh, Marubeni, and Sumitomo Shoji form the second strata of sogo shosha today.

In the past few decades, the number of companies in the top group has declined from about two dozens to nine. The rate of decline was not uniform, decelerating after the rapid pace of the 1950s. During the 1970s, only one company disappeared. Still, the trend is clearly toward decline. A question often raised in trading circles is whether all nine companies will remain throughout the 1980s. If any changes occur, the bottom three companies are most likely to be affected: they might be merged by larger companies, or their sales might lag behind so that they cease to be sogo shosha.

One conclusion which can be drawn from this and previous chapters is that trading is a competitive industry. A company might establish an advantageous position in some field and profit from it for a while, but other companies can imitate it and begin to cut into its profits. Thus, in order to grow, a company must continuously take risks. Still, a single company cannot be successful all the time, and when failure involves large capital losses, financial problems may be so great that a company might disappear from the trading scene altogether. Larger companies have advantages over smaller ones because of better credit ratings, more extensive trading networks, and special ties with manufacturers, but since they too face competition from smaller companies and manufacturers, they too must continue to take risks. Such a competitive situation has made the trading industry unstable and caused a number of bankruptcies.

1. Foreign trade in this period is described in a number of publications. For example, see Fukui Keizo, *Kaiko-roku: Waga Hanseiki*, 1974, p. 129, and Toyo Menka, *Tomen Shiju-nen Shi*, 1960, p. 197.

2. Fukui, p. 115.

3. Itohchu Shoji, *Itohchu Shoji Hyakunen*, 1969, p. 207.

4. Ibid., p. 236.

5. Nichimen Jitsugyo, *Nichimen Shichiju-nen Shi*, 1962, p. 164.

6. Mitsui Bussan, *Chosen to Sozo*, 1976, p. 120; and Mitsubishi Shoji, 'Mitsubishi Corporation', n.d., p. 35.

7. Mitsubishi Shoji, 'Who We Are, What We Do, Where We Are Going', n.d., p. 5.

8. Niizeki Yasutaro's recollection in *MBK Life*, June 1965.

9. This explanation was given by Takagaki Katsujiro in *Ryowa*, No. 11(1964), p. 21.

10. Mitsui Bussan, *Kaiko-roku*, 1976, p. 285.

11. Nakano Seishi, a former managing director of Kanematsu Gosho, recalls this period in *KG Monthly*, November 1972.

12. This is an estimate given by a bank. See *Daiyamondo*, 24 March 1956, p. 29.

13. Cho Toru later recalls his borrowing money from a black marketeer through one of his mistresses (an unpleasant memory to him) in *MBK Life*, January 1976.

14. The first major step toward strengthening trading companies was revealed in the statement issued on 16 July 1954. See *Daiyamondo*, 11 August 1954, p. 33.

15. Ibid., p. 34.

16. Ichikawa Shinobu's recollection which appeared in Noda Kazuo (ed.), *Sengo Keiei-shi*, Nihon Seisansei Honbu, 1965, p. 902; *Ekonomisuto*, 5 March 1955, p. 27; and Teijin, *Teijin no Ayumi*, Vol. 7, 1972, p. 190.

17. *Daiyamondo*, 24 March 1956, p. 29.

18. *Toyo Keizai Shinpo*, 3 April 1954, p. 15.

19. Small companies suffered. The problems they faced are described in Shinko Sangyo, *Wagasha Shiju-nen no Ayumi*, 1976, p. 7.

20. Ministry of International Trade and Industry, *Tsusho Hakusho 1955*, pp. 380–2.

21. Takagaki Katsujiro's recollection in *Ryowa*, No. 11 (1964), p. 31.

22. *Ekonomisuto*, 15 November 1952, p. 34.

23. The problems which needed to be settled before the merger are described in *Ryowa*, January 1980, p. 10.

24. The path to the rebirth of Mitsui Bussan is described in section 2, Chapter 4 of Mitsui Bussan, *The 100 Year History of Mitsui & Co., Ltd., 1876–1976*, 1977.

25. The post-war evolution of Mitsui Bussan is described in Mitsui Bussan (1977), Chapters 5–8. Mitsubishi Shoji began preparing its history in early 1980. In *Ryowa*, January 1980, the company published a preliminary report, which is at present the major source of information on its post-war evolution.

26. Interview with Kanbara Takeo in April 1980.

27. The way in which Mitsui Bussan made an unusually quick decision to merge Kinoshita is described in Mitsui Bussan (1977), pp. 229–32.

28. *Ryowa*, January 1980, pp. 127–8.

29. Ibid., pp. 109–21.

30. Seikei Tsushin-sha, *Sogo Shosha Nenkan 1978–79*, p. 281.

31. Mitsui Bussan, *Chosen to Sozo*, p. 312.

32. The major source of information on Daiken Sangyo is Marubeni, 'Marubeni Kessha no Zenya' (mimeographed), No. 1–4, 1964.

33. Unless otherwise specified, the following discussion on Marubeni is based on Marubeni, *Marubeni Shashi: Honshi-hen* (unpublished), 1975.

34. This paragraph relies in part on the files on Asano Bussan and Asahi Bussan in the archives section of Marubeni.

35. *Marubeni*, May 1961, p. 3.

36. This paragraph is based on an interview with Tajika Tokuzo of the archives section of Marubeni. The interview took place in October 1979.

37. The basic source of data on C. Itoh until the late 1960s is Itohchu Shoji, *Itohchu Shoji Hyakunen*, 1969.

38. *Daiyamondo*, 4 December 1971, p. 113.

39. Echigo's recollection in *C.I. Monthly*, July 1978.

40. This and the following paragraphs are based on an interview with Yajima Saburo, a former managing director of Toyo Menka. The interview took place in June 1980.

41. The basic sources of data on Toyo Menka in the post-war period are Toyo Menka, *Tomen Shiju-nen Shi* and a handwritten manuscript of Toyo Menka's history from 1960 to the mid-1970s, available at the public relations office of the Tokyo headquarters. As for Nichimen, Nichimen Jitsugyo, *Nichimen Shichiju-nen Shi* covers the period up to the early 1960s. The following period is covered by the company magazine, *Gekkan Nichimen* and Fukui Keizo, *Kaiko-roku: Waga Hanseiki*.

42. This paragraph is based on an interview with Fukui Keizo, a former president of Nichimen. The interview took place in February 1980.

43. This and the following paragraphs are based on an interview with Yajima Saburo.

44. Gosho's post-war history is described in Gosho, *Gosho Rokuju-nen Shi*, 1967, but many important questions are left vague. This source was supplemented by interviews with Kanbara Takeo, a former president, and Ogawa Kyoichi, a former managing director of Gosho. The interview with Kanbara took place in April 1980 and that with Ogawa in February 1980.

45. Iwai Sangyo, *Iwai Hyakunen Shi*, 1964, covers Iwai's post-war history up to the early 1960s.

46. This is based on an interview with Ushiba Naomichi, a former employee of Iwai. The interview took place in June 1980.

47. This view was expressed by several former Iwai employees in the interview in June 1980. Also, the same view appeared in *Toyo Keizai*, 11 May 1968, p. 12.

48. Interview with Ushiba Naomichi.

49. Ataka Sangyo, *Ataka Sangyo Rokuju-nen Shi*, 1968, covers Ataka's post-war history up to the mid-1960s.

50. Ataka's failure is documented in NHK, *Aru Sogo Shosha no Zasetsu*, Nihon Hoso Shuppan Kyokai, 1977; Nihon Keizai Shinbun-sha, *Hokai*, Nihon Keizai Shinbun-sha, 1977; and Shioda Nagahide, *Ataka Sangyo no Kenkyu*, Daiyamondo-sha, 1977. Also, though fictionalized, Matsumoto Seicho, *Ku no Shiro*, Bungei Shuju-sha, 1978, provides interesting insights into the process of Ataka's failure.

51. NHK, p. 71.

52. Nissho, *Nissho Shiju-nen no Ayumi*, 1968, covers Nissho's postwar history up to the merger with Iwai.

53. Takahata Seiichi describes the role of Nissho in Teijin's introduction of polyester technology in *Ekonomisuto*, 28 September 1971, p. 85.

54. Unless specified otherwise, this section is based on Sumitomo Shoji, *Sumitomo Shoji Kabushiki Kaisha-shi*, 1972.

55. Mainichi Shinbun-sha (ed.), *Nippon no Shosha—Sumitomo Shoji*, Mainichi Shinbun-sha, 1973, p. 33.

56. Kanematsu, *Kanematsu Kaiko Rokuju-nen*, 1950, covers the history of the company up to the late 1940s. The two major sources of data for the period after that are the company magazine and financial reports.

57. Interview with Miki Takuji, head of the planning and administration of Kanematsu-Gosho's Osaka office, in July 1980.

58. This is the view expressed by a managing director of the Bank of Tokyo, which appeared in *Boeki no Nihon: Kanematsu-Gosho Tokushu-go*, 1972, p. 34.

59. The basic source of data on Okura Shoji is *Boeki no Nihon: Okura Shoji*, 1978.

60. This paragraph is based on an interview with Sekine Shigenobu of Okura Shoji. The interview took place in November 1979.

61. Kishimoto's history up to the late 1940s also appears in Marubeni, *Marubeni Zenshi*, pp. 142–4.

62. The following discussion on steel traders is based on Sato Noboru, *Nihon Tekko Hanbai-shi*, Kyodo Kogyo Shinbun-sha, 1978; and interviews with Sato Noboru and Oki Tatsuji in May 1980. Hanwa Kogyo, *Hanwa Kogyo Sanju-nen Shi*, 1978 also contains a general discussion on steel traders.

63. The following discussion on the Senba Eight is based on Yagi Shoten, *Sogyo Hachiju-nen Shi*, 1972; and interviews with Ina Hajime, a former director of Iwata Shoji, and Iwasaki Takao of Toyoshima in April 1980.

64. This paragraph is based on articles on Chori which appeared in *Toyo Keizai*, 22 April 1965; 30 June 1969; and its investment edition, November 1960.

65. The following discussion on Itoman, Tamurakoma, and Yamaguchi is based on an interview with Asami Kazuya of Tamurakoma.

5

Cultural and Economic Background

1. THE DISMAL VIEW

IN the past several decades, the view that trading companies are bound to decline has gained currency. It has not been entirely unfounded. In the 1920s, a number of large trading companies, such as Suzuki, Mogi, and Takada, went bankrupt. Around 1930, Gosho and Nippon Menka, large cotton traders, experienced financial troubles, so severe that Nippon Menka managed to survive only by reducing capital and obtaining relief loans from its main bank (the Yokohama Specie Bank), and Gosho became a subsidiary of a spinning company, Toyo Boseki. In the 1950s and early 1960s, most of the Senba Eight and many steel distributors disappeared from the trading scene. These events undoubtedly gave credence to the pessimistic view of the future for trading companies.

It is not certain when such pessimism first appeared, but by the end of the 1920s, it had begun to affect even some members of giant companies such as Mitsui Bussan. Hashimoto Eiichi, chairman of that company in the mid-1970s, recalls that when he entered the company in 1930, he was asked by one of his seniors why he had joined a company which was bound to perish.[1] Undoubtedly, the man who posed this question had been affected by the events in the 1920s, but he may also have been influenced by the experience of European countries where trading companies had receded to the background with industrial progress. This European experience had been brought to public attention, especially by scholars who studied *Das Kapital*, in which Karl Marx discusses the supremacy of industrial capital over commercial capital after the Industrial Revolution. Many of the writers who expressed a pessimistic view regarding trading companies had been influenced by Marxism in one way or another.

There is some confusion about exactly what is meant by the statement that trading companies are bound to decline, i.e. the reasoning behind this pessimistic view. One interpretation is that the market does not need trading companies, so therefore, they are bound to perish. Experience has proven this to be unfounded, however. Even in the West, there exist a large number of wholesalers and foreign trading companies, though they occupy a less important position in the economy and are less visible than sogo shosha. In Japan, there are also numerous trading companies, in addition to sogo shosha and the other major trading companies discussed in Chapter 2. Only in a few products have manufacturers established exclusive trade channels. For all others, trading companies perform various functions, with no indication that they will disappear in the near future.

Table 5.1 illustrates types of distribution channels. Only in Type IV is there little need for trading companies. In this case, producers and buyers can trade directly. On the other hand, in Type I, the need for trading companies is most keenly felt —to have goods collected from the large number of producers

TABLE 5.1
The Types of Distribution Channels

Number of Buyers \ Number of Producers	Large	Small
Large	I	II
Small	III	IV

and distributed to the large number of buyers. Types II and III lie somewhere between the two extremes.

In all four types of distribution, trading companies have acted as intermediaries in Japan. Even in Type IV, trading companies still act as intermediaries in many transactions (for example, between steel producers and automobile assemblers), though they have become less important over time. In Type II, manufacturers could take the initiative in marketing, but in many cases defer to trading companies. Also in Type III, manufacturers or supermarkets could do purchasing on their own initiative, but in many cases choose not to do so. In Type I, where the need for trading companies is most keenly felt, numerous companies are involved in distribution.

The second interpretation of the view that trading companies are bound to decline is that they will lose control over distribution and come to play a role of only secondary importance. There is much evidence to support this interpretation. For example, in the case of the relationship between trading companies and spinners, trading companies had greater bargaining power at first and earned comfortable margins, but after 1920, the position was reversed. As a result of growth and merger, spinners improved their credit ratings with banks and no longer required the financial functions of trading companies; at the same time, by using oligopolistic or oligopsonistic power, they were able to dictate the terms of marketing or purchasing conditions. In the case of steel, from the beginning it was the producers who dictated the marketing conditions, and trading companies could operate only under their terms.

Although trading companies may not have been completely satisfied in their dealings with spinners and steel makers, these relationships were far more profitable than those with producers of consumer electrical machinery. In this case, producers eliminated trading companies from the distribution channel in the early stages. Consumer electrical machinery is not like steel or yarn, which are homogeneous in quality (making price the only major determinant of sales) and which do not need servicing after sales. To producers of consumer electrical machinery, marketing and servicing seemed almost as important as production, and thus it was difficult to leave these functions to other organizations.

It is true, in other words, that trading companies have been phased out in some areas, and in many others, have lost a leadership role in distribution. On this basis, it is tempting to conclude that although trading companies may not disappear altogether, they cannot play a leadership role in distribution. If such a conclusion is accurate, how can the existence of sogo shosha be explained? Does the pessimistic view exclude them?

In Misonoo Hitoshi's well-known article of 1961, the sogo shosha were clearly included as objects of the pessimistic view.[2] Misonoo was influenced by the Marxist interpretation that industrial capital would inevitably establish supremacy over commercial capital, but the thesis would not have attracted such wide attention at the time if it had had no empirical basis. In fact, the theory was reflected in the characteristics of the Japanese economy at that time. For instance, there were numerous bankruptcies of trading companies in the late 1950s and early 1960s. Also, the economy was shifting the centre of its activities from light industry to heavy industry in the early 1960s, and it was believed that since sogo shosha did not have the manpower to handle the technical knowledge required to market heavy industrial goods, they were destined to decline. Furthermore, the market gap, which was perceived to be large in the early years, had begun to shrink with the development of communications and transportation systems, and many manufacturers began to feel that they could market their products on their own.

As a matter of fact, some new export products in the early 1960s, such as consumer electronic equipment and cars, were handled by manufacturers themselves or their sales subsidiaries. In the case of consumer electronic equipment, sogo shosha were not much interested, since problems outweighed rewards. Many sogo shosha were interested in the automobile business, however. (Mitsui Bussan, for example, was interested in exporting Toyota cars.[3]) In this field also manufacturers decided to market on their own in major markets. Thus, either because trading companies did not want to or were not allowed to handle some of the major new exports, their relative importance in exports was adversely affected.

Despite problems and perhaps some degree of decline in the relative importance of trading companies in certain areas, Misonoo's prediction that they would disappear has so far not been realized. What accounts for the resilience of the sogo shosha?

One explanation which has been put forward is the cost consideration. It is expensive to maintain a sales office: rent must be paid; people must be hired or sent from the head office; a communications system linking the sales office to the head office must be set up, etc. Unless a manufacturer has a wide range of products or his products have high unit prices, the cost of distribution per unit becomes high. On the other hand, for sogo shosha, even if the volume of trading is not large for a particular product, because they handle other products as well, the cost of distribution decreases in many cases. A similar argument applies also to purchasing.

The cost consideration explanation first appeared in an article written by Obinata Yoshio of Toyo Menka, in which he argued against Misonoo's view.[4] Later, Kozo Yamamura put the argument in terms of transaction costs.[5] The cost of transaction, which is essentially the cost of searching out customers, negotiating with them and enforcing the terms agreed upon, was lower in many cases for a manufacturer when he used a sogo shosha than when he marketed on his own. Thus, the sogo shosha have remained as useful organizations.

Before we accept the cost of transaction argument as a valid explanation of the usefulness of sogo shosha, a few important questions must be answered. One question which remains, for example, is precisely why sogo shosha have continued to do better than many manufacturers in terms of transaction costs. And, if they are such efficient organizations, why have similar organizations not developed in other countries? That is to say, the cost of transaction thesis may be an acceptable (though it risks tautology) explanation of why the sogo shosha have been useful at a particular point in time, but it is a poor explanation of their evolution.

2. FINANCIAL POWER

Before the age of modern capitalism, trading and finance were not separated; many of the functions performed by banks today were performed by trading houses. In the Tokugawa period, the House of Mitsui, for example, was a banker as well as a trader, and often combined the two functions to expand its business interests. After the Meiji Restoration, however, since finance was separated from trading, the financial role of trading houses became somewhat obscure.

Japanese scholars have long noted the importance of the financial function performed by trading companies in the modern period, not being under the illusion that they performed a simple intermediary role. More recently, Shibagaki Kazuo, Umezu Kazuro, and Matsumoto Hiroshi, for example, described the essence of sogo shosha as their financial power and explained that this was the major reason for the resilience of sogo shosha.[6] Sogo shosha are considered vulnerable when they are regarded as trading companies, i.e., as part of commercial capital; if they are recognized as a segment of financial capital, there is no reason to think they will disappear.

Foreign observers who have studied sogo shosha have also noticed their financial role. For example, a British economic weekly, *The Economist*, noted some similarities between sogo shosha and merchant banks in Britain;[7] Peter Drucker, a noted American scholar on management, observed that in many ways, the sogo shosha 'is not a "trading company",' but a 'finance company'.[8] People within the sogo shosha also seem fully aware of the fact that the companies maintain their present positions in trading because of their financial power. For example, in a survey of approximately one hundred people at different levels in a sogo shosha, when asked to describe their company's business, the largest number of respondents replied that their company was 'a moneylender with knowledge about commodities'.[9]

Clearly, sogo shosha are not purely financial institutions, since they use money in connection with trading. If a merchant bank could be defined as a merchant-like bank or a bank-like merchant, sogo shosha would be merchant banks *par excellence*.

How large in fact is the financial power of sogo shosha? A glimpse of their strength is provided by the sum of the loans and net credits given by sogo shosha. At the end of March 1977 (the end of the 1976 financial year), the sum was estimated at roughly 9,000 billion yen.[10] This amount was greater than the loans of the largest city bank, Daiichi Kangyo Bank, and amounted to roughly 10 per cent of the total outstanding loans of city banks. In addition, sogo shosha spent another 2,000 billion yen to acquire the securities of other companies.

For what purposes was such a large sum used? Part of the money was spent in creating affiliated companies in various fields. Marubeni, for example, had 172 affiliated companies in Japan in mid-1975.[11] These companies were acquired or newly established primarily to obtain production bases. in the non-textile fields in which the company had been weak in the 1950s, and to create new distribution systems. Marubeni also has a large number of affiliated companies abroad. In March 1976, it had 213 affiliated companies in various parts of the world.[12] As shown in Table 5.2, they are spread over a number of manufacturing industries, distribution, etc. One noticeable difference between domestic and foreign affiliates is that a number of foreign affiliates are involved in resource development, while there are no such domestic affiliates. In 1976, Marubeni's companies were engaged abroad in fishing, coffee growing, pulp and chip production, logging, salt farming, iron ore mining, etc.

For all sogo shosha, foreign investment has become impor-

TABLE 5.2

The Activities of Marubeni's Affiliates Abroad

(As of 31 March 1976)

Industry	Details (products, etc.)
1 MANUFACTURING	
(a) Textiles	yarn, fabric, printing, blankets, towels, garments, synthetic fibres, etc.
(b) Metals	steel rods, galvanized iron sheet, steel sheet, steel pipe, special steel, structural steel, steel wire, aluminium, etc.
(c) Machinery	tape recorders, passenger cars, commercial vehicles, lamps, electrical appliances, televisions, radios, ball-bearings, agricultural machinery, ships, desk calculators, stereophonics, etc.
(d) Chemicals	agricultural chemicals, GMA, formalin, hexamin, polypropylene, synthetic resin, PVC pipe, etc.
(e) Foods	canned fish, canned vegetables, frozen fish, frozen vegetables, instant coffee, vegetable oil, raw sugar, soft drinks, etc.
(f) Others	tubes and tyres, rayon, rubber shoes, leather goods, paper, cement, etc.
2 RESOURCE DEVELOPMENT	fish, coffee, fruit, pulp and chip, logs, salt, coal, iron ore, bauxite, copper, zinc, etc.
3 DISTRIBUTION	
(a) Trading	textiles, steel, automobiles, elevators, ball-bearings, agricultural machinery, construction machinery, valves, textile machinery, chemicals, salt, coffee beans, etc.
(b) Physical Distribution	shipping, warehousing, packaging, cold storage, steel yards, log yards, grain elevators, etc.
4 OTHERS	finance, real estate (hotels, office buildings, housing), construction, factoring, restaurants, leasing, public utilities, travel agencies, etc.

Source: Marubeni

TABLE 5.3
Equity Investment
(Unit: billion yen)

31 March of the year	Mitsubishi Shoji		Mitsui Bussan		Marubeni		C.Itoh		Sumitomo Shoji		Nissho-Iwai		Grand Totals		
	Abroad	Total	Abroad	Total	Abroad	Total	Abroad	Total	Abroad	Total	Abroad	Total	Abroad	Total	Per Cent
1964	1.9	17.3	1.3	24.5	1.0	15.9	1.8	20.2	0.5	11.5	0.8	12.1	7.3	101.5	7.2
1966	2.2	22.7	3.4	30.6	5.4	21.9	3.0	26.2	0.6	13.7	1.5	15.3	16.1	130.4	12.3
1969	15.4	27.9	18.2	62.2	8.7	43.2	9.5	43.6	4.4	23.0	3.8	23.0	60.0	222.9	26.9
1971	23.3	42.2	28.3	93.9	12.8	65.3	13.2	69.2	6.0	33.6	7.3	34.8	90.9	339.0	26.8
1973	38.8	72.9	46.1	188.1	32.9	211.3	26.2	155.8	11.4	100.3	14.2	68.2	169.6	796.6	21.3
1974	68.2	110.2	94.3	259.4	55.8	224.1	49.6	207.6	13.0	109.3	18.2	83.7	299.1	994.3	30.0
1975	75.5	120.5	112.6	284.8	71.6	231.9	60.7	216.9	17.9	111.1	20.9	89.9	359.2	1,055.1	34.0
1977	101.7	149.6	142.3	257.8	87.7	172.5	75.3	232.6	32.4	101.7	28.2	49.1	467.6	963.3	48.5
1978	106.5	166.3	150.7	274.2	96.9	148.4	77.8	242.2	34.3	105.5	37.3	58.9	503.5	995.5	50.5

Source: *Yuka Shoken Hokokusho*

1. Nissho-Iwai was born in 1969 when Nissho and Iwai merged. Before 1969, the figure is the sum of Iwai's and Nissho's investments.

2. The holdings of stocks which are held temporarily and included in current assets are not included here.

tant recently. In the early 1960s, since Japan was still suffering from a chronic balance of payment problems, the government kept foreign investment to a minimum. As a result, as late as 1964, the ratio of foreign to total equity investment in the top six companies was only 7.2 per cent, as shown in Table 5.3. In the second half of the 1960s, since the balance of payments began to record surpluses, regulations on foreign investment became less strict. In the early 1970s, investment became virtually free. Sogo shosha were the first to take advantage of the removal of restrictions to undertake various foreign investments. Consequently, the ratio of foreign to total equity investment rose quickly.

Equity investment is only one part of investment. Unless the trend of loans is known, the picture of foreign investment by sogo shosha is not complete. Unfortunately, however, figures on the amount of foreign loans in the 1960s cannot be obtained from securities reports for most companies. Only in the case of Mitsui Bussan are data on loans available. When equity investment is taken alone, a gradual increase may be noted from the mid-1960s to the end of the 1970s, but when loans are included, as shown in Table 5.4, no such overall increase is shown. Either way, however, figures reveal a substantial increase in foreign investment in the second half of the 1960s.

One large component of foreign investment was resource development. Mitsui Bussan's acquisition of a 50 per cent interest in the aluminium division of AMAX (an American company) at $125 million has been the largest equity investment undertaken by a sogo shosha. Mitsui Bussan also extended about $100 million to the Robe River iron ore project in Australia, and with Mitsubishi Shoji, another $100 million to a copper mining company operating in Zambia. Other large projects include Mitsubishi Shoji's LNG project at Brunei, and Mitsui Bussan and Mitsubishi Shoji's copper mining project at Papua New Guinea. In addition, numerous less glamorous resource development projects were undertaken.

At home and abroad, sogo shosha give loans, trade credits

TABLE 5.4

Mitsui Bussan's Investment

(Unit: million yen)

31 March of the Year	Equity Investment			Long-term Loans			Total Investment		
	Abroad	Total	Per Cent	Abroad	Total	Per Cent	Abroad	Total	Per Cent
1964	1,276	24,657	5.2	164	11,670	1.4	1,440	36,327	4.0
1966	3,359	30,598	11.0	269	22,416	1.2	3,628	53,014	6.8
1969	18,161	62,216	29.2	28,458	55,348	51.4	46,619	117,564	39.6
1971	28,327	93,911	30.2	51,339	106,877	48.0	79,666	200,788	39.6
1973	46,080	188,068	24.5	58,446	233,999	25.0	104,526	422,067	24.7
1974	94,264	259,364	36.3	77,030	255,929	30.1	171,294	515,293	33.2
1975	112,569	284,780	39.4	106,919	280,360	37.8	219,488	565,140	38.7
1977	142,322	257,840	55.2	132,498	377,817	35.1	274,820	635,657	43.2
1978	150,686	274,274	54.9	123,346	379,128	32.5	274,032	653,402	41.9

Source: *Yuka Shoken Hokokusho*

and bank guarantees to their customers (unaffiliated companies) in order to gain a trade advantage. To small and medium-sized companies whose products they wish to handle, sogo shosha provide short-term and medium-term capital, and get in return agency rights or commitments for certain amounts of the goods for set periods of time. To those producers who are short of working capital, sogo shosha extend credit and let them postpone payments for their sales for a few months.

One recent development which indicates the willingness of sogo shosha to provide long-term capital is their entry into leasing. For example, the value of the lease contracts of Mitsubishi Shoji in 1976 amounted to $3 billion.[13] Its leasing business grew with the development of supermarkets in the 1970s. It leases refrigeration cases, packaging materials, cash registers, etc. Some of the capital goods it leases are expensive. For example, a mammoth refrigerated fishing ship costs more than a million dollars. Mitsubishi Shoji's future plans include leasing jumbo jet passenger planes, airport facilities, etc.

Where do sogo shosha get their working and investment capital? In the recent period, the bulk has been in the form of loans from financial institutions. In the 1976 and 1977 financial years, the average sogo shosha had about $3,400 million to spend, of which about $300 million was equity capital and $3,100 million was bank loans. That is to say, less than 10 per cent of the funds came from equity capital.

Such was not the case in the early years. As shown in Table 5.5, it was in the late 1960s that a sharp increase took place in the debt–equity ratio. Yet, even in the mid-1950s, the ratio was quite high on the international standard. What sogo shosha have been doing, in other words, is to get the bulk of their capital from banks and use it to create their own groups of companies at home and abroad, to participate in resource development abroad, and to provide credit to their customers— all in order to secure an advantageous position in trading.

How were the sogo shosha able to get such substantial funding from outside? One tempting hypothesis suggests that sogo shosha are subsidiaries of their main banks. If this is accepted, Mitsubishi Shoji may be regarded as a subsidiary of the Mitsubishi Bank; Mitsui Bussan, the Mitsui Bank; C.Itoh, the Daiichi Kangyo Bank; Marubeni, the Fuji Bank; Sumitomo Shoji, the Sumitomo Bank; Nissho-Iwai, the Sanwa Bank; Toyo Menka, the Tokai Bank; Kanematsu-Gosho, the Bank of Tokyo; and Nichimen, the Sanwa Bank.

TABLE 5.5

The Debt–Equity Ratio of the top Four Sogo Shosha

At the End of Financial Year	Mitsubishi Shoji	Mitsui Bussan	Marubeni	C.Itoh	Average
1954	5.80	*	3.10	5.45	4.92
1955	4.86	*	5.04	4.09	4.69
1956	3.99	*	4.76	3.60	4.08
1957	4.40	*	5.15	4.30	4.58
1958	4.47	4.51	4.86	4.21	4.50
1959	5.61	6.28	4.49	4.93	5.39
1960	3.75	6.79	5.01	4.12	4.84
1961	3.26	7.06	3.62	2.67	3.97
1962	3.41	6.52	4.44	3.01	4.23
1963	2.65	5.70	4.06	3.23	3.77
1964	3.31	7.54	4.79	3.82	4.66
1965	3.56	9.70	5.20	3.94	5.32
1966	4.11	8.17	7.10	3.93	5.62
1967	5.33	10.05	8.39	4.94	6.96
1968	7.08	11.80	9.11	6.13	8.40
1969	7.62	11.43	11.44	7.59	9.33
1970	9.24	13.36	10.22	8.57	10.45
1971	10.53	15.78	9.20	10.73	11.66
1972	10.96	12.29	11.66	9.67	11.25
1973	11.78	12.78	11.61	8.02	11.11
1974	10.56	12.66	10.53	8.75	10.81
1975	9.90	12.87	11.55	12.12	11.57
1976	9.61	11.66	12.14	12.81	11.29
1977	8.63	10.56	12.62	15.19	10.97

Source: *Yuka Shoken Hokokusho*

Notes: * indicates the years when the present Mitsui Bussan did not exist.

1. The debts in this Table are loans from financial institutions (mostly from banks), and thus do not include trade credits received. If debts are defined as the total liabilities on a balance sheet, the ratios become about twice as high as those in this Table.

Why did banks wish to make sogo shosha subsidiaries? Two reasons may be considered. Firstly, since banks were constrained in various ways by the regulations of the Ministry of Finance, they needed a company which could act freely on the bank's behalf (for example, extending loans and credits to small and medium-sized companies without collateral). Secondly, banks needed sogo shosha as their henchmen to create cohesive enterprise groups. Usually, banks have strong interests in creating enterprise groups, because if intra-group transactions increase, a loan to Company A in the group, for example, usually becomes a deposit by Company B in the same group, which enables the bank to make more effective use of its deposits. The sogo shosha can buy shares of member companies, which a bank can do only to a limited extent. They can also make their global networks available to member companies and perform liaison functions, some of which a bank may consider too degrading.

Much evidence may be cited to counter the hypothesis that trading companies are subsidiaries of banks. Firstly, although a company's main bank is one of its large shareholders, it does not have a controlling share (the holdings cannot exceed 10 per cent by law). Secondly, the main bank is the largest source of bank loans, but many other sources give loans, and the difference in the amount provided by the main bank and the second major bank is often not large. Thirdly, sogo shosha have often acted contrary to the wishes of their main banks in the past. For example, C.Itoh switched its main bank from the Sumitomo to the Daiichi Kangyo Bank, in the same way that Toyo Menka changed from the Mitsui to the Tokai Bank. As for Nichimen, when it was in financial trouble in the mid-1960s, it decided to reject the man whom the Sanwa Bank brought in as its president and to maintain 'pure blood'. Yet another example is the decision of Ataka in the mid-1960s to reject the arrangement by the Sumitomo Bank to merge with Sumitomo Shoji, strengthening, instead, its ties with the Kyowa Bank.

Although a certain degree of independence from the main

bank cannot be disputed, a few supporting argument should be given in defence of the 'subsidiary' hypothesis. With regard to stockholding, it is true that the bank does not by itself have a controlling share, but when the holdings of member companies are included, the voice of the main bank is influential on many issues (member companies often hold the shares at the request of the bank). Moreover, when considering the question of other sources of funds, one has to recognize that other banks usually have no more desire to lend money than the main bank. Since 'orderly finance' in Japan requires that the rank order of banks be observed, an increase in loans becomes possible only when the main bank agrees.

Obviously, the subsidiary hypothesis requires some modifications, but the fact remains that sogo shosha are under strong influence from their main banks. If this relationship is not recognized, it becomes difficult to explain why sogo shosha were able not only to survive but to grow at a rapid rate in the turbulent 1960s and 1970s. During this period, main banks served as umbilical cords for the sogo shosha.

3. MARKET SEPARATION

Main banks have been vitally important to sogo shosha but banking institutions did not found trading companies. As explained in Chapter 3, Mitsui Bussan was established by the Mitsui House around the same time the Mitsui Bank was founded; Mitsubishi Shoji was the marketing division of Mitsubishi's mines at first, and was disassociated around the same time as the Mitsubishi Bank; Nippon Menka was established by a group of spinners; Gosho was formed by merchants from Omi province; and C.Itoh, Marubeni, Iwai, Suzuki, etc., were set up by individual merchants. Since finance was an important part of trading, these companies maintained close relations with banks, but they were, in large measure, independent entities.

Another reason why too much emphasis should not be placed on the role of main banks is that if banks had in fact created sogo shosha, one would expect that similar organizations would have appeared in certain European countries (for example, Germany) where banks played an active role in economic development. Obviously, other factors must be included to explain the birth of sogo shosha in Japan. Most important among them, perhaps, has been the cultural separation of Japan from other countries.

The importance of market separation is well illustrated in the fact that European trading companies exist as links between Asia and Europe. European manufacturers did not depend much on intermediaries when trading in the Atlantic Basin where, because of cultural integration in the past, there was no large market gap. When they wanted to trade with Asian countries, however, the situation was very different. Having little knowledge of Asian languages, customs, and business practices, manufacturers were wise to trade through intermediary specialized trading firms. In Indonesia, Borneo-Sumatra Co. (Borusumy), Rotterdam Trading Society (Internatio), Jacobson van den Berg, and George Wehry acted as intermediaries; in Malaya and Singapore, Guthrie, Boustead, and Sime Darby were prominent; and in China, Jardine Matheson and East Asiatic played important roles. It is true that the import of tropical produce and other staple products from Asia was one of their important functions, but at the same time, these companies acted as agents for European manufacturers who wanted to sell their products in Asia.

To penetrate the Japanese market, Western manufacturers used Japanese trading companies. In the early phase of Japanese industrialization, a British company, Platt Brothers, relied upon Mitsui Bussan for the sale of its spindles to Japanese spinners. Around 1920, through Mitsui Bussan, General Electric was selling various kinds of electrical machinery; Caterpillar was selling tractors; Hoe and Co., printing machinery; Burmeister and Wain, diesel engines; Remington, typewriters; Otis, elevators; Babcock, boilers; and United States Rubber, tyres. On the other hand, Krupp, Goodyear, and Aluminium Company of America used Mitsubishi Shoji as their agent in Japan. As discussed in Chapter 3, the growth of other non-textile trading companies as well depended to a large extent on agency business from Western manufacturers.

This situation continued essentially without change in the post-war period. As explained in Chapter 4, Boeing granted agency rights to Nissho-Iwai; Lockheed contracted with Marubeni; Douglas dealt first through C.Itoh and then through Mitsui Bussan; Bendix, Rolls Royce, and Goodyear used C.Itoh; and so forth. In addition, there are numerous products from the West marketed in Japan by sogo shosha which were not discussed in Chapter 4. Examples include the products of Coca Cola, through Mitsubishi Shoji and Mitsui Bussan; Nestle, through Nissho-Iwai, *et al.*; Univac, through Mitsui Bussan; and General Electric, through Mitsui Bussan.

In trade with foreign countries, Japanese manufacturers have been confronted with even greater difficulties. One major problem was language. Foreign language ability is indispensable for obtaining information about foreign countries, carrying on negotiations, completing necessary documents, etc. It is also the basis for the understanding of foreign law, politics, economies and cultures necessary to conduct foreign trade smoothly.

Another problem was that foreign trade required knowledge of various business practices not common to domestic trade. Since foreign transactions involved multiple currencies, one currency had to be bought with and sold for another currency and there had to be a means of sending money from one distant place to another. Anyone who wanted to engage in foreign trade had to be familiar with the methods of settling financial claims. Also, he had to know the export and import regulations his government or foreign governments imposed. Furthermore, packaging, preparations for shipment, purchase of insurance policies to cover damages to or loss of the cargo during voyage, and the drawing up of contracts with shipping companies required an expertise different from that in domestic trade.

To understand the reluctance of manufacturers to venture into foreign trade and learn foreign trade skills, one has to understand the policy of the Japanese government towards foreign countries in the past. For slightly more than 200 years from the early seventeenth century, the government purposely closed Japan off from Western cultural influence in order to keep the country culturally distinct from the West. After the Meiji Restoration of 1868, Japan opened its doors to the West, but a strong ethnocentrism, whipped up by the government and elevated to the level of xenophobia in the pre-war period, made Western influence selective. For many years, it was confined to the area of technology. In the post-war period, the policy changed, but the cultural gap, artificially preserved over several centuries, could not be bridged in the matter of a few decades.

After the Meiji Restoration, since foreign trade was a *sine qua non* of the industrialization necessary for the country's economic development and military build-up, links had to be established between parochial Japanese manufacturers and foreign companies. Trading companies provided such links. They hired talented, adventurous young men, made them learn trade skills and foreign languages (not only English but also Chinese, South-East Asian languages, and other special languages), and created a pool of human resources who could handle foreign trade.

Because of the cultural gap, even producers who were marketing-oriented and handled domestic marketing on their own, had to depend on trading companies for exports. For example, when Mitsubishi Shoji returned agency rights to the ailing Mitsubishi Mining in 1924, it retained agency rights for export, since Mitsubishi Mining did not know how to handle this facet of its business. In the post-war period, Osaka-based steel producers (Sumitomo Metal Industries, Kawasaki Steel, and Kobe Steel) set up their own sales subsidiaries, but for the most part, they handled domestic marketing and left export largely to sogo shosha. These are but a few of the numerous examples of companies which used sogo shosha for export while undertaking domestic marketing themselves.

In other countries, the decline of once powerful trading

companies was often a result of the fact that as manufacturing companies grew in size, they became able to perform the functions trading companies had been performing. In Japan's case, a similar phenomenon took place in domestic marketing, but trading companies involved in foreign trade were able to use their expertise there to prevent manufacturers from establishing supremacy over them. For example, as discussed in Chapters 3 and 4, in the 1920s, spinners began dictating the terms of marketing conditions, and eventually drove most yarn dealers out of the trade, though trading companies which could export were not seriously affected. At one time, some spinners attempted to take over the export business by establishing offices abroad, but this tactic was not successful. Spinners were no exception in the fact that they faced difficulties in foreign trade. Most other manufacturers did also. Thus, it can be rationally argued that the inability of manufacturers to handle foreign trade was one major reason for the emergence of sogo shosha in Japan.

4. FOREIGN VERSUS JAPANESE TRADING COMPANIES

Foreign merchants were interested in filling the need for organizations which could act as links between Japan and other countries, and at first, they were very successful. In 1874, the first year for which data are available, foreign trading houses handled 97 per cent of Japan's total exports and 94 per cent of total imports.[14] Over the subsequent years, however, foreign traders were gradually replaced by Japanese trading companies; by the mid-1920s their existence was hardly noticeable.[15]

The rise of Mitsui Bussan illustrates well the gradual replacement of foreign companies. In 1897, the first year for which data are available (see Appendix 3), Mitsui Bussan accounted for 15 per cent of Japan's total imports and 6 per cent of total exports (about 11 per cent of total trade). At this point, its activity was already conspicuous, but since the sales volume of foreign merchants is not known, it is not possible to determine how Mitsui Bussan compared with them in the late 1890s. Around this time, foreign merchants were still strong in silk, the major export of pre-war Japan. It was not until 1907 that Mitsui Bussan surpassed the largest foreign silk dealer, Siber, Wolff & Co.[16] From this point, foreign merchant houses lost their leading position in all major exports and imports. Since Mitsui Bussan figured importantly in most major products, it must have surpassed all foreign merchant houses by this time at the latest, and possibly a little earlier.

How was this feat accomplished? There were three contributing factors. The first was government policy. From the end of the Tokugawa period through the early years of Meiji, imports by far exceeded exports, and specie coins flowed out of the country, causing great consternation in the government. At first, the government hoped to reduce the deficits by increasing tariff rates, but this did not work because Western countries objected. (Their consent was needed for such an increase, according to the commercial treaties signed at the end of the Tokugawa period.) The government's only alternative was to promote exports.

Because foreign merchants dominated foreign trade, export promotion would ordinarily have been left to them. From a purely theoretical point of view, the nationality of traders should not present a problem as long as they contribute to the common objective. The Meiji government, however, was distrustful of foreign merchants. In fact, a leading member of the government felt that if foreign trade was left to foreigners, export would decline. On account of such distrust, the government pursued a policy to promote direct exports. At the beginning, the government wanted to establish a state trading firm, but because of the lack of funds opted for protection of certain wealthy merchants who were willing to venture into direct foreign trade. As explained in Chapter 3, Mitsui Bussan was formed in accordance with this policy.[17]

The government contributed to Mitsui Bussan's growth in at least two important ways. It appointed Mitsui Bussan as exclusive agent for the coal in government-operated Miike mines. This made it possible for Mitsui Bussan to set up branches in Shanghai, Hong Kong, and Singapore in the early Meiji era and to have a basis for diversification in later years. Establishment of 'national policy' banks such as the Yokohama Specie Bank was also helpful in overcoming the capital shortage Japanese merchants encountered in foreign trade. This seems to have been a particularly severe blow to Western merchants since their major advantage lay in capital supply.[18] Since the government was so eager to help Japanese merchants, foreign merchants are quoted to have grumbled that 'in foreign trade the trader's nationality is of no importance. Even so, the Japanese government is so anxious to promote its direct exports and imports that it insists everything be handled by Japanese.'[19]

The government policy was undoubtedly prompted by a kind of xenophobia, but perhaps leaders were also aware of the benefits of direct trade to the economy. One government publication which had significant influence on the formulation of Meiji industrial policy compares the foreign trade situation in the early Meiji era to that of the Ryukyu Islands during the Tokugawa period, as follows.

Japan's foreign trade situation is very similar to the trade between the Ryukyu Islands and Satsuma [a province in southern Kyushu] in the old times. Although Ryukyu was a sovereign state abundant in products which enjoyed a large demand, it did not engage in direct trade. The prices of its products were controlled by merchants in Satsuma; such products as sugar and *kasuri* [cotton cloth with splashed pattern] were marketed as Satsuma products; and the commercial rights [of Ryukyu products in Japan proper] were in the hands of Satsuma merchants. As a consequence, Ryukyu incurred great losses. This relation is not different from what prevails in foreign trade today.[20]

Probably, having seen such disadvantages of 'trade by foreigners', Meiji leaders, in particular Okubo Toshimichi and others from Satsuma, could understand the need for promoting direct trade.

The second major factor affecting Mitsui Bussan's ascendancy was the Japanese work ethic. Masuda Takashi, who headed the company in its formative years, was convinced that Western merchants could not effectively compete with the Japanese because 'while the Japanese were diligent and satisfied with a low standard of living, the former lived in palatial houses, led luxurious lives, closed business at a set time in the evening, and took half day off on Saturday and all day off on Sunday, all of which cost them profits.'[21]

Masuda gives certain credit to Japanese women. According to him, Japanese women would accompany their husbands anywhere, and endure the same difficulties as their spouses. On the other hand, he had a poor view of Western women. Speaking of British women, he stated that 'they are domineering. Husbands . . . have to be back home by six thirty in the evening. After that, they have to be with their wives. While women have such power, husbands cannot devote themselves to their work. I feel that it is an easy task to beat such fellows.'[22] Masuda's view may be too ethnocentric, and may be an affront to the woman's liberation movement of today, but there is no doubt that the subserviency of Japanese women was an asset to Mitsui Bussan and other Japanese trading companies in their competition with Western merchant houses.

The third factor which contributed to Mitsui Bussan's rise involves the ability of the Japanese to build organizations based on merit. Mitsui Bussan was a family enterprise in terms of ownership, but not in terms of management. Masuda Takashi, who was not related to the Mitsui family, headed the company from 1876 to 1893, when it became a partnership. At this point, he stepped down from the presidency, and members of the Mitsui family occupied the top position thereafter. Nevertheless, they held the position only nominally and left management to Masuda Takashi and other professionals. This hands-off policy is intriguing, especially in view of the fact that today, in developing countries, for example, it is often difficult to separate ownership from management. Why such separation took place in Japan requires further investigation, but it seems related to the family's inability to cope with either the changes occurring during the politically turbulent era from the end of the Tokugawa period to the beginning of the Meiji era, or the rapid economic developments of the Meiji era.

Under Masuda's management, Mitsui Bussan recruited actively and invested in manpower training.[23] New recruits were taught business practices, the commodities they were to handle, and the company rules. Conscious efforts were also made to have new employees learn the languages of the countries with which the company traded. Language training was not confined to English or other Western European languages; the learning of Asian and other special languages was also strongly emphasized.

Mitsui Bussan became a large company because it delegated much authority to those who proved to be both trustworthy and in possession of business acumen.[24] As the company increased its offices abroad and diversified into new products, such people were promoted to positions as heads of new commodities or managers of new offices and given a considerable degree of freedom. Power had to be delegated if a company wished to grow, as it was impossible for one man or small group of people to have intimate knowledge of the varied commodities and new opportunities. Especially in the case of foreign branch offices, since communications and transportation were still undeveloped, considerable authority had to be given to branch managers abroad. Under such circumstances, merit could be the only basis for hiring and promotion, because if great power were delegated to incompetent managers, the company would fall rather than rise. Hence, the willingness to delegate power and use merit as the basis for hiring and promotion became one major factor in Mitsui Bussan's success.

At this point, it is important to recall that the second half of the nineteenth century was not the age of multinationals. According to Masuda Takashi, most Western merchants who came to Japan at the end of the Tokugawa period were mostly 'broken fellows'; few merchants had a good base at home.[25] Later, more respectable Western merchants came to Japan to trade in silk and tea, but the gap between them and Japanese merchants was not great. Thus, Masuda was building a modern organization at a time when there was virtually no such organization in the entire industry. When he succeeded, Mitsui Bussan towered above the Western trading companies in Asia, most of which were family enterprises.

5. IN THE WHIRLPOOL OF ECONOMIC CHANGES

In order to understand the strength of Japanese trading companies, one must look also at the economic environment in which they grew. Japan's modern economic growth began in the late 1870s, and in the following ninety-year period, Japan recorded the highest growth rate among developed countries. The growth rate was especially high in the 1960s and the early 1970s when approximately 10 per cent growth was recorded per annum. As a consequence of such high growth, Japan was transformed from a poor, agricultural country into a prosperous, industrial nation.

The rapid pace of the change can be better appreciated when the Japanese experience is contrasted with the British.[26] At the time Japan's modern economic growth began, its per capita income was at subsistence level (about $75 in 1965 prices). When British modern economic growth began in the second half of the eighteenth century, per capita income exceeded $200 in 1965 prices. Such a high per capita income was a result of slow growth prior to the mid-eighteenth century. It is not known exactly when the British economy broke away from the so-called low income equilibrium, but it must have been towards the end of the Middle Ages, thus about 200 years before modern economic growth began. Japan, in contrast, did not have such a long transition period; rather, it moved directly into modern economic growth with incomes at the subsistence level. And, in the next century, Japan caught up with Britain. In short, the road which Britain traversed for about four centuries was covered by Japan in one century.

The high rate of economic growth in Japan was accompanied by industrialization, population growth, structural change in the economy, increased import of raw materials, increased export of manufactured products, urbanization, foreign investment, changes in life-style, etc. The economy was always in a state of flux, and various problems arose which could not be solved by traditional methods. Such a fluid situation was an ideal environment for operation by trading companies.

One famous folk hero in Japan was a man called Zatoichi, a blind swordsman. In spite of the fact that he was blind, he was a master swordsman. The secret of his skill was that, determined at an early age not to be despised for his blindness, Zatoichi trained his ears to detect the slightest sound. Thus, as long as his attackers move and make noise, he can easily defeat them; but he becomes extremely vulnerable when attackers stop moving and produce no sound. The attackers are not, however, aware of this vulnerability of his. Trading companies seem to have many things in common with Zatoichi—when there are changes in circumstances, i.e., new problems (marketing, finance, purchasing, transportation, technology, etc.) are created, trading companies find new tasks, but when the situation is static, manufacturers and other companies begin to encroach upon trading companies.

Industrialization generated many tasks for trading companies. For example, when the cotton industry grew, raw cotton had to be imported from abroad since Japanese cotton proved to be insufficient in quantity and inferior in quality; new machines, especially spindles, had to be imported; and products had to be marketed. In the case of products such as fabric, which varies by kind and requires quality control, trading companies played an especially important role: they instructed weavers as to which kind of fabric was needed, and ensured that output was of uniform quality. When the steel industry emerged, similar problems arose. In the case of Yahata Steel, since iron ores were not available in Japan in sufficient quantity, it was necessary to import them from China. As steel production increased, surpassing the demand from armament factories and other state enterprises, marketing problems emerged, and the assistance of trading companies was solicited.

When new goods were produced, manufacturers faced special difficulties in marketing. In the case of chemical fertilizer, for example, towards the end of the Meiji era (around 1910), marketing was a problem because peasants, used to traditional, organic fertilizers, resisted the introduction of new types of fertilizer. Trading companies found it necessary to demonstrate to peasants the usefulness of the new fertilizers, and, at the same time, help them overcome psychological barriers. In the case of synthetic fibre, at first it was not quite clear what it was good for, except socks (in which nylon had proven to be useful abroad). The quality of synthetic fibre had to be studied; the percentage at which it should be mixed with other fibres had to be experimented with; weavers had to be told what kind of fabric was needed. Garment manufacturers could have performed all these tasks, but they were busy with production problems, and welcomed the help of trading companies.

In the petrochemical industry also, manufacturers preferred to concentrate on production and depend on trading companies for marketing. Since this industry was capital intensive, large sums of money were required for plant construction, and manufacturers usually did not have funds left to spend on the marketing of large quantities of the various products to be produced at the new plants. They usually appointed large trading companies as primary wholesalers and the organization of exclusive marketing channels was left to them. As a consequence, the so-called 'train formula' emerged, into which outsiders could not break (for example, a foreign buyer could not buy a Japanese petrochemical product except from an appointed agent in his country).

In the 1960s, when industrial production became substantial, one major problem was how to ensure a long-term supply of raw materials. Until then, it had been possible for trading companies to buy raw materials on the spot market, but as demand became great, the spot market could no longer be relied upon. The only way to obtain raw materials was to secure long-term contracts with foreign suppliers by investing large sums of money. Though this was not as risky a venture as oil exploration, it was far from being risk-free. Trading companies took the risks, however, and participated in various resource development projects.

Trading companies have also played an important role in changing the sources of energy in Japan. Wood and charcoal were Japan's traditional fuels, but when coal emerged as an important source of energy, Mitsui Bussan, for example, acted as agent for the Miike and other mines. For some time, coal was one of Mitsui Bussan's major products. After coal was replaced by oil in the post-war period, importation was handled at first primarily by the majors, but recently, especially since the oil crisis of 1973, because direct oil deals have increased, the share of sogo shosha has risen. In 1978, they handled about 35 per cent of Japan's total oil imports, and in 1980 are expected to handle more than 50 per cent.[27] Sogo shosha were in a good position to meet the requirements of oil producing countries (for plant construction, etc.), and they used this as a leverage to increase oil transactions.

The sogo shosha's activities in fuel importation have not been restricted to oil. When liquefied petroleum gas (LPG) began to be imported in the early 1960s, they set up distribution centres in various parts of Japan and became major importers. When LNG became an attractive energy source in the late 1960s as pollution became a major social issue, sogo shosha took an active interest in forming the consortium necessary for its import. Today, all LNG imports pass through sogo shosha (Alaska, Brunei, Indonesia and Abu Dhabi are the only sources today). Recently, since oil prices have increased, coal has become an attractive fuel again, and sogo shosha are involved in coal development in Australia, the United States, Canada, etc.

As industrial production increased, the distribution sector became a bottle-neck. Japanese distribution is fragmented, and is known to be 'long'. One measure of this is the ratio of wholesale transactions to retail transactions. In the United States, this ratio was 1.51 in 1972, whereas in Japan it was 4.05 in 1970.[28] These figures indicate that a commodity passes through a greater number of wholesalers (for example, primary, secondary, tertiary wholesalers) in Japan before it reaches a retailer than it would in the United States. It is estimated that the costs of distribution in Japan account for as much as 50 to 60 per cent of retail prices on commodities.[29]

One method by which distribution costs may be reduced is to integrate the distribution channel vertically. Sogo shosha helped supermarkets financially (for example, by providing loans and leasing buildings and equipment), but to a large extent, necessary funds could probably have been raised without such aid. A more important function of sogo shosha was the establishment of a more efficient channel to supply goods to supermarkets. It might be supposed that supermarkets were in a better position than sogo shosha to set up new channels, but since they had to spend large sums of money to acquire land (which is very expensive in Japan) and construct buildings, and also because they did not have enough manpower capable of planning products and organizing manufacturers and distributors (as a result of their short history), supermarkets were forced to depend on sogo shosha and other trading companies. At the time when they were multiplying rapidly in the 1960s and early 1970s, supermarkets simply did not have the extra resources for backward integration.

One example of a new distribution channel being opened was the establishment of food combinats along the coast. At the waterside processing and storage points of the combinats, various foodstuffs (such as sugar, wheat, soybeans, maize, etc.) brought from abroad are unloaded, and then 'either stored in bulk or passed through pipes and other appropriate conveyances to processing plants. In the case of soybeans, the oil is first extracted and the by-products are passed to a nearby feed processing plant. Wheat is converted to flour, then passed on either to the distribution center or first to producers of secondary products, such as confectionery products and then to the distribution center.'[30] From the distribution centre, the products are transported directly to supermarkets and other large-scale marketing outlets. This new channel of trade not only reduced the costs of land transportation through integrated operation but also eliminated the commissions of many wholesaling intermediaries.

In various other less revolutionary ways, sogo shosha have contributed to the reduction of distribution costs. Unnecessary intermediaries have been by-passed; new systems of transportation (containerized transportation, refrigerated ships, specialized carriers of bulky cargo—such as ore carriers—and combination carriers to reduce 'ballast sailings') have been introduced; and distribution centres (steel distribution and processing centres, log distribution centres, etc.) have been established in various parts of Japan to minimize delivery time and transportation costs. Sogo shosha are also involved in food and other manufacturing industries in order to streamline the distribution system. Broiler integration may be cited as one such example.

There have been numerous other activities undertaken by sogo shosha in order to cope with changing circumstances. When Japanese wages became high, sogo shosha were among the first to invest in Taiwan, Korea, Hong Kong and Singapore to create production centres to supply Japan. From these centres, a large quantity of garments and other labour intensive products are imported. When Japanese began to be fashion-conscious, as the standard of living rose, sogo shosha tied up with foreign manufacturers to produce their products in Japan under license. When Japan encountered difficulties in negotiating with the Soviet Union over fishing rights, sogo shosha invested in Alaska to create supply bases to Japan. They also moved into the fast food business by tying up with foreign firms, such as Kentucky Fried Chicken, Pizza Hut, International Dairy Queen, etc., in order to meet the demand created by urbanization and the growing number of working housewives.

Rapid economic changes generated two major problems for Japanese manufacturers. One, as discussed above, was the need to raise funds for plant expansion and replacement investment (as a result of rapid technological changes). Because funds were required for these purposes, unless marketing was difficult to separate from production (as in the case of consumer durables) manufacturers tended to devote most of their resources to production, leaving little for marketing and necessary manpower training.

The second problem was that of underwriting new risks. For example, when large quantities of raw materials came to be required because of increased industrial production in the 1960s, participation in resource development projects became unavoidable. It, therefore, became necessary for someone to raise funds and then assume the risks that such investments might either go down the drain, or if they did yield some returns, these would be small compared with the costs involved, and the investments might not be worth undertaking. Often, manufacturers did not want to take such risks. Even when they did, they invited sogo shosha to participate in order to help spread the risk.

There was another kind of risk involved in marketing products as the economy expanded. When production increased, greater quantities of output had to be sold, and to ensure sales, it was the normal practice to extend credits. If cash payments were insisted upon, there was a great possibility that the desired quantities of goods would not be sold, or that large discounts would have to be granted. Manufacturers could have extended credits on their own, but to do this they needed additional working capital and had to assume the risk of defaults. They often preferred that trading companies assume such risks, being content with slightly lower prices if they could get paid in cash.

The financial status of customers changes all the time, especially when the economy is changing rapidly. It is a reasonable policy to extend more credits to customers who are succeeding, and limits credits to those who are facing financial problems. Yet, it is extremely difficult to identify changes in financial status. Trading companies visit their customers often in order to observe any significant changes, but they often make mistakes and end up with bad debts. Since profit margin is only a small percentage of sales, if the ratio of bad debts to total sales exceeds 1 per cent, the situation would have reached a dangerous point, for out of this small percentage must come large interest payments and wages and other expenses. Companies which have done poorly in credit management have gone bankrupt (as Ataka did recently), while those which have managed credits well have grown by leaps and bounds.

As the economy developed, increased production meant increased sales, which, in turn, meant increased credit sales. Manufacturers were reluctant to take the risks involved in credit sales, and thus, trading companies found a role to play. This, however, was not an enviable task, for it placed a considerable burden on them. A manager of the Thai factory of a Japanese synthetic producer stated that 'we might be getting less than what we could, by depending on Japanese trading companies, but at least, I sleep well. I do not have to worry about the possibility that our customers might suddenly go bankrupt and we would end up with large bad debts.'[31] In developing countries such as Thailand, the financial status of customers is extremely difficult to comprehend; even relatively large firms sometimes go broke. By assuming the risk of credit management, many trading company managers spend sleepless nights worrying about the sudden collapse of their customers' business.

To sum up, rapid economic changes in the past brought about many problems which manufacturers were not able or were reluctant to handle by themselves—for example, marketing new products, finding new suppliers, securing resources on a long-term basis, streamlining the distribution system, and increasing credit sales, etc. Economic changes also generated the emergence of supermarkets, for which new, more efficient distribution channels were required, and new demands and new imports, which required new investors and channel leaders. Sogo shosha were able to grow because they had the financial resources, the manpower and the networks to deal with many of the new problems. If economic change had been much slower, or, worse, if the economy had been at a standstill, sogo shosha might have been vulnerable to the encroachment of manufacturers and supermarkets, just as Zatoichi, the blind swordsman, is vulnerable when his attackers stop moving.

6. CONCLUDING REMARKS

Certain Japanese trading companies have become large and have played an important role in the economy because Japanese producers were insular and needed organizations which could act as links between them and foreign countries. These trading companies sold Western products to Japanese producers, acting as agents for Western manufacturers, and acquired cotton, iron ores, and other raw materials for Japanese manufacturers. When the demand for such products became so great that it became necessary to invest in resource development abroad, Japanese trading companies did so, and played an important role in securing the long-term supply of raw materials. They have also played an active role in exporting Japanese products. In the pre-war period, all major exports (fabric, etc.) passed through their hands. In the post-war period, manufacturers of consumer durables (chiefly, cars and electronic equipment) established their own networks abroad, but manufacturers of steel, chemicals, industrial machinery, and many other products have depended on trading companies.

In the post-war period, major city banks have found ties with major trading companies to be convenient. Trading companies were able to help banks solidify the enterprise groups they had been promoting, by making global networks available to member companies, or by acquiring shares in member companies, etc. Trading companies were also able to undertake numerous activities banks could not because of regulations and guide-lines imposed by the supervisory authority for banks, the Ministry of Finance. By establishing ties with major banks, large trading companies have been able to obtain large loans (exceeding their equity capital by ten to one since the late 1960s), which they have used to establish various trade advantages. Such financial power has been important to them in maintaining and even enhancing their positions in the last two decades, as Japanese manufacturers have become less insular and have begun to make some inroads into foreign trade.

The two factors which greatly influenced the growth of trading companies—market separation and financial power—would have been less significant if the economy had changed much less rapidly. Fortunately for trading companies, change was so rapid that manufacturers were kept busy trying to assimilate new technology and investing in plant expansion, and supermarket and other new industries felt the urgent need for new investors and channel leaders. Large trading companies developed manpower, networks, and the financial capability to reckon with many of the problems created by rapid change. Essentially, they threw themselves into the whirlpool of changes, and grew with it.

One interesting development in the pre-war period was that although foreign merchants provided the initial links between Japan and other countries, they gradually declined in importance and became inconspicuous by the mid-1920s. The rise of Japanese trading companies may be attributed to government assistance, the Japanese work ethic, and organizational ability. This last factor is clearly discernible when assessing its contribution to the growth of Mitsui Bussan. It became a large, decentralized organization by using merit as the primary basis for hiring and promotion and by delegating considerable authority to qualified personnel, at a time when family enterprises were the most common form of organization even in the West.

1. *MBK Life*, April 1973.

2. Misonoo Hitoshi, 'Sogo Shosha wa Shayo de Aruka', *Ekonomisuto*, 23 May 1961.

3. Mitsui Bussan, *Kaiko-roku*, 1976, p. 329.

4. *Ekonomisuto*, 18 June 1963, p. 35.

5. Kozo Yamamura, 'General Trading Companies in Japan: Their Origins and Growth', in H. Patrick (ed.), *Japanese Industrialization and Its Social Consequences*, Berkeley, University of California Press, 1976.

6. Matsumoto Hiroshi, *Mitsui Zaibatsu no Kenkyu*, Yoshikawa Kobun-kan, 1979, pp. 2–3; Umezu Kazuro, *Nippon no Boeki Shosha*, Nippon Hyoron-sha, 1971, p. 65; and Shibagaki Kazuo, *Nippon Kin'yu Shihon Bunseki*, Tokyo Daigaku Shuppan-kai, 1960, relevant chapters.

7. *The Economist*, 3 June 1967, p. xxvi.

8. Quoted in Mitsubishi Shoji, 'Who We Are, What We Do, Where We Are Going', n.d., p. 20.

9. *Ryowa-β*, January 1978, pp. 3–4.

10. *Nihon Keizai Shinbun*, 24 June 1977.

11. Marubeni, *Kankei Kaisha Yoran 1975* (unpublished), July 1975.

12. Marubeni, *Kaigai Jigyo Yoran 1976* (unpublished), June 1976.

13. *Tokyo Newsletter*, February 1978.

14. Mitsui Bussan, *Mitsui Bussan Shoshi*, 1951, p. 12.

15. Nagai Minoru, *Jijo Masuda Takashi-o Den*, 1939, p. 473.

16. Togai Yoshio, 'Kiito Shoken o Meguru Naigaisho no Kakuchiku', *Senshu Daigaku Shakai Kagaku Kenkyusho Geppo*, No. 66, 20 March 1969.

17. Iwasaki Hiroyuki, 'Seisho Hogo Seisaku no Seiritsu', *Mitsui Bunko Ronso*, 1967, p. 179.

18. Mitsui Bussan (1951), p. 91.

19. Ibid., p. 92.

20. Ministry of Agriculture and Commerce (ed.), *Kogyo Iken*, quoted in Mitsui Bussan (1951), pp. 51–2.

21. Chucho-kai Nakamigawa Sensei Denki Hensan Iin, *Nakamigawa Sensei Den*, 1939, p. 206. The quotation is of Tanaka Bunzo, one-time managing director of Mitsui Bussan.

22. Nagai, p. 500.

23. For further discussion on this, see section 1 of Chapter 7 of this volume.

24. For further discussion on this, see sections 1 and 2 of Chapter 7 of this volume.

25. Nagai, p. 120.

26. For further discussion on this, see Yoshihara Kunio, *Japanese Economic Development*, Tokyo, Oxford University Press, 1979, pp. 31–5.

27. Seikei Tsushin-sha, *Sogo Shosha Nenkan 1978–9*, pp. 280–1, and *Asahi Shinbun*, 7 May 1980.

28. Murata Shoji, *Nihon no Ryutsu Kozo*, Zeimu Keiri Kyokai, 1978, p. 76.

29. Ibid., p. 241.

30. Mitsui Bussan, 'Mitsui & Co.', 1977, p. 28.

31. These are the words of Kobayashi Masahiko of Teijin Polyester (Thailand) Ltd., in an interview in Bangkok. The interview took place in July 1979. Mitsui Bussan makes a similar point in Mitsui Bussan, *Chosen to Sozo*, 1976, p. 26.

6

Role in Industrialization

1. INDUSTRIAL INVESTMENT

THE theory that commercial capital does not turn into industrial capital seems to be incorrect, for when the investment behaviour of large trading companies is examined, it becomes clear that numerous industrial investments have been undertaken. Towards the end of the pre-war period, Mitsui Bussan, for example, had a number of manufacturing subsidiaries and also had large holdings in many established companies. Relatively well known among its subsidiaries were Yuasa Battery Manufacturing, Onoda Cement Manufacturing, Toyo Rayon, Sanki Kogyo, Toyo Carrier, Tama Shipyard, and Toyo Precision Machinery and Engineering. It also held large shares of Nippon Steel Works, Electro-Chemical Industrial, Nippon Flour Mills—companies of the Mitsui zaibatsu.

In the 1910s and 1920s, Suzuki was by far more aggressive than Mitsui Bussan in industrial investment. When it was at its peak, Suzuki had about fifty subsidiaries and affiliates in the manufacturing industry, spreading over such industries as textiles, cement, flour, steel, and chemicals. Teijin (formerly Teikoku Jinken), Kobe Steel, Mitsui Toatsu Chemicals, and Honen Oil—Japan's representative manufacturers today—were either created by Suzuki's investment or grew out of its subsidiaries. Probably, no trading company has ever exceeded the scale of Suzuki's industrial investment (relative to equity capital). By the late 1910s, it had ceased to be a simple trading company, evolving in the direction of becoming an industrial-commercial combine.[1]

Today, all sogo shosha have numerous manufacturing subsidiaries or affiliated companies. For example, in mid-1975, C.Itoh had 108 companies in its group (C.Itoh Group), out of which 31 companies were in manufacturing (7 in textiles, 2 in machinery, 9 in foods, 3 in plywood, 8 in chemicals, 1 in metals and 1 in paper).[2] In addition, C.Itoh held minority shares in many other manufacturing companies. Among C.Itoh's industrial investments at that time, the largest went to an oil refinery called Toa Oil: C.Itoh spent 4.7 billion yen to acquire about 60 per cent of its shares.

Many manufacturing investments by trading companies were undertaken to set up new companies. One such investment was Suzuki's to establish an ammonia factory by importing technology from abroad. In the early 1920s, Suzuki bought the patent for the method of fixing nitrogen from the air invented by a Frenchman, G. Claude, and began ammonia production based on this patent. After Suzuki went bankrupt in 1927, the company was taken over by Mitsui to become Toatsu Chemicals, which subsequently merged with Mitsui Chemicals to become Mitsui Toatsu Chemicals, a leading chemical company today. Suzuki's import of the ammonia production technology, which cost a fortune (£500,000)[3] made an important contribution to the development of the Japanese chemical industry.

Trading companies entered into the manufacturing industry also as a spin-off effect of trading activities. For example, Mitsui Bussan added shipbuilding and ship repairing to its activities, and constructed a shipyard in 1917. The purpose of establishing this industry was to repair a fleet of ships it possessed (about twenty ships totalling about 100,000 tons in the early 1910s) to facilitate its transportation requirements, and also to build new ships (all shipyards were, at this time, operating to the maximum capacity due to the war boom, and it took a long time to get a new ship built). In the mid-

1920s, Mitsui Bussan concluded a licensing agreement with a Danish firm, Burmeister and Wain, to manufacture diesel engines, and then attached an engine plant to the shipyard. In 1937, the shipyard was separated out from Mitsui Bussan and became Tama Shipyard (subsequently Mitsui Engineering and Shipbuilding).

A more common pattern of entry into manufacturing was through import substitution, that is, production of a product formerly imported. An example of this pattern is Mitsui Bussan's establishment of Toyo Rayon in 1926. The company had been importing rayon from a British company called Courtaulds, and had developed a marketing network in Japan. Using this as leverage, Mitsui Bussan hoped to begin rayon production. At first, it negotiated with Courtaulds and then with Du Pont for a technological licensing agreement, but since neither was much interested, it decided to import the necessary machinery, employ foreign engineers, and begin production on its own. Apparently, rayon technology was embodied in machinery to a large extent, and it was not absolutely necessary to buy patents. Until the mid-1920s, Teikoku Jinken, under the financial support of Suzuki, had made some progress in rayon production without relying on foreign companies. What Toyo Rayon did then was to follow the path of Teikoku Jinken. It faced difficulties at the beginning, but within several years (by the early 1930s), it had become a successful rayon manufacturer.

In this connection, it is interesting to note that two of the major rayon producers in pre-war Japan were set up by trading companies, and that these two companies became the major synthetic producers in the post-war period. During the Pacific War, Toyo Rayon began experimenting with nylon production with the know-how acquired in rayon production as a base, and after the war, it became the first company to produce nylon. Teikoku Jinken was unprepared for nylon, but began production of polyester early, and split that market with Toyo Rayon. As will be explained in the next section, both Toyo Rayon and Teikoku Jinken were helped by their ties with trading companies in the import of the technology necessary to produce the synthetic fibres.

Mitsui Bussan was not alone in undertaking import substitution investment. Iwai was also a vigorous investor of this type. For example, in 1918 it established a company to manufacture soda ash and caustic soda (Nihon Soda Kogyo). Katsujiro, who headed the company at that time, saw great opportunity in soda production since its prices were high due to the reduction of imports from the West during the First World War.[4] He is the one who made the decision to produce soda domestically. Unfortunately for him, the war ended soon, and in 1920 the post-war depression set in, so it was rough going until the early 1930s when the economy began to improve again. Today, the company, known as Tokuyama Soda, is a leading soda manufacturer in Japan.

In studying industrialization in developing regions, such as South-East Asia, one gets the impression that a typical pattern for a trading company's entry into manufacturing is through a tie-up with a foreign company. At first, the trading company becomes an agent for the foreign company, and when it becomes advantageous to establish a production base in the market, the trading company sets up a joint venture with the foreign supplier. In a way, this is an ideal tie-up, for the foreign company supplies technology and the trading company, marketing know-how. For example, most Japanese industrial investments in South-East Asia are joint ventures, and their partners are often Chinese and South-East Asian trading companies (or merchants).

Did Japanese trading companies also tie up with foreign suppliers? Though this pattern was much less common in Japan, there were a number of such cases. For example, in the pre-war period, Mitsubishi Shoji set up a joint venture with Associate Oil (an American company) for oil refining, and Mitsui Bussan tied up with Carrier Engineering (an American company) for the production of air-conditioners. In the post-war period, Coca Cola and Pepsi Cola set up bottling plants with Mitsubishi Shoji and C.Itoh, respectively, and

Mobil Oil established a refinery with Mitsui Bussan.

A large part of trading companies' industrial investments have been directed to already existing companies. In some cases, this was forced on the trading companies. Such situations arose when manufacturing companies to which credits or loans were extended faced financial difficulties and the trading company converted part of the credits or loans to equity capital. Sometimes, when the financially-troubled company was rehabilitated with assistance from the trading company, the latter withdrew by selling its holdings. Often, however, trading companies retained holdings, and used the company as a supply base. In other cases, the acquisition of a manufacturing company's shares was necessitated by strategic considerations. For example, trading companies often acquired, or established partial control over manufacturing companies in fields in which they wanted to increase sales, when they faced financial problems, or when they needed an investor to finance plant expansion.

A trading company might prefer not to undertake industrial investment, if the same objective could be achieved without it. In the early years of the Meiji era, Masuda Takashi, the man who built the foundation of Mitsui Bussan, insisted that the company should stick to agency business and that the company should avoid using its capital for industrial investment since that slowed down the turnover of capital.[5] It became increasingly clear over time, however, that in order to maintain or enhance its position in trading, a trading company must undertake industrial investment. Otherwise, it would likely be pushed out from trade channels. For this reason, Mitsui Bussan has invested in numerous manufacturing companies.

2. INTERMEDIATION IN TECHNOLOGY TRANSFER

Japanese trading companies have functioned as a conduit of technology transfer from the West to Japanese manufacturers. When technology was embodied in machineries—which was typical of technological imports in the early years of industrialization—trading companies collected information on machinery producers as well as on technological changes in the West, and helped Japanese manufacturers import necessary machinery. For example, in the Meiji era, Mitsui Bussan imported spindles from Platt Brothers in Britain for most of the large-scale spinning companies. More recently, trading companies have gathered relevant information for capital intensive manufacturers in Japan and acted as consultants as well as purchasing agents when manufacturers needed to import machinery. Since machinery accounted for a large part of production cost and determined the quality of output, the extent to which they were well chosen had important bearing on the business.

In closing the technological gap between the West and Japan, trading companies played a by far more important role by importing new, advanced machinery than by mediating in technological licensing agreements. Especially in the early years of Japanese industrialization, they widened the technological spectrum of Japanese manufacturers by informing them about various technological opportunities available in the West, and took the initiative to materialize the interests they developed as a consequence, thus contributing to the technological progress of Japanese industry. This function of trading companies, however, can be considered as marketing intermediation (discussed in section 4), and thus, will not be discussed further here. The remainder of this section will deal only with the role of trading companies in mediating technological licensing agreements.

One group which trading companies assisted in importing technology was their subsidiaries and affiliates. In Suzuki's case, for example, technology import led to the establishment of the ammonia factory. In most cases, however, technology was imported for subsidiaries and affiliates already established. For example, Mitsui Bussan noticed the superiority of diesel engines over steam reciprocating engines in the early 1920s, and drew up licensing agreements with Burmeister and Wain,

a major diesel engine manufacturer in the West, for its shipyard.[6] In the post-war period, Mitsui Bussan imported the
floating glass process for Central Glass, from a British company, Pilkington, and helped its diversification into sashes.[7]
Also, Marubeni mediated licensing agreements between Yutani
Heavy Industries and a French company, Poclain, and enabled
Yutani to become a major producer of hydraulic shovels.[8]

Trading companies have also mediated technological licensing agreements for the companies with which they had close
business relations. In the post-war period, Mitsui Bussan established contact between Du Pont and Toyo Rayon, and enabled
the latter to import nylon technology. In particular, the good
reputation Mitsui Bussan established among Western manufacturers in the pre-war period was a decisive factor in Du
Pont's decision to accept Toyo Rayon as a trustworthy licen-
see.[9] In the case of Teikoku Jinken's import of polyester
technology from ICI, Nissho got wind of the information first
and used its trading relations with ICI to explore the possibility
of a licensing agreement.[10] In the case of Showa Denko's
diversification into polyethylene production, Marubeni played
a pivotal role by importing necessary technology from Phillips
Petroleum.[11] Marubeni also mediated a licensing agreement
between Hitachi Shipbuilding and Engineering and a Swiss
company, L. De Roll (now Von Roll), a major company in
the field of waste disposal plants.

Mitsubishi Shoji has also been busy with mediating licensing
agreements for member companies. In the pre-war period, it
helped Mitsubishi Electric tie up with Westinghouse for production of electric generators; aided Mitsubishi Kakoki (established in 1935) in importing necessary technology from
Krupp and several other European machinery producers;
mediated for Mitsubishi Aircraft in drawing up licensing agreements with various European and American aircraft producers
(Henriot, Hispano-Suisa, Junkers, Rohrbach, Curtiss Aeroplane and Motor, etc.); and helped Mitsubishi Shipbuilding
produce diesel engines under license from a Swiss company,
Sulzer Brothers, motor-boats under license from a British

company, Thornycroft, and various other marine-related products under license from European companies.[12]

In the post-war period as well, Mitsubishi Shoji has been active in mediating licensing agreements between Mitsubishi companies and Western manufacturers. When Mitsubishi Heavy Industries tied up with American and European manufacturers to produce new machines (such as bottling machines and power shovels), Mitsubishi Shoji acted as its contact abroad. From the late 1950s to the early 1960s, when petrochemicals became an important industry in Japan, Mitsubishi Shoji imported polyethylene technology for Mitsubishi Petrochemical from BASF, and imported polypropylene technology from Montecatini. For Edogawa Kagaku (now Mitsubishi Gas-Chemical) it imported polycarbonate (plastic) technology. More recently, the company imported technology related to satellites for Mitsubishi Heavy Industries and Mitsubishi Electric from American companies (such as Rockwell and McDonnell-Douglas).[13]

In a relatively small number of cases, trading companies acted as organizers of industrial projects and functioned not only as intermediaries for technology transfer, but also as investors. Such cases lie between establishment of a new company (as in Suzuki's establishment of the ammonia factory) and pure technological intermediation. In such cases, the projects depend significantly on the import of technology from abroad, and trading companies undertake investment as well, but unlike Suzuki in the ammonia case, the trading company is not the sole investor. For example, when Mitsui Aluminium was set up in 1968, Mitsui Bussan acted as its organizer and contributed slightly over 20 per cent of its equity capital. At the same time, it located suitable technology abroad and finally succeeded in drawing up a licensing agreement with a French company, Compagnie Pechiney.[14]

In intermediating in the transfer of technology, the bulk of the activities of trading companies has been related to imports, which reflects the fact that Japanese industrialization has progressed by importing technology from abroad. Furthermore, as Japan's technology level rose with industrial progress, some companies developed technologies which could be exported. Trading companies arranged the exports of some such technology. For example, in 1926 Mitsui Bussan sold the patent for Toyota's power-loom to Platt Brothers (from which it had imported a large number of spindles). More recently, Mitsui Bussan exported Toyo Rayon's synthetic fibre technology to E.N.I. of Italy (in 1971) and the technology of Nippon Steel Works to a Spanish company for production of large-sized steel forgings (in 1976).[15] In the future, since Japanese industry is now one of the most advanced in the world, technology exports will rise, and the opportunities for trading companies to export technology from Japan will increase. Up to this point, however, imports have been the major function of trading companies.

3. FINANCIAL INTERMEDIATION

In order to understand the financial intermediation of trading companies, one must understand the dual structure of the Japanese manufacturing industry. One sector consists of large companies: for example, in the field of consumer goods, there are such giants as Toyota Motor, Nissan Motor, Sony and Matsushita Electric Industrial, and in the field of intermediate and investment goods, Mitsubishi Heavy Industries, Nippon Steel and Mitsui Toatsu Chemicals. The other sector consists of a by far larger number of small and medium-sized companies, which range from midget companies relying on family labour to companies employing a few hundred persons. One interesting feature of Japanese industrialization was that these small and medium-sized companies made an important contribution to exports and the increase of productivity. Trading companies have been especially important to this sector of the manufacturing industry.

One might argue that the existence of small and medium-sized companies is by no means a phenomenon unique to Japan. In the manufacturing industry, there can be ample room for them, if, for example, there is no economy of scale in production. What makes the Japanese case unique is that such companies have played a large role in the manufacturing industry. In 1955, they numbered about 500,000, or 99.6 per cent of the total, and accounted for about 73 per cent of the workers and 56 per cent of the output in the Japanese manufacturing industry.[16] As the economy grew and the heavy-chemical industry gained importance in the following years, their relative importance declined. Yet even in 1970, their share of employment and output were about 68 per cent and 50 per cent, respectively. These shares are considerably higher than, for example, in the United States. In 1967, the share of employment of American companies of comparable size was about 40 per cent.[17]

The availability of cheap labour has been one major reason for the importance of small and medium-sized companies in Japan. This explains why a great majority have specialized in labour intensive production. In contrast, production in small and medium-sized companies in the United States has tended to be more capital intensive. In the United States, capital intensity in small and medium-sized companies may be slightly lower than in large companies, but the difference is at most 20 to 25 per cent. In the Japanese case, capital intensity in the companies which employ four to nine workers is about one-fifth that of those which employ a thousand workers, steadily increasing as the size of employment increases.[18] For the very small companies which employ less than four workers, no data is available, but it is a safe guess that their capital intensity is even lower.

The export market has supported the relatively large number of small and medium-sized companies in Japan. In the 1950s and 1960s, they exported such labour intensive products as garments, toys, plastic goods, rubber products, and ceramic ware to the United States and Western European countries, which were at a disadvantage in labour intensive production because of higher wages. In the period 1956–8, small and medium-sized companies accounted for about 60 per cent of Japanese exports and were the chief foreign exchange earners.[19] In a way, Japan found in the production of labour intensive exports an outlet for over-population.

As Japanese wages rose, it became increasingly clear that the cheap labour argument had to be modified. Large companies enjoy economy of scale in production and various monopolistic advantages (such as lower interest rates), but suffer from a number of disadvantages, such as higher wages (direct and indirect) and difficulties in organization control. These disadvantages can be overcome by smaller organizations, and if the increase in cost due to a smaller scale of production and loss of the monopolistic advantages can be outweighed by the savings (made possible by overcoming the disadvantages), smaller organizations will be preferred. The vitality of small and medium-sized companies in Japan even today has to be attributed to such cost advantages, but one wonders why this has been the case in Japan more than in other industrial countries.

One reason is social. About one hundred years ago, when Japan started modernization, the country was integrated enough to function as a nation state, but there were many social divisions, and each community had its own identity. Legally, barriers to mobility and economic exchanges within the country were removed, but social barriers remained high, and each community had a sort of nationalism of its own. However, since the country was modernizing its economy, it became imperative that communities also modernize if they wished to preserve their identities. To accomplish this, communities expected certain people to act as organizers and set up factories and other modern economic organizations where people in the community could earn a livelihood. When such community need combined with the spread of education and money economy which had taken place during the Tokugawa period, many production centres comprising small and medium-sized companies emerged in Japan.

The other reason for the existence of large numbers of small and medium-sized companies is the existence of other organizations which enabled them to overcome a number of disadvantages associated with small size. One disadvantage lay in obtaining necessary funds at reasonable rates of interest. Since the capital market was imperfect, it was extremely important that their disadvantages in fund raising *vis-à-vis* large manufacturing companies not be too great. Their second major disadvantage lay in marketing and purchasing. Large companies were in a better position than small companies to establish trading networks to undertake these activities because their volume of trade was much larger. The existence of large trading companies was extremely beneficial to small and medium-sized companies in overcoming these disadvantages. The remainder of this section will deal with the financial role of trading companies in relation to small and medium-sized companies, and the next section with their role in marketing and purchasing.

If small and medium-sized companies had been satisfied with growth using their own funds, there would have been no financial role for trading companies to play, but as it was, the latter functioned as conduits for the flow of money from banks to small and medium-sized companies. These companies could borrow a certain amount from banks on their own by offering their assets as collateral, but not nearly enough to meet their demand for capital. In a high growth setting, there were many opportunities to exploit, and they were willing to pay the prevailing rate of interest, or a rate slightly higher. But banks were not willing to lend money beyond a certain percentage of the value of the collateral.

One problem for banks was that they were supervised by the Ministry of Finance, which strongly discouraged them, in the interest of depositors, from undertaking risky (that is, unsecured) lending. The Ministry did not want to see a repetition of the experience in the pre-war period when banks often went bankrupt and runs on banks occurred; thus the Ministry urged banks to establish a conservative lending policy. The Ministry had the power to impose penalties on banks which were recalcitrant (it had set up a web of regulations for banks under the pretext of protecting their depositors). As a consequence of such guidance by the Ministry, major banks dealt mainly with large companies (where risk of bankruptcy is slight), and when small and medium-sized companies asked for loans, they requested collateral and gave loans amounting to a certain percentage of its value.

A second problem was that major banks were not allowed to set up branches freely, and thus their contacts with small and medium-sized companies were limited. This would not have caused major problems if local banks had been more willing to take risks, but since they were under stricter supervision (since small banks tended to face financial troubles), they requested even larger collateral from small and medium-sized companies. Given the fact that major banks have staffs more qualified to undertake credit evaluation, if they had been allowed greater freedom, they might have been a little more amenable to requests from small and medium-sized companies. As it was, however, a large part of the latter's demand for capital was left unfulfilled.

In spite of the fact that small and medium-sized companies needed capital, banks maintained a 'surplus fund'. The Japanese have almost always put their money in banks (and post offices) rather than in stocks. Banks used their deposits to make loans to the companies which could offer collateral, and made some unsecured loans to large companies, yet still had a large surplus.

In the 1950s, banks were slightly more aggressive in making unsecured loans, but as certain trading companies re-emerged as healthy, dynamic companies, banks recognized that the trading companies were much better in risk management, and therefore used them as intermediaries. This relationship is reflected in the fact that in the 1960s banks decreased their bad debts whereas the percentage of bad debts of trading companies increased.[20]

Trading companies did not face the same regulations banks did, and thus could establish contacts with small and medium-sized companies freely. Through buying from and selling for them, trading companies came to possess knowledge of their credit worthiness, and were willing to take the risks involved in granting them unsecured credits and loans. Because small and medium-sized companies go bankrupt from time to time, a premium was necessarily added to the rate of interest at which they borrowed. Since trading companies did a fairly good job of avoiding unsound companies, however, the premium was low enough to be attractive to many of them.

The outcome of the involvement of trading companies in financial transactions was that they functioned in roles that normally would be fulfilled by financial intermediaries. A financial intermediary shifts money from one place to another and reduces the gap in interest rates among regions or sectors, thus contributing to a better allocation of capital. In the Japanese setting, trading companies borrowed money from banks, and lent it to the small and medium-sized companies which had high growth potential but could not obtain capital because of the imperfection of the capital market. Such a function is usually performed by banks in foreign countries; had aggressive banking been allowed, Japanese banks would have performed the same function. In a high growth economy, however, trading companies seem to be in a better position to locate growth points or identify companies with growth potential because of their flexibility and intimate trading relations with various firms.

One advantage trading companies had over banks was that they were more perceptive in forecasting demand because they were involved in day-to-day transactions. If, for example, there were a promising opportunity for exporting a certain product (as in the case of silk, cotton fabric, matches, etc., in the Meiji era), trading companies investigated which companies had the best potential as suppliers, and gave credits and loans to promising companies. Banks, on the other hand, especially local banks, did not have intimate knowledge of the marketability of products made by small and medium-sized companies and, thus, were not in the position to evaluate effectively their growth potential.

One interesting recent development in the area of trading

companies' contributions to export is that they have begun to use foreign banks for export promotion. In plant export, foreign buyers usually prefer to pay in instalment over several years since sums involved are large, but Japanese manufacturers hesitate to accept such a scheme because of the foreign exchange risks involved (the Japanese yen has been floating since early 1973, and normally it is difficult to hedge the risk beyond six months). When a trading company is involved as the organizer of plant export, it can arrange financing for foreign buyers and make it possible for Japanese manufacturers to obtain immediate payments (thus, avoiding the foreign exchange risk). Large trading companies have high credit standings in financial circles throughout the world, and can become intermediaries between foreign banks and purchasers of plants in developing countries, the area to which most plant export is directed.

4. INTERMEDIATION IN THE GOODS MARKET

The large, modern companies which emerged in the trading sector became a tremendous blessing to Japanese industrialization, for thanks to them, wide, long-range distribution channels were created through which various kinds of information criss-crossed and numerous deals were consummated. Within Japan, they made possible the movement of goods from one place to another, thus contributing to a better allocation of resources. This function was especially important in the early Meiji years when the Japanese economy was not well integrated and there was a large discrepancy in prices. In international trade, they made it possible for Japanese manufacturers to export to places where there was a potential demand and to import necessary goods with proper timing and in sufficient amounts.

In order to establish such distribution channels, the first job of trading companies was to set up offices where there was a market or source of supply. They first established a few bases in Japan, and then gradually expanded their networks domestically and internationally. As Japanese industrialization progressed, it became particularly important to establish trading networks abroad. As discussed in Chapter 3, Mitsui Bussan and Mitsubishi Shoji's overseas offices essentially covered the world already at the end of the pre-war period. In the 1940s, because of the Pacific War and Japan's subsequent defeat, trading companies lost all foreign assets, but beginning in the early 1950s, they began to move abroad again, and today, the average sogo shosha has about one hundred offices abroad.

Offices spreading throughout the world had to be connected by some means. In the pre-war period, the telegraph was the most important means. Mitsui Bussan, for example, spent a large amount of money on a telegraph system, becoming a major customer for foreign telegraph companies (such as Western Union). Today, overseas offices are connected by a modern communications network. The Japan Foreign Trade Council describes this network as follows:

One sogo shosha lends an entire floor, thousands of square feet of floor space, to its communications center. It is jammed with telex and facsimile machines and computer terminals linking 187 offices scattered throughout 77 countries. Another sogo shosha has over 3,500 employees reporting from around the world through computer linked exclusive lines. It is linked between Tokyo and New York by 11 lines, and New York offices are linked to London by six lines.[21]

This telecommunications system is supplemented by telephone, mail, and frequent air travel by employees.

In international trade, it is also important to set up an efficient system of physical distribution, for if the cost of distribution is high, or if there is no means of transportation or no storage place at a time when there is demand, trading is impeded. In order to prevent this from occurring, trading companies have invested in physical distribution, established close relations with companies in this field, and developed manpower with the necessary expertise. In many cases, the costs of transportation (for example, in the case of trampers), storage, and insurance are negotiable, so large trading companies have often been in a favourable position to minimize costs, for their experience and the volume of goods they handled gave them considerable bargaining power. In cases where it appeared more advantageous to own the means of transportation or warehouses, trading companies have often made the necessary investment.

For trading companies to function as intermediaries, they must possess an experienced staff. In international trade, language barriers had to be overcome first. In addition, it was important to have intimate knowledge of the products involved and to be able to establish contact with possible suppliers and buyers. When the trade was not on a letter of credit basis and Japanese exporters assumed the risks of default, the credit status of potential buyers had to be evaluated for them. In order to build up a large staff of traders who could handle this type of work, trading companies hired competent people and assumed the costs of training them.

Trading companies have also made efforts to win the trust of customers. With this in mind, one area to which they paid close attention was that the terms of contracts be executed, no matter what happens between the time of signing the contract and that of delivery or receipt. Especially in the early phase of economic development, business morale was generally low, and there were many merchants who wanted to make short-term gains when prices moved in their favour, despite initial promises.[22] All of the sogo shosha of today established business principles at the beginning to prosper along with their customers, and highly valued the trust they received in turn.

What they have tried to accomplish by extending their networks to various parts of the world, establishing communications networks to link them, setting up efficient distribution systems, creating large staffs of experienced traders, and gaining trust from customers, was to create trade channels which a large number of people could find useful and dependable. Since the trading sector is fragmented abroad, trading companies are usually too small to be useful or too risky to inspire much confidence. In Japan, several trading companies have succeeded in building large, modern organizations, and have served as useful intermediaries for many manufacturers.

Trading companies may be contrasted with banks. Both play the role of intermediary: banks handle money, whereas trading companies handle goods, and both match up supply and demand. The more confidence people place in them, the more effectively they can function as intermediaries. When they do function effectively, those who deal with them are either enhanced in economic welfare or move closer to their maximum potential. In one respect, large trading companies have been more active in intermediation. Because capital flow was subject to strict regulation by the government, the international networks of banks have tended to be weak. But international trade was regulated much less severely, allowing trading companies greater degree of freedom than banks in foreign operations; thus, they were able to establish more extensive networks.

Japan's advantage over other industrial countries is, then, the existence of effective intermediaries in the goods market. Trade channels, especially the ones connecting Japan and foreign countries, are more efficiently used because they are open to many manufacturers; they function as if they are 'public highways', and thus distribution margins are lower. At the same time, because the channels are extended to various parts of the world as integrated units, numerous exchanges have taken place which would have been hampered if the channels had been disconnected and information had not passed through from one end to the other.

In order to understand how intermediation by large trading companies operates, consider the case of the export of orange juice to the Middle East in the mid-1970s.[23] The hot and dry climate, and the presence of oil money, raised the market potential for non-alcoholic beverages in this region. With the help of a sogo shosha, producers of mandarin oranges (who had been suffering from over-production) succeeded in exporting canned juice to this market.

What role did the sogo shosha play in making this export possible? The first important contribution was transmission of the information to orange producers that their products might be marketable if canned as orange juice. Before this, also, the sogo shosha made the necessary preliminary market research, studying the tastes of the people in the area, the availability of substitutes, f.o.b. prices in Japan, transportation costs, tariffs, etc. When it was found that Japanese orange juice might enjoy substantial demand, such information was transmitted to Japanese orange producers.

This kind of information was valuable in promoting export, but before actual trade could take place, further problems had to be solved. The first problem was to find an importer who had a good distribution network in the area, enough capital to act as a primary distributor, and who at the same time was trustworthy (that is, would not cause a lot of trouble on purely technical grounds). When such an importer was located, the sogo shosha presented its proposal with a persuasive case for its economic viability. Without the intermediation of the sogo shosha the deal would not have been consummated, for the producers and the importers would not have come to know each other; even if by some chance they did, they might not have trusted each other because of the uncertainty involved in shipping over such long distances.

The export of canned orange juice is just a single example. There have been numerous other commodities which have been exported from Japan as a result of the efficient intermediation of trading companies. For example, textiles were first exported to China, and then to South-East Asia, South Asia, the Middle East, Africa, and Latin America by trading companies.[24] As early as the 1930s, Japanese companies were busy convincing local distributors in these areas of the advantages of Japanese textiles. More recently, they skilfully persuaded numerous distributors and manufacturers in both developed and developing countries to use Japanese products, such as steel, chemicals, and machines. Undoubtedly, some of these exports would have been effected anyway because of the price advantage Japanese manufacturers enjoyed, but a large portion of the exports were due to the marketing skills, efficient physical distribution systems, and reputation for reliability which trading companies possess.

The contribution of trading companies has also been important in imports. As pointed out earlier, Japanese industrialization relied on the importation of raw materials and up-to-date machines. It may seem that import is an exceedingly simple activity but in fact a great deal of skill is involved in importing necessary products with proper timing and in sufficient amounts. Unless these requirements are met efficiently, the manufacturing industry in a country like Japan, where the dependency on foreign countries is high, tends to suffer. In the Japanese case, trading companies enabled manufacturers to take various precautionary measures (such as stock-purchase when prices were expected to rise, and postponement of purchase when they were expected to decline) by transmitting relevant information to them. In some cases where the price of a raw material continued to rise, driving Japanese manufacturers into difficult positions, trading companies were successful in locating cheaper substitutes. Or, as in the case of the cotton industry, because trading companies imported raw cotton from such diverse sources as China, India, the United States, East Africa, and Egypt, Japanese spinners were able to develop a blending method to minimize the cost of cotton for a certain quality of yarn.[25] These services to Japanese manufacturers helped them improve their efficiency, and have contributed indirectly to their competitiveness in the international market.

Some activities of trading companies went beyond the normal definition of intermediation. In many cases, financing accompanied intermediation. For example, when a Japanese manufacturer was short of capital to increase production of a product for which demand had increased abroad, the trading company which sought to handle the export advanced credit, and made the trade flow possible. Or, if a foreign importer was short of capital, the trading company performed a similar function so that import could be realized. In these cases, the role of the trading companies as financial intermediaries cannot be neatly separated from their roles as intermediaries in the goods market, but it is useful to keep them separate, for in a large number of cases, finance was either not involved at all or was subservient to intermediation in the goods market.

Even when finance is separated out, combination deals, counter-purchases, and plant export still constitute more than simple intermediation in the goods market. Combination deals are cases where the country to which a good is exported from Japan suffers from lack of foreign exchange, and, therefore, allows import only on the condition that the Japanese exporter buys goods equivalent in value in return. If the Japanese exporter is a manufacturing company, purchasing is usually limited to inputs for production, so it is highly unlikely that the condition can be met. If a sogo shosha is involved, however, it can buy enough goods from the country to offset the export, and then market them either in Japan or abroad. In such a case, two transactions must take place in order to realize one. In the past, the ability of sogo shosha to undertake this type of deal was useful in exporting Japanese products to developing countries and Socialist countries which tended to suffer from lack of foreign exchanges.

Counter-purchase is sometimes involved in plant export. When a plant is exported to a developing country, for example, its output capacity may be greater than the domestic demand; hence, for the plant to be a viable economic proposition, a certain portion of the output must be exported. Usually, in such instances, the country in question is inexperienced in export marketing, and thus, requires the prime contractor of the plant to promise to market the excess. This condition is extremely difficult for Japanese manufacturers to meet, since they usually do not handle the output of plants. When such a condition is imposed, the involvement of sogo shosha becomes valuable.

What exactly is plant export, and what other roles do sogo shosha play? Plant export is usually understood to be the export of manufacturing plants, but it can include the export of non-manufacturing facilities, such as power plants and telecommunications systems. Plant export differs from conventional export in two respects: (1) more than one manufacturer is required to supply plant equipment; and (2) designing and construction (and/or assembling) on site are necessary. This requires someone to coordinate the work, and in Japanese plant exports, coordination is often done by the sogo shosha.

The sogo shosha qualified well for the organizing role in plant export. Their global networks promptly pick up information on the planning of new projects abroad, making it possible for groups of Japanese manufacturers to prepare in advance. When certain machines cannot be obtained at competitive prices in Japan and this jeopardizes the chance of winning a project, a sogo shosha may use its network to locate better suppliers abroad. Also, in comparison to Japanese manufacturers, sogo shosha have far richer experience in operating abroad, a *sine qua non* of plant export where on-site construction is involved. Experience becomes especially important in that plant export usually goes to developing countries where the methods of rational business planning used in Japan cannot be easily transferred.

In 1976, plant export amounted to about $8 billion, becoming an important single component of Japanese exports (about 10 per cent of total exports). This is a rather large figure, considering that in 1973, when plant export was already receiving considerable attention, the value was only about $2 billion. Plant export is expected to increase further in the future in view of the fact that developing countries, including China, are increasing industrialization.

5. CONCLUDING COMMENTS

Considering the large role trading companies plays in the establishment of manufacturing companies in South-East Asia and certain other developing regions, it is possible to infer that trading companies were also an important investor in the Japanese manufacturing industry. As discussed earlier (see section 1), trading companies have undertaken numerous investments and contributed capital and entrepreneurship. This aspect of their contribution to Japanese industrialization must be clearly recognized. At the same time, however, it must be admitted that their relative importance as industrial investors was not as great as in the case of some developing regions of today. Most Japanese manufacturing companies were established and grew without financial and entrepreneurial contributions from trading companies.

The role of trading companies as intermediaries in the transfer of technology was relatively more important. Their offices abroad closely monitored the situation of technology in the West, and passed relevant information to their customers, or searched for the kinds of technology their customers required. In the course of these activities, trading companies often mediated a number of important licensing agreements. Yet, it must be acknowledged that they were constrained in this role, because in order to become a really effective intermediary, it was imperative that they possess sophisticated technical knowledge, and this was often beyond the comprehension of trading companies. Nevertheless, many manufacturers depended on trading companies because of their information networks, contacts with Western manufacturers, and negotiation skills.

Intermediation in the capital and goods markets was a more significant contribution to Japanese industrialization. In financial intermediation, trading companies were greatly assisted by the policy of the Ministry of Finance which made banks adopt conservative lending policies. In this respect, the role of financial intermediation reflects the uniqueness of the Japanese situation. Yet, in almost any country, government regulations exist (to protect depositors), causing commercial banks to adopt more or less conservative policies; in many countries there is thus the need for organizations able to undertake risky investments. In the Japanese case, because trading companies were involved in actual transactions, they were often ideally situated to find companies to which such investments should be directed.

Intermediation in the goods market was perhaps the most important contribution to Japanese industrialization. Trading companies have endeavoured to build efficient, wide, long-range channels by establishing offices wherever there was either a demand for Japanese goods or supplies of raw materials for Japanese industry; by setting up communications systems to link them; by developing contacts and expertise in the field of physical distribution; and by building up staffs of experienced traders. Through such channels, information criss-crossed between Japan and major business centres throughout the world, and goods were traded with distant places.

In the capital market, large intermediaries frequently emerge in almost any country. In the goods market, however, intermediation is much more difficult because the trading industry is more competitive and because manufacturers tend to usurp the functions of trading companies as they grow in size. Still, there is a need for large, efficient intermediaries in the goods market as there is in the financial market. In Japan's case, such intermediaries have emerged, and as a result, numerous exchanges have materialized which would not have taken place otherwise.

1. For further discussion on Suzuki's involvement in industrialization, see Katsura Yoshio, 'The Role of Sogoshosha in Japanese Industrialization: Suzuki & Co., 1877–1927', in Herman Krooss (ed.), *Proceedings of the Business History Conference*, Indiana University, 1975, second series, Vol. 3.

2. C.Itoh, *Itohchu Gurupu*, 1973.

3. Takahata Seiichi, 'Watashi no Rirekisho', *Nihon Keizai Shinbun*, 30 October 1972.

4. Iwai Sangyo, *Iwai Hyakunen Shi*, 1964, pp. 315–23.

5. Mitsui Bussan, *Mitsui Bussan Shoshi*, 1951, p. 38.

6. Mitsui Bussan, *The 100 Year History of Mitsui & Co., Ltd., 1876–1976*, 1977, p. 99.

7. Mitsui Bussan, *Kaiko-roku*, 1976, p. 324.

8. Marubeni, *The Unique World of the Sogo Shosha*, 1978, p. 48.

9. Mitsui Bussan, *Chosen to Sozo*, 1976, p. 209.

10. Takahata Seiichi describes the role of Nissho in Teijin's introduction of polyester technology in *Ekonomisuto*, 28 September 1971, p. 85.

11. Marubeni, p. 53.

12. Mitsubishi Shoji, *Ritsugyo Boeki-roku*, 1958, the part on machinery.

13. *Ryowa*, January 1980, pp. 180–203.

14. Mitsui Bussan, *The Mitsui Story*, n.d., p. 59.

15. Mitsui Bussan, *Chosen to Sozo*, p. 410 and p. 419; and Togai Yoshio, *Mitsui Bussan no Keiei-shi teki Kenkyu*, Toyo Keizai Shinposha, 1974, p. 72.

16. Ministry of International Trade and Industry (MITI), *Chusho Kigyo Hakusho 1973*, p. 51.

17. Ibid., p. 53.

18. Ibid., p. 59.

19. MITI, *Chusho Kigyo Hakusho 1963*, p. 3.

20. *Chuo Koron Keiei Mondai*, Fall 1977, Special Number on General Trading Companies, p. 152.

21. Japan Foreign Trade Council, 'The Sogo Shosha: What They Are and How They Can Work for You', 1978, p. 5.

22. Many foreign merchants also broke their promises when things became unfavourable, and lost the trust of their customers. See Mitsui Bussan (1951), p. 50.

23. Mitsui Bussan, *Chosen to Sozo*, p. 25.

24. The first major export of cotton fabric was organized by Mitsui Bussan. See Mitsui Bussan (1951), p. 75; and Yamamoto Jotaro-o Denki Hensan-kai, *Yamamoto Jotaro-o Denki*, 1942, pp. 132 and 308.

25. This point was made by Abe Fusajiro, president of Toyo Boseki, in his tribute to Kita Matazo, which appeared in Nippon Menka, *Kita Matazo-kun Den*, 1933, p. 2.

7

People and Organization

1. THE TRADING COMPANY IS PEOPLE

THE best way to understand the importance of people in a trading company would be to think about a sales company somewhere which sells consumer products of a large manufacturing company. This sales company would grow if its sales increased, but would lose agency rights and disappear from the trading scene if its sales stagnated or, even worse, declined. In that event, what should the company do to increase the sales? The answer would be to hire many competent salesmen, for the sales of the company are the sum of individual sales. Unlike manufacturing companies, in sales companies machines are not involved in achieving corporate objectives—only people are involved. In this sense, the sales company is people.

The trading companies which we have been discussing in this book are not like our imagined sales company. A Japanese trading company handles many products (not just one product), and thus deals with many suppliers. Purchasing is often as important as selling, for a certain product might not be available in sufficient amounts at the time needed, or prices might fluctuate so widely that profits depend on purchasing at a time when prices are low. Furthermore, since team-work is much more important in a trading company, individual contributions are not clear cut, as they are in a sales company.

Yet, trading companies share the basic feature of sales companies: it is the people who sell, buy, and coordinate various activities which contribute to the corporate objective. Unlike manufacturing companies, which are essentially joint ventures between people and machines (for machines are an important determinant of the cost of production and the quality of output), people are the sole determinant of the success or failure of trading companies.

The pattern of hiring qualified people varied from one trading company to another in the early years. Itoh Chubei, for example, recruited people mostly from his birthplace, the Omi province; and because his early business was domestic trade, there was no particular need for hiring college graduates. Stress on higher education did not begin until the 1910s when the second Chubei took over the business and began emphasizing foreign trade.[1] The second Chubei was much more open-minded than his father about the birthplace of the people to be hired, recruiting a number of college graduates from outside his province, but even he had a preference for college graduates from his province. In some cases, he gave financial support to poor, but able young men in his province and enabled them to attend college (Echigo Masakazu, who headed C.Itoh for about fifteen years from 1960, went to Kobe Commercial College—the present Kobe University—with Chubei's support).[2]

Mitsui Bussan, under Masuda Takashi, had already adopted a modern hiring policy in the Meiji era. At that time, it was generally felt that higher education was not necessary for merchants, but Mitsui Bussan recruited college graduates actively, and did not pay much attention to their birthplaces. Tokyo Commercial College (the present Hitotsubashi University) was its major hunting ground. In fact, these graduates so dominated the top echelon of the company later on that it was said that 'Tokyo Imperial University was established to produce government officials, and Tokyo Commercial College to produce Mitsui Bussan's cadres'.[3]

Over time, as Japan's modernization progressed, Mitsui Bussan's recruitment policy became the standard. Today, all sogo shosha hire a large number of college graduates, specialists not only in business, economics and law but also in engineering and science. Their birthplaces are hardly important. The only major change from Mitsui Bussan's recruitment policy in the early Meiji era is that sogo shosha today recruit college graduates from much more diverse sources (not concentrating on one college, as Mitsui Bussan did). This change occurred as the local colour of trading companies disappeared, as their needs for manpower became more diverse (some recruited from engineering colleges), and as the number of colleges increased.

Newly recruited people have to be trained before they can function effectively as members of a company. They have to be taught the company rules and the skills required for their tasks, and introduced into the network of human relations into which their work will involve them. Training is done both on-the-job and off-the-job. Recent training at Mitsubishi Shoji is described as follows.

On-the-job training is conducted under the 'instructor system'. The recruit is assigned as an assistant to a staff member who already has several years of professional experience and who has a specific task to perform in the business of the company. This senior does not hold a managerial position yet, but he gives man-to-man instruction to the recruit not only on practical routines but also on deportment as a business man. Particular attention is paid to attitude and manners. Personal relationship is stressed, and the instructor, thus, is at the same time a friend and a big brother to the new employee. This relationship continues for a year.

During the period he is under the 'instructor system', the new employee also undergoes off-the-job training. This consists of schooling conducted within working hours. About an hour a day are [sic] devoted to schooling throughout the year.

The schooling courses are the same for all and are designed as basic training in practical matters. They learn about foreign exchange, trading procedures and regulations, sales accounting, etc. Foreign language, too, is included to give them practical speaking ability which is neglected in the curriculum of schools in Japan.

During this on-the-job and off-the-job training, the new employee's aptitudes and qualities are evaluated and his preferences noted. On the basis of this, when the year of training is completed, the employee is assigned for the first time to a specific business task. This is the beginning of the process to fit him into a field of specialization.[4]

Mitsubishi Shoji also has overseas training for those who have been on its staff for two or three years. Each year it sends about thirty of these people to other countries to learn foreign languages and, in some countries, to attend schools. In addition, each year it sends several of its most promising young people for a two-year study of business administration and corporate management at top American and European business schools. In all, about sixty to seventy employees were studying business and language in twelve countries in the mid-1970s.[5]

Off-the-job training was first emphasized by Mitsui Bussan in the Meiji era. Its main feature was language training. Since English and some other Western European languages were the major media of communication in international business, these were naturally emphasized, but Mitsui Bussan also encouraged its employees to learn Asian and African languages. Masuda Takashi explained the reason why it was necessary to learn Asian and African languages in the following way.

To do business in a foreign country, it is important to know its language. For example, in Manila the Manilan language [sic], in Africa the African language, and in India the Indian language must be learned. Japanese learn English and French, but do not like to learn Chinese and the Manilan language. They question the usefulness of learning such 'inferior' languages. But this is a wrong attitude, for in business, there is no use in arguing whether the language of a trading partner is inferior or superior.[6]

Language training was not only for the purpose of mastering a foreign language but also for acquiring a means of understanding the business practices and psychology of the trading partner. In China, trainees were required to wear pigtails and Chinese clothes, live with Chinese families, and work at Chinese stores in order to assimilate the culture as well as to learn the language. At some point in time, they were even encouraged to marry Chinese women, and Mitsui Bussan promised bonuses to those who did.[7]

Mitsui Bussan's training programme in China began in the early 1890s. At this time, it was probably intended to train China specialists who would work at middle to low management levels, for trainees were 15 to 20 years old and their only educational background was the mastering of subjects up to the third year of junior high school. In 1899, a higher level programme was started. Those who could qualify under this programme were to have had a high school education. This programme was a direct result of Masuda's tour to China which led to the decision to get rid of compradores. In the early years of the programme, about twenty trainees were sent to China, and as they mastered the language and business practices of China, they replaced the compradores who served Mitsui Bussan. The latter were told either to quit or to work as Mitsui Bussan employees.[8]

Information on training programmes in other countries is scanty, though it is certain that overseas training was not confined to China. In 1904, Mitsui Bussan set forth a language training rule in order to encourage learning of the languages in the countries where it had branches. One source states that 'trainees were sent not only to China but also to India, Southeast Asia, South America, and Australia'.[9]

Mitsui Bussan and other trading companies have paid for the costs of manpower training. In a way, this is a risky investment, for they have no legal power to keep the people they have trained. In most developing countries today, where job hopping is common, it is particularly difficult to incur large training costs.

In order to minimize the risk, Japanese trading companies have provided various incentives to their employees. When profits were earned, employees were given bonuses. Itoh Chubei, for example, initially gave one-third of the profits to his employees (another third went to the family, and the remaining third to the company as retained earnings).[10] In 1891, since the size of capital had become large, the employees' share was reduced to 20 per cent, but this was still a large share at that time.[11] In the case of Kanematsu and Ataka, employees were made shareholders, and enjoyed part of the fruits of the common endeavour.[12] In trading companies where management was separated from ownership, employees who performed well were promoted to management posts and earned greater monetary as well as psychic income commensurate with those posts.

The management of trading companies realized early enough that their business was a joint venture with their employees, and made efforts to establish fair systems of incentives. This was one reason why it was possible to keep many of the trainees until their retirement. Another reason was the lack of horizontal movement in the Japanese labour market. In a way, people were locked into the company and not expected to leave as long as the company was doing reasonably well. This lack of horizontal movement lessened the risk involved in manpower training.

It should be pointed out, however, that training is not a unique Japanese practice. Major trading companies in the West have their own training programmes, and tend not to recruit people from outside for management posts. Some companies have an apprentice system and the management posts are restricted to those who have gone through this training. There seems to be, however, a difference in willingness to incur training costs between Western companies and Japanese companies. This is reflected particularly in the off-the-job training, which Japanese trading companies have undertaken far more extensively. In this, undoubtedly, Japanese trading companies were aided by the lack of horizontal movement in the labour market.

Hiring and training are not completely separate problems. In the Tokugawa period, merchant houses hired boys and taught them the three R's (reading, writing, and arithmetic) as well as necessary trade skills. After compulsory education was established in the Meiji era, the teaching of the three R's was left to schools, and training involved primarily the teaching of trade skills.

Primary education was sufficient at first for employment in most trading companies. Higher education was considered even dangerous. For companies engaged in foreign trade, however, higher education was important, for foreign trading required language ability (especially, in Western languages) and the knowledge of foreign countries, the teaching of which was carried out more effectively in schools. In addition, over time, the demand for college graduates rose because trading increasingly required people who had technical knowledge, general economic understanding, financial knowledge, etc., which could more easily be acquired in college.

For many years, college graduates were a scarce 'commodity', and trading companies which employed a large number of college graduates enjoyed a sort of monopoly profit since they undertook activities which required a combination of foreign language ability, legal, and technical knowledge. On the other hand, domestic trading companies, which relied on people with primary or, at most, secondary education, faced severe competition because there was no shortage of people who could undertake domestic trading.

There was one other advantage enjoyed by trading companies with foreign dealings. These companies offered a dream to young, adventurous people: the dream of going to the United States and Western European countries, countries which Japan considered models for its modernization, or of visiting exotic places such as India, Africa and Latin America, areas which appeared often in books. Until very recently, foreign travelling was confined to the élite; for able, ambitious young men who did not have money, work at trading companies with offices abroad was one of the few avenues for foreign travel. For example, when Kita Matazo (who built up Nippon Menka in the 1910s and 1920s) was still a junior member of the company, he was asked by his father to marry the daughter of a fairly well-to-do family and become its adopted son (and thus resign from the company to take over that family's business). He declined, however, citing as one reason the possibility that he might have the chance to travel to the West on company business in the future. Such a prospect was entirely lacking in the family business, or the business of the family whose daughter he was asked to marry.[13]

When trading companies were unable to build up manpower sufficient for the pace at which they wished to expand, it became necessary to recruit already trained traders. As pointed out above, however, this was difficult under normal circumstances (because of the lack of horizontal movement in the Japanese labour market). If companies persisted, several people were perhaps recruited, but not more than a few at one time. Sometimes, however, financially troubled companies were forced to release some employees, and this presented an opportunity for rapidly growing companies to recruit large numbers of experienced people at one time. For example, when Daiichi Bussan merged the financially troubled Nippon Kikai Boeki, the main attraction of the latter was that it had 300 to 400 college graduates with technical competence. (Nippon Kikai Boeki specialized in machinery).[14] The net liabilities taken over from Nippon Kikai Boeki were less than the amount Daiichi Bussan would have spent in order to recruit and train a technical staff of that size. In many other mergers, also, the acquisition of experienced traders was an important motive for carrying out the mergers.

When companies expanded their business without qualified personnel, they often incurred disasters. Practically all cases of failure in diversification can be explained by such reckless management. For example, Kinoshita collapsed because of mistakes in textiles, a new field for the company; and Kuhara and Furukawa incurred large losses because their traders were young and inexperienced. It may seem that trading is so simple an activity that any reasonably competent person can become a trader without much training. In fact, however, a great deal of skill is involved in buying, selling, coordinating activities, raising money, negotiating with shipping and insurance companies, and judging the credit worthiness of customers. Since such skills are invisible, they are sometimes underestimated; new companies have often burnt their fingers—sometimes so badly that they disappeared from the trading scene (as did Kinoshita, Furukawa and Kuhara).

2. TWO FOUNDERS IN CONTRAST: ITOH CHUBEI AND TAZUKE MASAJIRO

Itoh Chubei, who laid the foundation for Marubeni and C.Itoh, and Tazuke Masajiro, who founded Tazuke (one of the Senba Eight), were related. Chubei was Masajiro's uncle. Both amassed large fortunes during their lifetimes, were respected in the Osaka business world, and shared a number of other business distinctions, but they had different approaches to business. Masajiro was an individualist, whereas Chubei was an organization builder.

Masajiro was born in Omi province (as was Chubei), and apprenticed to Chubei's store in Osaka early in the Meiji era. Later, he recalled this time as follows.

There were 16 clerks in total in the store—five apprentices and 11 head clerks (*banto*). In addition, there was one cook, and the apprentices took turns every day assisting him. I served 6 months. When this was finished, I pulled the baggage cart. Piling on bags, I'd make the rounds every day to Kawaguchi, Tosabori, Nagahori and Matsushima.

I got up early in the morning and went to draw the day's drinking water. I didn't consider it painful because my body had been hardened by having been a peasant when I was a child. Still, I recall that because I was short of stature I had shortened the ropes of the water carrier and carrying it up the stone steps was painful.

Also, there were only two places where there were telegraph stations— Koraibashi and alongside the Osaka prefectural government building at Kawaguchi. Every day, I went to send telegrams. This was just one year before the outbreak of Saigo's war in the ninth year of Meiji (1876). In the morning, I'd go to Koraibashi to send telegrams and on the way home I'd loiter for twenty or thirty minutes on top of the bridge watching the movements of the side-wheel steamboat Suiryomaru going to and from Fushimi. The ship's arrival was interesting—I looked forward to it every day when I went to Koraibashi.

In summer, I took loads to Kawaguchi. I'd set my load alongside Nagahori bridge, wash out my summer outfit (*jinbe*), lay it out to dry on top of lumber, and go swimming while it dried. We'd work at night until eleven o'clock at the earliest, and get up about eight o'clock in the morning, as was the custom in all the shops in Motomachi. The area had a reputation for this morning sleep; indeed, only the person who went to draw water got up while it was still dark.[15]

As seen from Masajiro's recollection, in the early Meiji era, Chubei's store was small and traditional—there were no indications that the present Marubeni and C.Itoh would spring up from this store.

Masajiro did not stay with his uncle for very long. He became independent and started his own business. By the time the Sino–Japanese War ended (the mid-1890s), he had made some money and was confident that he would become as successful a merchant as his uncle. Around this time, he told Chubei, 'Uncle, I do not set up many stores and train people as you do. I am not very good at such things. But I will make more money than you will.'[16] Probably, he made more money than his uncle. He was adept at speculation (his line of business, yarn, involved speculation to a considerable extent), and he made a large fortune. In fact, he was so skilful at it that he was called Tazuke shogun [general Tazuke] by his fellow merchants in Osaka.

Although he was immensely successful in making money, Masajiro was not talented in the area of organization building. He was fully aware of this shortcoming, and warned his son not to follow his example. Maybe, because of his rivalry with his uncle, he did not tell his son to follow Chubei's example. Instead, he cited as a model his friend and sometime business associate, Abe Fusajiro, who came from the same province (Omi) and built up Toyo Boseki, a large spinning company. Masajiro instructed his son as follows.

I do everything by myself. It is not good. And I seem to be too strict with other people. This seems to put them off. This is my deficiency. You should not follow my example. Mr. Abe Fusajiro is a great man. He is broad-minded enough to train people. You should follow Mr. Abe's example.[17]

Itoh Chubei was far better at building an organization. He made great efforts to attract talented men to his stores, especially those from his birthplace, and he promoted people who proved themselves to be competent and trustworthy. In order to train his employees and at the same time keep an eye out for promising ones, he introduced discussions, personally chairing two large meetings each year. Meetings held once every month were chaired by managers. In these meetings, opinions were sought from employees on the economic forecast, future price movements, selection and quantities of goods to be handled, etc.[18]

Promoting competent employees to higher posts required a willingness to trust them. In many developing countries today, lack of trust acts as a barrier to organization building. Yet it is only through the delegation of power that an organization can grow. Japan was by no means an open society during Chubei's time, but in one respect, he was fortunate: the sense of regional togetherness that characterized much of later Tokugawa society made his chances of being betrayed by employees from his birthplace small.

Dedication and loyalty on the part of employees is not, however, a one-way process. As pointed out earlier, Chubei considered his employees business partners, and shared profits with them. At first, one-third of the profits went to the Itoh family, another third was kept as retained profits, and the remaining third was divided among employees as bonuses. In 1891, as the size of capital invested became large, the employees' share was reduced to 20 per cent, but this was still a large share at that time. In Chubei's view, the business should not only support his family but also enhance the welfare of his employees.

Chubei's management philosophy paid off. When he died in 1903, his son was just 17 years old and a student of a commercial high school in Omi. Immediately, the son succeeded to his father's name (thus, becoming the second Chubei), and in 1904, he joined the family business. In 1909, he went to England to study, and in his absence, his brother-in-law acted as head of the family. Actual management was left to Tanaka Ryozo who had joined the store in 1877 and become manager of the head store in 1893. In the several years before the first Chubei's death, because of his poor health, management had been delegated to his top employees. The founder had succeeded in building a management team which could handle the business without the presence of the Itoh family head.[19]

The success of Marubeni and C.Itoh today may be traced to many events which took place after the death of the first Itoh Chubei, while the failure of Tazuke in the post-war period can be attributed, in large measure, to factors beyond that company's control. Nevertheless, the predilections for the founders seem to have had important bearings on the evolution of their respective businesses. Because Chubei made great efforts to attract talented people and train them, the business prospered even after his death. On the other hand, since Masajiro was not good at human relations, the fortune of his business rose and fell with him. The money he left was a poor substitute for a solid organization.

3. DELEGATION OF POWER

When a trading company is small, all major decisions can be made by the head of the company, but as the size increases with growth in the number of goods handled and the area covered, it becomes necessary to delegate power to other people. Hence, whether or not a trading company is willing to delegate power bears significantly on its growth.

Mitsui Bussan is known for being a company in which considerable power was delegated to managers in the pre-war period. This practice was necessitated in part by the underdeveloped state of transportation and communications. Unlike today when a mere day or two is sufficient to travel from Japan to any place in the world, and when all offices are connected by telex on a 24-hour basis, in the pre-war period much more time was required for travelling and sending messages. It took over a month to reach Europe, and about half a month to get to the West coast of the United States. A trip from San Francisco to New York required an additional four days. It was possible to communicate with overseas offices by telegraph, but this was expensive and time consuming. Under such circumstances, if new business opportunities were not to be missed, it became necessary to allow branch managers to make various decisions on-the-spot without obtaining approval from the headquarters each time.[20]

We might conclude that Mitsui Bussan grew to become a large company because the leaders delegated considerable power to managers, and, on the basis of this, recommend to stagnant or only slowly growing companies that if they want faster growth, they should delegate greater power to managers. Certainly, more and more power must be delegated as a company grows in size, but the delegation of power involves risk. If power is delegated unwisely, a company will decline rather than prosper. In the history of Japanese trading companies, a number of companies have gone bankrupt because of mistakes like this. Considering this possibility, many trading companies are reluctant to delegate power.

Herein lies the basic dilemma of trading companies. If power is not decentralized, the risk of a manager misusing his power and bringing down the whole organization is minimized, but the chances of exploiting new opportunities are also reduced, and to that extent, growth slows down. On the other hand, if power is decentralized, there is greater risk, but at the same time, greater opportunity for growth. The trend over time for companies which have become sogo shosha has. been decentralization, but the amount of power to be delegated at a particular point in time has been decided by trial and error. No set formula for this can be derived.

When power is delegated, it is important to establish a check system to ensure that there is no unauthorized use of power. Of course, if the check system becomes elaborate, the cost becomes prohibitive, so trust has to be placed in people to whom power is delegated. To be able to do this, trading companies have to cultivate loyalty, build up *esprit de corps*, and provide proper incentives. As back-up, a check system, though it may be used only randomly, must be set up as an additional deterrent.

Limits are usually set on the extent of stock purchases and short sales, the amount of credits to customers, and the amount of money which can be borrowed from banks. If these limits need to be exceeded, approval has to be obtained from higher levels of authority or the departments which set such limits (for example, the credit evaluation department). One important function of the check system is to ensure that set limits are not violated.

Another purpose of the check system is to prevent people from resorting to illicit practices. One recurrent problem of trading companies in the early days was that traders did business for themselves by using the name and money of the company. They might speculate in commodities or foreign exchange markets for their own gains; they might handle goods on their own and earn extra commissions; or they might collaborate with customers and withdraw large sums from the company by forging the receipts of goods, and then disappear. Numerous other problems, such as stealing cash, using the company seal to withdraw money from banks, and so on, also arose in many companies.

One effective system for preventing some of these illicit activities was the so-called 'separation of three powers'. The three powers are: (a) buying and selling; (b) shipping and receiving; and (c) actual handling of money. Under this system, at least three persons have to collaborate in order to trade for individual gains. Deriving individual profits thus becomes much more difficult than when one person has all three powers. Mitsui Bussan instituted this type of check system in the pre-war period, and Nissho adopted it in the post-war period. In other companies, this system has not been adopted *in toto* because it would increase paper work.

The problems of exceeding the limits of power, trading for individual gains, and undertaking other illicit acts were not minor in the history of trading companies. Many people were fired in the pre-war period for such acts. Approximately half of the people who entered major textile trading companies in Osaka left for such reasons.[21] In the post-war period (1952–76), one sogo shosha took disciplinary actions against workers on eighty-seven occasions (with penalties ranging from warnings to firings). Some of the causes involved problems of negligence and lack of discipline, but violation of rules and illicit acts were the dominant causes.[22]

Even Mitsui Bussan encountered difficulties with employees not obeying company rules. One frequent violator in the Meiji era was Yamamoto Jotaro (manager of the Shanghai branch, who later became an executive managing director and resigned in the early 1910s because of involvement in a political scandal). Masuda Takashi frequently had to warn him not to violate the rules. Such violations often involved speculation (in both commodity and foreign exchange markets), and sometimes caused heavy losses in some branches. Nakamigawa Hikojiro, who managed the Mitsui zaibatsu in the 1890s, felt unfavourable toward Mitsui Bussan because he believed that if Masuda lost control of the company, people would go wild in speculation and cause great losses to the company, so great in fact that the whole Mitsui zaibatsu would find itself in financial quagmire.[23] This turned out to be groundless fear on Nakamigawa's part, but the fact remains that Mitsui Bussan had to make constant efforts to enforce company rules.

4. THE LESSONS OF SUZUKI

As discussed in Chapter 3, Suzuki grew rapidly in the 1910s and surpassed Mitsui Bussan in sales sometime during the First World War boom. Kaneko Naokichi, who directed the growth of the company, wished to make Suzuki an industrial-commercial combine and create a Suzuki zaibatsu comparable in size to the Mitsui and Mitsubishi cliques. If the post-war recession had come several years later, he might have succeeded. As it was, before he could close the ranks, the recession hit hard, and his achievements up to that time came to nothing.

From the viewpoint of organization theory, there are two interesting lessons which can be learnt from Suzuki's failure. First, as discussed above, is that when the size of a trading company increases, it becomes impossible to manage unless power is delegated. If a company is too centralized, it becomes difficult to follow closely new developments in many commodities and areas, and mistaken or uninformed orders are inevitably issued. This impairs the mutual trust between the superior and his subordinates, and causes a breakdown of the command system.

The other interesting lesson is that when such a breakdown occurs, a serious organizational crisis develops, a solution to which is extremely difficult to find. To Kaneko, who built his firm up from a small, local company into a world famous company, Suzuki was his whole life, and he resisted any attempts to displace his personal power. After the company encountered financial difficulties, it became necessary to wrest power from Kaneko and set up a decentralized structure, but he fought back, not wanting to step down. Certain trading companies may have to depend on autocratic rulers in the initial phase of their growth. In these cases, future growth depends on the smooth transfer of power. Suzuki's organizational problems are discussed in more detail below.

In the 1910s, as the business expanded, Suzuki hired a large number of personnel and established new offices, but the command system was not able to keep up with this growth. After the late 1910s, Kaneko could no longer hold together and command his subordinates by his own strength. He explains this situation as follows.

Towards the end of the First World War, judging that business policy had to be radically and rapidly changed, I was getting ready to retreat. I told people of my new policy but to my surprise, they would not act as I ordered. I was amazed. In retrospect, it is clear that the command system of Suzuki had collapsed by that time. . . . It is possible to command when the number of workers is 50 or 100, but when it increases to 500 or 1,000, it becomes impossible to do so. A large number of bright graduates were hired, and they became overconfident after meeting and working on equal terms with leading figures in the London and New York business world. As long as my' predictions were borne out, they listened, but were I to make an occasional mistake, then all order was lost. They would mutter, 'The old man has lost his mental strength' or 'the old man is showing signs of senility'.[24]

A large part of the responsibility for the breakdown of command can be attributed to Kaneko himself. He may have been a brilliant merchant, but he was not an organization builder, for he was not willing to delegate power to his subordinates. He ran the company in the 1920s the same way he did in the late 1890s when it was still small. In the 1920s, since the company had grown into a large concern with numerous related companies, it was simply beyond his capacity to make all major decisions. Yet, he was still not willing to relinquish power. As a result, he made a number of mistakes and alienated some of his subordinates. The Bank of Taiwan, which became the financial caretaker of Suzuki in the 1920s and made various attempts to rescue the company, described the situation in the following way, '[The reorganization plan] was troubled by the dictatorial attitudes of Kaneko, who ignored systematic management. Institution of clearly laid down rules on the function of each post was of no use now, and new large losses resulted from the breakdown of the chain of command.'[25]

If Kaneko had resigned early enough, the collapse of Suzuki might have been prevented. The company included young college graduates, like Takahata, who had a sense for modern management as well as experience in trading, so that Kaneko was not only dispensable but a downright burden for the company. Nevertheless, he would not step down, for it was his company, the company he had built. The Bank of Taiwan, resorting to its power as a major supplier of credits, tried to force him out, but he fought back. This situation is described as follows.

Mr. Kaneko was urged to take responsibility for the reorganization of related companies as director of the unlimited partnership and to leave the management of Suzuki Shoten, Ltd., to new men. At the end of last year, when Suzuki Shoten suffered from an acute shortage of funds, it presented a reorganization plan, dated December 22, for the partnership and Suzuki Shoten, Ltd. According to this plan Mr. Kaneko was to remain as director of the partnership and the limited company was to be managed by the other directors. We were asked for approval as well as for financial assistance. At the same time, Mr. Kaneko promised that he would withdraw from the limited company, taking full responsibility for the present difficulties, and presented a letter of petition for our assistance. We approved the plan on the whole. In January of this year, when Mr. Kaneko gathered the employees of Suzuki and told them of the decision, some of them misinterpreted his remarks to mean that the reorganization would force Mr. Kaneko to withdraw completely from Suzuki, and a protest movement was started. Their complaint was that his withdrawal was unnatural, and so they began to whip up antipathy against our bank. If Mr. Kaneko had felt heavy responsibility, as he stated in his letter of petition, and been willing to improve the general situation, he should have explained to the employees the reason why such actions were disloyal to the cause of Suzuki Shoten and convinced them of their mistake. Instead, by utilizing this protest as an excuse, he asked us to allow him to remain as director of the limited company, or to postpone the time of his resignation by saying that it would cause the loss of public confidence. . . .

If he is not uprooted, it will be forever impossible to straighten out the twisted financial relations with related companies, eliminate favoritism, impose discipline, mete out rewards and punishments justly, and expect the tension of the employees and the performance of the company to improve. Therefore, Mr. Kaneko's request to stay on in Suzuki Shoten, Ltd., whether nominal or not, should be rejected absolutely since it impairs our policy and shakes the basis of the reorganization plan.[26]

Kaneko stayed on too long. Before the reorganization plan was given a chance, Suzuki collapsed. In a way, Suzuki was inextricably tied to him, and the only way to remove him was to destroy the company he built. This was eventually what the Bank of Taiwan was forced to do. A year after Suzuki's collapse, about forty of the traders Kaneko had trained joined together and established a small trading company (Nissho). Since this company considered itself to be the heir of Suzuki, it might be argued that the transfer of power did take place. In the process, however, a trading company with an extensive international network was reduced to a small, obscure company.

5. ORGANIZING PRINCIPLES

Trading companies may be organized by area or by product. In the case of Mitsui Bussan, for the first thirty years or so, it was organized by area, each branch functioning as if it were an independent company. As the volume of sales increased and the number of products multiplied, however, this organizational structure began to cause problems. The most serious problem was lack of coordination in promoting the sale of a particular commodity. In order to cope with the problem, in 1894 a system of common account was introduced for strategic commodities. This system allowed branch managers to charge the expense of their sales against the account but since there was no particular incentive for branch managers, it did not work. As a consequence, from the late 1890s to the early 1910s, commodity divisions were gradually created to coordinate purchase and sales, and the power of branch managers was reduced. In other words, the previous organizational structure based on branch autonomy was gradually replaced by a structure organized along commodity lines.[27]

The restructuring in Mitsui Bussan began in the late 1890s when business operations were separated from administration, and railroad machinery, coal, raw cotton, and miscellaneous products divisions were created. The number of commodity divisions increased further in subsequent years. In 1907, the division of machinery was created, and in 1909, when Mitsui Bussan became a joint stock company, wood and sugar divisions were set up. During the First World War, grain and fertilizer, and metals divisions were set up. Silk, petroleum and chemicals divisions were established in 1920, 1925, and 1926, respectively. Towards the end of the pre-war period, there were grain and vegetable oil, textiles, food, cement, chemicals, machinery, coal, petroleum, metals, wood, and silk divisions.[28]

A considerable amount of power was delegated to division heads, so that each division functioned as if it were a specialized trading company. As the number of commodity divisions increased, it became difficult for one person to supervise all of them, so the job came to be shared by managing directors. In the early 1910s, there were four managing directors. One was in charge of the administrative division, and the other three jointly of the commodity divisions. One was in charge of the machinery division, the second of the coal and wood divisions, and the third of the raw cotton and sugar divisions. Each managing director had virtual autonomy over the divisions he supervised. He was, in turn, answerable to the chief managing director, who functioned, in reality, as the president, although the post was nominally held by a member of the Mitsui family. Roughly from the time when Mitsui Bussan became a joint stock company to the 1930s, though the number of managing directors varied slightly, the organizational structure remained essentially the same.[29]

Today, all sogo shosha are divided into administrative and product divisions. The administrative divisions are engaged in support activities (finance, shipping, etc.) and house-keeping activities (accounting, auditing, etc.). The product divisions undertake business operations. Their number varies somewhat from one sogo shosha to another, but most sogo shosha have ten to fifteen divisions (iron and steel, iron and steel material, textiles, non-ferrous and light metals, machinery, energy, chemicals, agri-marine products, etc.). Each division is further divided into departments (for example, the chemicals division is divided into inorganic chemicals, organic chemicals, fine chemicals, plastics, etc.).

In most sogo shosha, product divisions are profit centres, and division heads manage their divisions as if they were independent companies. Division heads are held responsible to either executive managing directors or vice-presidents, and the president presides over all. Thus, the chain of command is from the president to executive managing directors or vice-presidents, to division heads, and then to department heads. This organizational structure of sogo shosha is the one Mitsui Bussan developed in the beginning of this century. Certainly, the number of products handled and the volume of trade have increased, and the organizations have become much bigger, but the essential organizational features have remained the same.

One problem for sogo shosha is determining the degree of independence to be given to product divisions. If they have complete autonomy, two major problems arise. One is the loss of organizational flexibility, a necessity at times when the structure of the economy changes. For example, when Osaka-based textile companies diversified into non-textile products, it was essential for the top management to divert profits and manpower from textile to non-textile divisions, even if it involved losses on a short-term basis. Also, since Japanese economic changes have been fast, to maintain organizational flexibility was important for the growth of trading companies. To maintain this flexibility, the autonomy of product divisions had to be curtailed considerably from time to time.

The other disadvantage of giving complete autonomy to product divisions is that their activities become difficult to coordinate. In order to take full advantage of the organizational set-up of a sogo shosha, it is important to be able to undertake combination deals or counter-purchases by co-ordinating sales and purchases (activities involving more than two divisions). Furthermore, many new projects require expertise from various divisions, and the objections of one product division have sometimes to be overruled if the projects seem profitable for the company as a whole.

In view of these problems, top management has had to have staffs to help them obtain an overview of the various activities being undertaken throughout the company. This role is usually fulfilled by the planning and coordination department of the administrative division. The power of this department seems to have varied by time and by company. In the case of C.Itoh, the planning and coordination department was headed for many years in the post-war period by Sejima Ryuzo (a general staff member during the Pacific War recruited to the company after detention in Siberia for about eleven years) who wielded considerable power.

The basic organization principle of sogo shosha today is by product, but areas cannot be completely ignored because of their geographical spread. In Table 7.1, a person X_{ij}, who is in charge of commodity i at the office in area j, is responsible to both the manager of office j and the head of commodity i. Usually, office j is a profit centre, and thus, the

TABLE 7.1

The Organization of a Sogo Shosha by Commodity and Area

Commodity \ Office	1	2	$\cdots$	j	$\cdots$	n
1	X_{11}	X_{12}		X_{1j}		X_{1n}
2	X_{21}	X_{22}		X_{2j}		X_{2n}
. . .						
i	X_{i1}	X_{i2}		X_{ij}		X_{in}
. . .						
m	X_{m1}	X_{m2}		X_{mj}		X_{mn}

hierarchical structure has to be built also on office j. Furthermore, since X_{ij} serves two masters, the unity of command, an important organization principle in classic management theory, breaks down.

It is possible to consider that office j is a place where representatives of various product divisions gather, and that the office manager simply supervises them so as to prevent them from exceeding the limits of power delegated to them by their bosses (the heads of commodity divisions). Then, the chain of command still runs along product lines, and product remains the basic principle of organization.

Sogo shosha have historically, however, given some weight to area. Especially in the recent period, some overseas offices have become large (e.g., New York offices) and have begun to take initiatives in business on their own. In order to increase offshore trade (which has become important especially because with the slowdown in economic growth after the oil crisis, trade based in Japan has not been growing rapidly) it has become imperative to give more independence to offices abroad. Such a situation is bound to increase the importance of area as an organizing principle, and some sort of compromise between area and product will have to be worked out in a new structure.

6. THE PLACE OF FAMILY ENTERPRISES

Most of the trading companies which have become sogo shosha began as family enterprises. The major exceptions are Gosho and Nippon Menka. In the case of Gosho, Omi merchants pooled their resources, whereas in the case of Nippon Menka, four spinners joined together with domestic cotton traders to undertake international cotton trading. Apparently, the amount of capital required to establish a purchasing network for raw cotton abroad and to supply sufficient quantities to spinners was more than one merchant was willing to risk by himself. In other cases, growth could be gradual, and the family enterprise was the common form of organization.

There was considerable variation among family enterprises in the Meiji era. Mitsui Bussan, for example, was a family enterprise in terms of ownership, but from the very beginning, management was separated from ownership, and the owner family (the Mitsui) rarely interfered with management. In most other family enterprises, however, the owner family dominated top management and there was no separation of management from ownership.

At first, employees in family enterprises were treated as members of the owner family in many ways. For example, they slept and ate in the house of the owner family, and the head of the family supervised their social life as well. They did not get paid for their work; only occasionally were they given pocket money. The labour practice was different then: they worked not for money but for training and to become, eventually, independent merchants. On completion of their pupillage, they were given financial assistance and the permission to use the family name in their own stores, which, as branch stores (like branch families), owed allegiance to the head store for a few generations.

A person who entered the head store of the Itoh family around 1910 later recalled his life at that time as follows.

As far as our livelihood was concerned, all employees—no matter where they worked—slept at the store and were given three meals; it was a set-up whereby we didn't need much spending money. The chiefs lent us two or three yen a month of petty cash and we managed by using as much as possible things we could buy on account, and by going into debt. The system was that at the end of the year we received bonus type payments in the form of notes, and debts would be balanced. It was this kind of age, so in the first year I was with the store, at New Year's there was a three-day holiday and spending money was 50 *sen*; in summer, at the festival for one's ancestors, vacation was two days with 50 *sen*; Emperor Jimmu's Festival and the Emperor's Birthday were holidays, 30 *sen* each; in total, one yen, 60 *sen*. This was one year's total income.[30]

In two decades from the mid-1890s, changes began to take place in family enterprises. As the number of employees increased, it became impractical to grant all of them independence, for the amount of financial assistance required became large, and at the same time, it was necessary to increase the size of the trading company to keep pace with the growth of industrial capital. It was better to pool as much resources as possible and not to use funds to establish autonomous branch stores for employees and family members.

In order to meet the new situation, employees were socially separated from the owner family, and made into wage earners (who sold hours for wages). The working hours and holidays were specified—in off-hours, employees could now have time to themselves—and the formula for wages and bonuses was set down. More and more people began to commute from their own homes. By the early 1920s, what had emerged were family enterprises in terms of ownership and management, but relations between the owner families and the employees had become predominantly economic.

A family enterprise is bound to lose in competition over the long run, for when top management posts are hereditary, the management cannot continue to be as competent as ones based on meritocracy. All trading companies which have become sogo shosha from family enterprises were assisted by the dispersion of holdings imposed by the GHQ during the Occupation period as part of economic democratization. In the case of Ataka and Iwai, some family influence remained and that weakened the companies. They were later merged by other companies.

Small trading companies were not affected by the occupation reforms, and the separation of management from ownership did not take place. Tamurakoma and the Senba Eight are examples of such. Their decline in the post-war period can be attributed to the continuation of family control. In the confusion of the early post-war years, Tamurakoma, for example, grew rapidly; by the early 1950s, it had become comparable in volume of trade with the 'Five Cotton Traders of the Kansai Area'. Tamurakoma had the chance to surpass these five and become a sogo shosha; but, it did not. Instead, it came under the control of the Sanwa Bank, and was made an affiliate of Mitsui Bussan. If the company had been freed from the control of the Tamura family, its fortune would have been quite different.

Given the conclusion that a family enterprise is bound to decline over the long run, an interesting question will be, 'How many generations can such a company prosper?' Apparently, in many cases, three generations constitute one cycle. There is a saying in Japan that 'the father toils, his son enjoys life and his grandson is a beggar'. Though this may be true as a general principle, there are cases where a company has prospered with an hereditary top management for a few generations.

In the case of Iwai, it was not until the fourth president that the company got into financial trouble. The second generation president (Katsujiro) developed the company, and the third generation president (Yujiro) maintained the position his predecessor had established. In the Itoh family likewise, it was the second generation which played an important role in developing the business.

When these two companies (Iwai and Itoh) are examined closely, a sharp difference in business philosophy between the founder and his successor may be observed. In both cases, the founder became successful in domestic trade, but was inward looking, whereas the successor was more outward looking, initiating direct foreign trade and thereby creating a wide range of new business opportunities. In changing business strategy at Itoh, the second Chubei did not have to fight with his father (who had died before the son entered the family business), but he did have differences with the seniors his father had taken into confidence.[31] In order to begin direct foreign trade, Chubei wanted to go abroad for study and also to recruit college graduates. The seniors, on the other hand, felt that since the business had been functioning smoothly, they did not want to change the established policy. So, Chubei divided the family business into two, and brought more flexible employees into the foreign trade branch. Then, when the crash occurred in 1920 and the business ran into difficulty, he fired some older employees and started rebuilding the foreign trade branch (C.Itoh) with young people.[32] Thus, by the early 1920s, Chubei had been able to crush all his opposition.

In the case of Iwai, the second president, Katsujiro did not have much problems with employees but he had to contend with Bunsuke, the founder. Bunsuke was innovative in the sense that he saw the opportunity to make a profit by handling Western goods and established a business to realize it, and he was successful since he managed the business better than his contemporaries. But he was also a rather traditional merchant who, instead of dedicating himself to the expansion of his business, looked forward to the time when he could lead a comfortable existence on the rent from his properties. He was quite content with the way he conducted his business.

Katsujiro was more of an empire builder. In his memoirs, he explained that the schism was a result of the difference between his business philosophy and Bunsuke's.

... when I was 16, three employees senior to me resigned, so that I took over their work. The period from that time until I was 30 was spiritually the most difficult in my life. Partly influenced by the instruction of my mother, I held a positive business philosophy, but Bunsuke, who was my master as well as my father-in-law, held a passive one. Thus, always there were differences of opinion, and I suffered indescribable pain.[33]

Katsujiro seems to have felt that in order for the business to grow, it was necessary to put new ideas into action and that even if he succeeded in following the path laid down by Bunsuke, the business would not grow much. For the growth of the business, it was more important to gauge the direction in which overall business conditions would move, and to launch new businesses accordingly, rather than pushing efficiency in the established business to an extreme. It was also important to him for such businesses to be started early. In 1931, he stated in a speech that 'I have the peculiar habit of wanting to venture into areas of businesses that have scarcely been explored.'[34]

It is difficult to imagine the growth of Iwai and C.Itoh in this century without direct foreign trade. Both Bunsuke and the first Chubei laid the foundation by making money in various new opportunities made available by economic progress in the Meiji era, but without the new policy of their successors, what they had accomplished would have come to nothing, for competition became keener in domestic trade as time went on. In the case of Iwai and C.Itoh, two generations were required to put the family business on a firm base.

7. TOP MANAGEMENT

The importance of top management cannot be overemphasized. Though top managers are not involved in actual trading, they make decisions affecting the present and future overall performance of the company, and if such decisions are injudicious, no matter how competent the traders may be, the performance of the company declines. On the other hand, if the decisions prove sage, even if some traders are mediocre, the company's fortunes improve.

In the history of Japanese trading companies, there have been a number of top executives who had particularly important influence on the evolution of their firms. For example, without the foresight and organization skill of Masuda Takashi, Mitsui Bussan would not have grown to become a large international trading company in the pre-war period. In the post-war period, without the vision and determination of Ichikawa Shinobu, Marubeni would have faded away from the trading scene or become an obscure trading company (like Inanishi in the Senba district of Osaka, Marubeni's rival around 1910). On the other hand, the failure of Ataka, Iwai, Suzuki, Gosho, and others may be attributed to the bad judgement of their top management.

In large organizations, top management is a group, not a single individual. Any person who makes important decisions or participates in a meeting to make such decisions may be considered a member of the top management, and exactly who constitutes the top management is often not clear cut. In Japanese trading companies, all product division heads, executive managing directors, vice-presidents, presidents, and chairmen normally constitute the top management (the number exceeds twenty in most sogo shosha).

Within the top management, there is a hierarchical structure. Usually, the president is at the apex of power, executive managing director and vice-presidents at the second level, and division heads at the third level. This is a typical structure, but it is often not clear who holds the ultimate decision-making power. In part, this is a result of the fact that, although the president is supposed to have ultimate power, major problems are discussed in top management conferences, the decision of which the president often simply follows. Who is actually most influential in reaching a decision varies from one case to another.

Another reason why it is not clear exactly who holds the ultimate decision-making power is that the power of the president is sometimes shared. Most large trading companies have both a chairman and a president, and the division of power is ambiguous. The chairman is usually supposed to deal with external affairs (by becoming members of committees in economic organizations, participating in government-sponsored business conferences, meeting with high government officials, etc.), and the president is expected to deal with internal management. But the chairman sometimes has vested interest in internal affairs, and exerts his influence on these matters; likewise, the president must participate in external activities from time to time.

The sharing of ultimate power may cause a certain amount of confusion in the chain of command and damage the hierarchical structure, but it has certain advantages. In the case of C.Itoh, the second Chubei was active in the business community and established liaisons with the political world, while his brother-in-law (Takenosuke) took charge of the actual business. Yagi, the only survivor of the Senba Eight, had a similar arrangement. Sugi Michisuke, who married a daughter of the Yagi family, became a leading figure in the Osaka business world and established important political connections, but rarely touched the actual management of the company. In the case of Mizukami and Niizeki of Daiichi Bussan and later Mitsui Bussan, Niizeki played a role similar to that of Sugi Michisuke and the second Chubei, being more involved in external affairs. It was Mizukami who made decisions concerning trading matters. Sometimes who was in charge of what became confused and the two clashed. On the whole, however, the growth of Daiichi Bussan (and later Mitsui Bussan) was made possible by the complementary team-work of these leading figures.[35]

What these cases indicate is that since the job of top executive is a demanding one, if it can be shared by two persons who complement each other, the job can be performed much better than by a single individual. A single person often cannot perform effectively both inside the company and in external affairs. If he does not realize this, his over-confidence is likely to cause his company to decline. The failure of Gosho, for example, may be attributed to the fact that although

Komamura Sukemasa, its first president in the post-war period, was successful in establishing liaisons outside the firm, he performed poorly internally.[36] On the other hand, the presidents of many Osaka-based trading companies were skilful at managing their trading businesses, but because they did not make serious attempts to establish contacts with the government or did not participate much in business meetings or on government committees which dealt with matters beyond their immediate interests, they were unable to forecast accurately the direction in which the economy was moving and the possible effects on their businesses.

Despite the importance of top management, there are no set rules for determining what qualifies people for top management posts. Fukui Keizo, president of Nichimen in the mid-1960s, considered *kenshiki* to be the qualification necessary to be a top manager. *Kenshiki* is one of those Japanese words difficult to translate into English. Literally, it means 'sound thinking'. Perhaps 'wisdom' is an appropriate translation, if wisdom is considered to include the qualities of insight and perception as well. Fukui explains the importance of *kenshiki* as follows.

In the teachings of Saigo Takamori, which Matsushita Konosuke often quotes, there are these words.

'Let us give stipends to people who render meritorious service to the country. We should not give them positions because they do good deeds. To be granted a position, a person must naturally possess the *kenshiki* appropriate to being granted a position. Bestowing position on a person who lacks *kenshiki* just because he has rendered meritorious service will be the source of the nation's downfall.'

This quotation deals with the world, i.e., the nation, but I think it is a wise saying which applies well even in the case of present day corporate management. In the operation of a company, there are many occasions when before you know it, this kind of mistake occurs. A certain person may make the company a lot of money, or make connections with good clients, or locate good jobs, and thus contribute greatly to business. He might therefore become section chief, or be promoted to director. In this situation, it would be better to reward him with a prize; bestowing position should automatically be separate.

It is also often said that 'a good salesman would not necessarily be a good manager'. It's the same thing: if a person is given a higher position just because he is skillful at his trade, it might prove to be the case that the person is not at all useful in the higher position. In fact, he might bungle everything and be treated coldly even by subordinates. This would be a tragedy for the person in question, and even more tragic for the subordinates. Subordinates will be happy and a company will prosper if people who truly possess the *kenshiki* to be directors are made directors. When many people with this kind of appeal are directors, a company's prospects will be bright—it will prosper.[37]

Fukui is correct in emphasizing *kenshiki* as the basic qualification for top management, and the candidates should be examined as closely as possible as to whether they have this qualification. However, a major problem with this standard is that determining whether or not a person has *kenshiki* is basically a subjective judgement. Hence, more objective standards, such as contribution to profits, tend to be emphasized. If objective standards are the only criteria, however, qualities which are not important at the actual trading level but which become indispensable at the top management level tend to be ignored. Fukui is quite correct in emphasizing a subjective qualification like *kenshiki*. Still, it is not easy to find people who have such a qualification.

8. CONCLUDING REMARKS

The recipe for ensuring the success of a trading company is relatively simple. The first step is to recruit competent people, the second to give them the necessary training, and the third to organize them properly. As long as the people and the organizational set-up are well chosen, a trading company prospers. It is never certain, however, who constitutes the best person for a particular job, or what constitutes the perfect organizational scheme. Accordingly, there have been various paths taken by successful trading companies (i.e., sogo shosha).

The problem of people and organization has not been settled yet; what companies are doing these days to deal with it will be different from what will be done in the future. For example, it is not yet determined on what principle (area or product) or on what combination of the two an organization should be built. At present, the pendulum of the organizing principle is swinging toward area. How much power should be delegated to product division and branch managers is not certain either, because the advantage of a sogo shosha sometimes depends on a certain degree of centralization of power to enable it to build a system out of its diverse activities. Furthermore, as discussed in the earlier section, although it is recognized that people in top management must have a qualification like *kenshiki* which transcends actual trading, identifying such people is not easy. It is largely a matter of trial and error.

Conclusions which may be drawn with some certainty from the examination above are: firstly, that if a family enterprise wishes to keep growing, it must rely more and more on a meritocracy system for filling its top management posts, and beyond a certain point, the owner family must stop interfering in management; and, secondly, that as a trading company grows, the top management must become a team, so that at a certain stage, power must be decentralized. (As we saw in the case of Suzuki, the company failed because Kaneko continued autocratic rule even after the company grew in size.)

The trading companies which became successful regarded their employees as a partner in the business (not as the objects of exploitation), and instituted proper incentive systems. Even in family enterprises, where workers may have been treated somewhat unfairly, bonuses were paid in profitable years. For example, Itoh Chubei gave one-third of the company's profits to his employees in the early years. Although companies could not completely open high positions to non-family members, they were liberal in providing monetary incentives and in allowing employees to share in the fruits of their activities. Without such incentives, trading companies would not have prospered.

1. Itohchu Shoji, *Itoh Chubei-o Kaiso-roku*, 1974, p. 155.

2. Echigo Masakazu, 'Watashi no Rirekisho', *Nihon Keizai Shinbun*, 19 September 1975.

3. Sato Kiichiro, 'Watashi no Rirekisho' in *Watashi no Rirekisho, No. 26*, Nihon Keizai Shinbun-sha, 1966, p. 39.

4. *Tokyo Newsletter*, May 1975, p. 4.

5. Mitsubishi Shoji, 'Who We Are, What We Do, Where We Are Going', n.d., p. 25.

6. Nagai Minoru, *Jijo Masuda Takashi-o Den*, 1939, p. 487.

7. Hoshino Yasunosuke, *Mitsui Hyakunen*, Kajima Kenkyusho Shuppan-kai, 1968, pp. 134–5.

8. Mitsui Bussan's training in China is discussed in Togai Yoshio, *Mitsui Bussan Kaisha no Keiei-shi teki Kenkyu*, Toyo Keizai Shinposha, 1974, pp. 54–6; Mitsui Bussan, *Mitsui Bussan Shoshi*, 1951, pp. 54–66; Nagai, pp. 329–31; and Hoshino, pp. 134–5.

9. Chucho-kai Nakamigawa Sensei Denki Hensan Iin, *Nakamigawa Sensei Den*, 1939, p. 206. Hereafter referred to as *Nakamigawa Sensei*.

10. Marubeni, *Marubeni Zenshi*, 1977, p. 18.

11. Itohchu Shoji, *Itohchu Shoji Hyakunen*, 1969, p. 12.

12. Ataka Sangyo, *Ataka Sangyo Rokuju-nen Shi*, 1968, p. 104; and Kanematsu, *Kanematsu Rokuju-nen no Ayumi*, 1960, p. 41.

13. Nippon Menka, *Kita Matazo-kun Den*, 1933, p. 59.

14. Mitsui Bussan, *The 100 Year History of Mitsui & Co., Ltd., 1876–1976*, 1977, p. 185.

15. Itoh Teizo (ed.), *Tazuke Masajiro Den*, 1935, pp. 239–40.

16. Ibid., p. 262.

17. Ibid., p. 133.

18. Marubeni, pp. 21–2.

19. Ibid., p. 39.

20. *MBK Life*, December 1964, p. 72.

21. This information was provided by Tajika Tokuzo of the archives section of Marubeni and Ina Hajime, a former director of Iwata Shoji.

22. An appendix to a handwritten manuscript of the post-1960 history of Toyo Menka (the first forty-year history was published in 1960) available at the public relations department of the company lists the causes and years of disciplinary actions in the period 1952–76.

23. Yamamoto Jotaro-o Denki Hensan-kai, *Yamamoto Jotaro-o Denki*, 1942, pp. 61 and 138 (hereafter referred to as *Yamamoto Jotaro*); and *Nakamigawa Sensei*, pp. 316 and 322.

24. Nissho, *Nissho Shiju-nen no Ayumi*, 1968, pp. 28–9.

25. Ibid., p. 74.

26. Ibid., pp. 75–6.

27. Morikawa Hidemasa, 'Meiji-ki Mitsui Bussan no Keiei Soshiki',

Keiei Shirin, April 1972; and 'Taisho-ki Mitsui Bussan no Keiei Soshiki', *Keiei Shirin*, April 1973.

28. Takahashi Toshitaro, *Mitsui Bussan no Omoide*, Kyobunkan, 1934, p. 9; Wada Hidekichi, *Mitsui Kontserun Tokuhon*, Shunju-sha, 1937, p. 240; Morikawa (1973), p. 20; and Ajia Shobo, *Mitsui Tokuhon*, Ajia Shobo, 1943, p. 255.

29. *Yamamoto Jotaro*, p. 287; and Mitsui Bussan (1951), pp. 189–92.

30. *Senba Konjaku Monogatari*, 1967, p. 75.

31. Itohchu Shoji (1974), pp. 123–5; and Itohchu Shoji (1969), pp. 142–63.

32. *Daiyamondo*, Shinshun Tokubetsu-go, 1966, p. 56.

33. Iwai Sangyo, *Iwai Hyakunen Shi*, 1964, p. 97.

34. Ibid., p. 191.

35. Mitsui Bussan (1977), p. 156.

36. This point was made in an interview by Kanbara Takeo, the last president of Gosho. The interview took place in April 1980.

37. Fukui Keizo, 'Juyaku', *Gekkan Nichimen*, January 1967.

8

Public Criticism

1. SPECULATION AND PROFITEERING

IN the 1970s, sogo shosha came under severe attack in Japan. The first sign of this appeared in 1972 when it was revealed that some sogo shosha were involved in buying up glutinous rice. Then in early 1973, sogo shosha were accused by leftist politicians and the mass media for causing price increase and other economic evils. In April, the heads of the top six sogo shosha were summoned to the Diet and grilled for several hours about many of their activities. Then in January 1974, the Fair Trade Commission (FTC) issued an unfavourable report on sogo shosha, which fuelled the mass media to launch another attack.[1] Under public pressure, even top government officials began to talk about the need to curb the activities of sogo shosha.

The one and a-half year period from early 1973 was an ordeal for sogo shosha. They were reviled as 'traitors', 'wicked traders', 'parasites', 'Shylocks of Tokyo', and 'Dracula sucking the blood of the public'. They were attacked by consumer groups which levelled emotional charges. Senior citizens staged sit-ins in front of their headquarters. They also faced criticism from the right. One right-wing newspaper warned them that it might become necessary to take 'direct action' against them for the sake of social justice.[2]

For one thing, they were accused of speculation on land and stock. According to the data they submitted to the Diet,[3] the top six sogo shosha increased their land holdings from 27 million to 42 million square metres (in terms of value, from 73 to 129 billion yen) in the 1971 and 1972 financial years. As a result, their holdings came to exceed those of real estate companies whose main business is in land transactions. Sogo shosha's stockholdings also increased sharply in the same period, and their profits from stock transactions became comparable to those of security brokers. One sogo shosha, Marubeni, made substantial profits in stock transactions, and came to be called 'Marubeni Securities, Inc.'[4]

For another thing, sogo shosha were accused of speculating on commodities (wool, yarn, soybeans, wood, etc.). In particular, the price of wood (which affected the cost of housing construction) increased sharply in 1972 and 1973, and sogo shosha were held responsible. Their critics considered the large profits made in this period to be strong evidence in support of their case. In the first half of the 1971 financial year, sogo shosha recorded some losses, but reaped large profits in the following three periods: their profits were 1,578 million yen in the second half of 1971; 2,243 million yen in the first half of 1972; and 5,935 million yen in the second half of 1972. Such great profits provoked the antipathy of a public suffering from a housing shortage.

Probably, sogo shosha did undertake speculation on stocks, land and commodities in this period, and made large profits from it. The report of the Fair Trade Commission issued in early 1974 could not find strong evidence concerning commodity speculation, but found sogo shosha guilty of stock and land speculation. The report of the Ministry of International Trade and Industry issued in early 1973 said that there was a strong possibility that sogo shosha had speculated on wool and a few other commodities, a large part of the imports of which they handled.[5]

Sogo shosha denied these charges. Regarding the charge of land speculation, they replied that land was needed for constructing houses, buildings, warehouses, and industrial estates (it should be remembered that all sogo shosha have a construction division). In reply to the charge of stock speculation, they noted that stockholdings were necessary to strengthen ties with the member companies of the groups to which they belonged, as well as to form their own groups of companies. For example, Marubeni, charged with massive speculation in the stock-market, argued that since the Fuyo group was a loose group, it was necessary for the company to increase the holdings of the member companies and strengthen group solidarity.[6] As for the charge that sogo shosha undertook commodity speculation, causing price increases on daily necessities, they replied that there was no sharp increase in their inventories and that profits were made because prices increased between the time when commodities were bought abroad and the time when they were sold in Japan.

Speculation is not illegal, it is part of trading activity in various commodities. However, sogo shosha did not want to admit to speculating for the following two reasons. One was the market power they possessed. In the five-year period from 1968, the ten sogo shosha accounted for about a quarter of the sales of all incorporated wholesalers, about half of the country's exports, and about two-thirds of the imports.[7] When such large companies undertake speculation, the influence is bound to be felt on prices. In the long run, what is bought has to be sold, so speculation does not have long-run effects, but it can cause price instability. This is especially the case at times when it is generally believed that prices are moving rapidly in one direction (up when inflation is occurring).

In fairness to sogo shosha, it should be pointed out that the charge that they colluded for price increases does not seem to be accurate. On the basis of past price trends and future projections, sogo shosha may find themselves following identical courses in buying and selling, but in view of the competitive environment, it is unlikely that they consulted each other, jacked up prices, and made off with handsome profits. Sogo shosha usually compete with each other fiercely; even if a collusion existed, outsiders would try to undersell them, so it would be difficult to maintain their position. In the pre-war period, yarn dealers, for example, tried to form a coalition to counter the power of the spinners who had formed a cartel and regulated production, but the attempt failed because some dealers did not want to join and the agreements could not be enforced. Similar difficulties would have arisen if sogo shosha had attempted collusion.

Another reason why sogo shosha did not want to admit to speculation was that speculating is considered an 'evil', an activity a respectable person or company should not undertake. This can be seen from the fact that speculation in goods is always made distinct from trading, and speculating in land and stocks distinguished from investment. Hence, if a certain degree of speculation is necessary, trading companies regard it as an integral part of trading, and try to draw the attention of the public away from their speculative activities. If this is not done, they lose not only respectability but also public trust (and thus, endanger their chances of raising additional capital).

Speculating in stocks is usually considered to be an activity any respectable trading company should avoid if at all possible. Some sogo shosha which undertook speculation in commodities shied away from speculation in the stock-market, and criticized those which did not. For example, the head of the finance department of Mitsui Bussan said that even if the company had excess liquidity, it would not speculate in the stock-market; the most it would do would be to buy fixed interest bonds or deposit money with trust banks. He rebuked other companies which acted like stockbrokers and brought shame to all sogo shosha.[8] A former high official of the Ministry of International Trade and Industry compared stock speculation to drug addiction, and warned sogo shosha not to get involved in it because it was 'habit forming'.

Even if sogo shosha did speculate, why did they alone become the target of criticism? Many other companies, including manufacturers, bought stocks and land, increased inventory, and made large profits in the early 1970s. Sogo shosha may have gained more from price increases than other companies, but it was not merely a matter of degree that distinguished them. Beneath the public criticism of sogo shosha lay a normally dormant distrust of trading companies.

The exact origin of such distrust is difficult to determine; it probably dates back to many centuries ago. Already in the Tokugawa period, trading was not considered a very honourable occupation, as seen from the fact that merchants formed the bottom of the social strata. Confucian scholars, such as Ogyu Sorai, wrote disparaging things about merchants and trading, in order to justify the social system of the period. In the modern period, the social value system changed and economic activities became more respectable, but commercial activities did not fare as well as industrial activities. The premodern view which looked down upon trading has remained strong (even in the business world).

Such distrust surfaced in the early 1970s when inflation caused anxiety among the public, while sogo shosha earned large profits. Mass media, always on the look-out for sensational news, and politicians of minority parties, always distrustful of big business, made the most of this opportunity. The government should have taken measures to defuse this emotionally charged atmosphere, but since it did not want to take full responsibility for the on-going inflation, it offered sogo shosha as a sacrificial lamb.

2. THE FAIR TRADE COMMISSION ATTACKS

When public criticism was rising in early 1973, the Fair Trade Commission became concerned with the activities of sogo shosha and began investigating. The results were published in January 1974. Then, to probe the matters more deeply, the FTC continued its investigation in 1974, and published a second report in early 1975.[9] In these two reports, the FTC argued that the government should take measures to curb the activities of sogo shosha if a competitive economic environment were to be preserved.

One area of the FTC's concern was control by sogo shosha of numerous companies. Japan's Anti-Monopoly Law prohibits

holding companies; thus, if sogo shosha are acting like holding companies, they should be ordered to dispose of their
holdings. This does not mean, however, that companies are
not allowed to own shares of other companies. Except for financial institutions, all companies are allowed to set up subsidiaries and to own controlling shares of other companies as
long as such investments are necessary as vertical extensions
of their activities. On the other hand, horizontal investments
which restrict competition are prohibited. For example, a
manufacturer can own sales subsidiaries but is not allowed to
own another company in the same industry, without the permission of the FTC.

The size of the holdings of sogo shosha is large (relative to
their equity capital) and their investments spread over many industries. At the close of the 1972 financial year, the top six
sogo shosha held stocks in 1,848 listed and 3,542 unlisted companies.[10] Out of a total of 5,390, they held majority shares in
506 companies and had controlling shares in another 551 companies. The total capital of these companies amounted to 440
billion yen, three times more than that of the six sogo shosha.

Sogo shosha's investments range throughout various fields.
They have subsidiaries and affiliates in manufacturing (foods,
chemicals, steel, metal processing, machinery, textiles, etc.),
warehousing, trading, shipping, real estate, etc. The FTC's
concern was whether these numerous investments were actually a necessary part of trading activities, or whether sogo shosha had in effect become holding companies.

The second area of the FTC's concern was the financial
role of sogo shosha. As discussed in Chapter 5, a large amount
of funds are channelled from banks to sogo shosha, and the
latter use them to undertake investment and give credits to
small and medium-sized companies. Such activities raise two
questions. First: should sogo shosha, essentially trading companies, be allowed to act as financial intermediaries? If the financial system is not functioning properly to channel funds
from banks to small and medium-sized companies, it may be
better to rectify the situation and let banks handle all fi-

nancial intermediation. A second question is whether sogo shosha function as subsidiaries of banks (or if they act as banks tell them to do) and undertake activities banks are not allowed to engage in (such as owning large stockholdings). If so, the activities of sogo shosha should be controlled in the manner that banks are controlled.

The FTC feels that the financial power which enabled sogo shosha to undertake various investments and extend large credits is endangering the competitive environment. One problem has been the elimination of the competition which existed between sogo shosha and certain customers which they brought under their control. For example, among the 2,559 affiliates of the ten sogo shosha, 2,057 of them had some trading relations with their parent sogo shosha in the 1973 financial year. About half of them depended on their parent companies for both the marketing of their products and the purchasing of raw materials, while the other half were dependent for either marketing or purchasing.[11] On the basis of this information, it may be argued that competition was reduced to the extent that affiliates were not free to choose marketing and purchasing agents.

The FTC reports a number of unfair business practices which arose because of the financial power of sogo shosha. The following are several examples.[12]

1. Company A borrowed money from a sogo shosha on mutually agreeable conditions. Later, the sogo shosha demanded to become the purchasing agent for A's raw materials. Because of its indebtedness, A accepted the demand. The raw materials came directly from a company A had previously been dealing with, but A now had to pay a commission to the sogo shosha. The commission is called *nemuri kosen* (sleeper's fees).

2. Company B received loans and investment from a sogo shosha. By using its power as a major stockholder and financier, the sogo shosha forced B to appoint it as the sole agent of its products. Before this, B had been marketing its products on its own.

3. A sogo shosha bought a majority share of Company *C*, and brought it under its control. Sometime after this, this sogo shosha found itself with an excess inventory of a good which *C* had been using as one of its raw materials. The sogo shosha dumped the product on *C*, causing *C* to incur substantial losses, and when *C* got into financial troubles, secretly sold its holdings, and took the factory and land as compensations for its loans.

4. Company *D*, an affiliate of a sogo shosha, was almost certain that the price of a certain raw material would go up, and wanted to buy it from the sogo shosha, but the sogo shosha refused. *D* was forced to buy the product after the price went up.

5. Company *E* received both encouragement and financial assistance for plant expansion from a sogo shosha. Later, the market for its product turned out not to be as lucrative as initially expected. Even after this, the sogo shosha continued its support. Then suddenly, it decided to terminate relations with *E*, forcing *E* to sell its properties to pay the money it owed to the sogo shosha.

The third area of the FTC's concern was the increasing influence of enterprise groups and the role of sogo shosha in these groups. The FTC's second report shows some alarming results. At the end of the 1973 financial year, the member companies of the six groups accounted for 22 per cent of capital and 23 per cent of assets in the corporate sector of Japan. If their affiliated companies are included, the percentage of capital and assets goes up further. If affiliated companies in which member companies own more than 50 per cent are included, the percentage of capital goes up to 26 per cent and that of assets to 25 per cent. If the percentage of shares owned in affiliated companies is lowered to 25 per cent, the figure for capital goes up to 33 per cent and that for assets to 28 per cent. If the percentage of shares owned is lowered further to 10 per cent, the corresponding figure for capital becomes 41 per cent, and that for assets 31 per cent.[13]

Compare this situation with that at the time when zaibatsu

were dominant in the Japanese economy. At the end of the Pacific War, the four largest zaibatsu—Mitsui, Mitsubishi, Sumitomo, and Yasuda—controlled 544 companies directly or indirectly, and these companies accounted for 24.5 per cent of the capital in all industries. The FTC report reveals that the recent situation has apparently become more alarming than that in pre-war Japan.

Of course, there are differences between enterprise groups and the pre-war zaibatsu. One obvious difference is the absence of an overall organization in the enterprise group. In the pre-war period, the holding company was such an organization. In the post-war period there have been no such organizations, though there were ways to make up for this. Meetings of presidents' clubs, mutual stockholdings, the interlocking of directorates, the undertaking of common projects, etc., have all contributed to the solidarity of the various enterprise groups.

In particular, banks and sogo shosha play an important role in promoting group solidarity. Banks provide loans, and main banks take moral responsibility for the loans other banks extend to member companies. The sogo shosha undertake various activities to solidify their groups, some of which banks are not allowed to engage in (such as increasing holdings beyond 10 per cent). Functioning as links with foreign countries, sogo shosha export the products of member companies, import the raw materials they need, gather information on technology, and perform many other activities required by their member companies. Furthermore, they act as organizers for member companies in projects which are beyond the capacity of a single company to undertake.

The FTC has been criticized for putting all six groups in the same basket. Clearly, there are differences in group cohesiveness between the former zaibatsu groups (Mitsubishi, Mitsui and Sumitomo) and the other post-war groups. For example, the Fuyo group is the most cohesive among the latter three, but compared with the former zaibatsu groups, it is loose. One indication of this is Hitachi's relative independence in the group. Hitachi is, above all, a 'group' in itself, comprising Hitachi, Hitachi Metals, Nippon Mining, Nissan Motors, Nissan Chemicals, etc. Secondly, it has maintained close relations with the Industrial Bank of Japan and the Sanwa Bank as well as the Fuji Bank. Also, Marubeni, the sogo shosha of the Fuyo group, maintains active relations with competitors of the Fuyo members. For example, Marubeni works closely with Minolta (camera producer), a competitor of a Fuyo member, Canon. It also does business with Koyo Seiko (producer of ball-bearings), a competitor of a Fuyo member, Nippon Seiko, and with Nippon Electric (a member of the Sumitomo group), a competitor of a Fuyo member, Oki Electric.[14]

The FTC is fully aware of the differences in cohesiveness among the enterprise groups, but is concerned with the possibility that the loose groups may strengthen mutual ties in order to counter the former zaibatsu groups, and that this may set off inter-group rivalries. If such a situation occurs, the competitive environment of the economy would be seriously impaired, for it would become extremely difficult for non-member companies to break into the groups. At present, data on intra-group transactions do not show strong ties even within the former zaibatsu groups. However, this is primarily a result of the fact that a number of commodities needed by member companies are not produced in the groups. If these commodities are excluded, intra-group transactions become very important,[15] thus, to the extent that intra-group transactions will increase, the level of competition be reduced.

In order to protect the competitive environment of the economy, the FTC recommended that: (a) the stockholdings of sogo shosha should be limited; and (b) the flow of funds from banks to sogo shosha should be restricted. As to stockholdings, the FTC revised the Anti-Monopoly Law (effective December 1977) to the effect that the holdings of a company whose net assets exceed 30 billion yen or whose capital exceeds 10 billion yen shall be limited to the larger of its net assets and capital. Since as of March 1977, the holdings of the top eight sogo shosha exceeded their net assets by 40 per cent, it might be presumed that this revision would have a significant effect on the role of sogo shosha. Actually, however, since part of their holdings is financial investment, to dispose of these would not have much effect on their role in enterprise groups or their own groups of affiliated companies. Furthermore, since a transition period of ten years is allowed, if it appears that disposing of present holdings is likely to affect their operations, sogo shosha can increase capital and net assets within that period.

Restriction on bank loans was not within the jurisdiction of the FTC. This was a matter to be decided by the Ministry of Finance. Under political pressure demanding that banks make their funds more easily available to small and medium-sized companies, the Ministry decided to put a ceiling on bank loans to individual companies. In December 1974, the Ministry issued a circular notice to all financial institutions to the effect that within five years, banks must bring loans to individual companies to within 20 per cent of their equity capital; long-term credit banks and trust banks, to within 30 per cent; and foreign exchange banks, to within 40 per cent.

It is believed that this restriction will have wide repercussions on sogo shosha, banks and enterprise groups. First of all, since banks now cannot provide capital to companies as freely as they used to, the leadership role they have played in enterprise groups will be weakened. Secondly, member companies, such as sogo shosha, which have depended on member banks for large amounts of funds, must find new sources. In doing so, they may have to develop close relations with other city and local banks.

Although the FTC feels that the strengthening of enterprise groups will reduce competition and, therefore, impair economic efficiency, this view is not well accepted. Supporters of enterprise groups would argue that the existence of strong groups might reduce internal competition but would intensify competition between groups or independent companies; thus, it would raise rather than lower the level of competition. Furthermore, the need exists for information exchange, the undertaking of joint projects which are too large for a single company, and the creation of a business system by coordinating various companies. These needs can be met better if enterprise groups exist.

Some supporters of enterprise groups go so far as to say that holding companies should be legalized. If enterprise groups are indispensable for the above reasons, they can be coordinated better by holding companies. The problem with the holding companies of the pre-war period was that they were family-dominated companies. If holding companies were public companies, without ties to any particular families, they might be justified even on equity grounds.

The FTC is correct in warning that if enterprise groups become too powerful, it will become extremely difficult for small companies to grow independently, and the basis for economic democracy will be seriously eroded. For this reason, there was considerable support for restrictions on large bank loans and stockholdings. On the other hand, because there are merits in forming enterprise groups, these restrictions should not be pushed to the extreme.

3. POLITICAL INVOLVEMENT

The government is able to influence the outcome of the activities of sogo shosha in many ways. First of all, it has the authority to approve or not approve certain projects. For example, in the 1950s and early 1960s when the government controlled imports because of the tendency of the balance of payments to record deficits, the government evaluated import applications case by case, and allocated foreign exchanges only to those approved. Also, when exports or imports involved politically sensitive countries, sogo shosha had to seek approval in advance, and the government exercised discretionary power in decision-making.

The government is also a large purchaser of goods and services. If public corporations, such as the Japan National Railway, are included, government expenditures amount to 15 to

20 per cent of the gross national product. A large portion of government expenditures is on goods and services sogo shosha do not handle, but such expenditures as military procurements have been an attractive source of profits for them. In the pre-war period, the Army bought many weapons from trading companies, and the Navy bought ships, while in the post-war period, the Defense Agency has bought aircrafts and spare parts through sogo shosha which represented Western manufacturers and competed with each other for government contracts.

Furthermore, the government is an important source of funds. In the post-war period, the Export and Import Bank of Japan and the Overseas Economic Cooperation Fund have given numerous low interest loans to trading companies to finance projects abroad or plant exports. Many of these projects would have been unprofitable without such loans. The Bank of Japan has also intervened in the capital market occasionally, and has given relief loans to certain trading companies, usually indirectly through city banks. It is also possible for the government to rescue a project by taking over part of the equity share and converting it to a 'national' project, as was done recently for Mitsui Bussan's petrochemical project in Iran.

The government has the power of taxation, and in certain cases, can use it at its own discretion. Sogo shosha are engaged in many transactions involving foreign exchanges, and particularly in the past several years, while the exchange has been fluctuating, the problem has sometimes arisen as to which exchange rate should be used in calculating profits (which is the base rate of corporate income tax). There is also the question of to what extent expenses must be documented. This becomes important at times, since sogo shosha pay commissions to people in foreign countries who cannot issue receipts. If such payments cannot be deducted as costs, profits increase to that extent on paper, and more taxes have to be paid.

Reparations and economic aid decided upon by the government have been an attractive source of profits for sogo shosha.

In many cases, projects had already been determined when sogo shosha became involved, and their main task was to offer the best deal to the Japanese government and the governments of the recipient countries. What constituted the best deal was often vague, so there was a considerable degree of manoeuvring possible by sogo shosha. In cases where projects had not been decided, sogo shosha proposed attractive ones to developing countries and negotiated with the Japanese government.

The government has information which has considerable value to sogo shosha. For example, if a change in the value of foreign exchange can be predicted in advance, a considerable amount of money can be made. The Japanese government has made decisions regarding exchange rates a number of times, and also received information through diplomatic channels which had bearings on foreign exchange rates. Sometimes also the government may plan public works projects which will affect the value of land in the surrounding area. If this type of information is transmitted to sogo shosha by high government officials, the companies can take appropriate actions in advance and make huge profits.

In the pre-war period, Mitsui Bussan and Mitsubishi Shoji had close ties with the government and made it part of the 'business environment'. For this reason, they were called *seisho* (privileged merchants). Osaka-based companies, on the other hand, stayed away from the government for the most part. Many of them even thought that it was shameful to involve the government in business. In the post-war period, however, this attitude has changed greatly.

From the late 1930s, government regulations became pervasive, at first because the government was forced to impose regulations as a wartime measure. Then after the Pacific War, the GHQ set up a government-controlled distribution system to prevent the economy from collapsing. Many of these regulations remained for a considerable period after Japan's independence in 1952. Added to this was the shift of the economy to heavy industry, in the development of which the government played an active role as financier and project evaluator.

For Osaka-based trading companies, establishing liaison with the government became an important matter in the postwar period. Some were more aggressive than others in pursuing this goal. For example, Ichikawa Shinobu was convinced that Marubeni had to become a *seisho* if it wanted to be a sogo shosha; he approached politicians with great enthusiasm.[16] The first important link was established with Kono Ichiro, and Marubeni used him to win a contract from the Defense Agency for Lockheed's fighter planes, for which Marubeni had been the exclusive agent. Next, Marubeni approached Tanaka Kakuei. It is not entirely clear when relations between the two became close, but it seems that by the mid-1960s, the relationship was cemented. In 1964, Ichikawa took charge of Fujikoshi, a manufacturer of ball-bearings and machinery based in Niigata (Tanaka's constituency) at the request of Tanaka, then Minister of Finance.[17] (The company was in financial trouble.) Tanaka's first favour to Marubeni to become public knowledge was the preference he gave to the Marubeni group in Japan's joint project with the Soviet Union for developing natural gas in Sakhalin.[18] Later, after the disclosure of the Lockheed scandal, it became known that Marubeni had been able to sell Lockheed aircraft to All Nippon Airways thanks to Tanaka's intervention on its behalf.

Itoh Chubei's political connections were important for C.Itoh. One of Chubei's close political associates was Kishi Nobusuke, one-time Prime Minister. Chubei first came to know Kishi in the pre-war period when he was still a division head in the Ministry of Commerce and Industry and their relationship continued until Chubei's death in the early 1970s. Chubei's friendship must have been appreciated greatly by Kishi when he came out of Sugamo Prison (Kishi was a class A war criminal). Later, he recalled that at that time Chubei had entertained him, his brother Sato Eisaku (who also became Prime Minister), and one other brother in a Japanese restaurant.[19] Also, Chubei and Kishi had once been together

on the board of directors of a pulp making company. Furthermore, they met each other frequently at Atami, where their
villas were next to each other.

Chubei's relations with Ichikawa of Marubeni were warm
on the surface, but not close, for Ichikawa resented Chubei's
treatment of him in the early 1940s when Marubeni and
C.Itoh were merged as a wartime measure. So, probably,
Marubeni did not make much use of Chubei's connections.
Chubei was closer to C.Itoh, particularly so after Echigo became president in 1960 (it will be remembered that Echigo
came from Omi province and went to college with Chubei's
financial support). Echigo's predecessor, Kosuga, also came
from Omi province and owed a 'debt' to Chubei, so relations
between the two were fairly close.[20]

In the early 1950s, C.Itoh was very anxious to establish
close ties with the government and become a full-fledged sogo
shosha. One of C.Itoh's directors at that time wrote on the
importance of Tokyo (i.e., Japan's political and business centre) as follows.

When Itoh Chubei was still a young businessman of a little over 30, he
enjoyed the favor of Inoue Junnosuke, president of the Bank of Japan.
This made it possible for C.Itoh to become the first recipient of the
Bank's relief loans and tide over the crash following the First World War.
I came to know this fact recently from a man in the Bank. After hearing it, I changed my belief that self-reliance was the honor of Osaka
merchants. For large trading companies, especially at a time when prices
are rising rapidly, good management is impossible without friends in the
central government and the business world. Chubei made a great contribution to the company [in the pre-war period] by transforming it from
a wholesaler in Osaka to a company known nationwide. Unless we are
satisfied with the fact that ours is a sound, profitable company representative of the Kansai economy, and if we want to establish a reputation
that we will occupy the place of Mitsui and Mitsubishi and play a leadership role in the foreign trade necessary for the reconstruction of the
Japanese economy, we have to make greater efforts than Chubei did,
toward expanding our interests in Tokyo.[21]

Besides Chubei, there was another person in C.Itoh who had
important political connections: Sejima Ryuzo. Many of his
friends and acquaintances from the Pacific War period, when

he was a general staff member of the Army, came to occupy important positions in the Defense Agency and other government offices in the post-war period. C.Itoh lost two major defense contracts (the first to Marubeni and the second to Nissho-Iwai), but maintained close relations with the Defense Agency as supplier of parts and equipment. What role Sejima exactly played in establishing C.Itoh's ties with the Agency is not known, but his role is generally believed to have been important.[22]

Nissho (and later Nissho-Iwai) was also aggressive in establishing contacts with the government. In the early post-war period, it had better connections than Marubeni or C.Itoh. In the first place, Nagai Kotaro, who had run the company together with Takahata Seiichi, became director of the Foreign Trade Agency in early 1947. Also, Oya Shinzo of Teijin, who had been Nagai and Takahata's junior at Suzuki, became Minister of Commerce and Industry. Later, Nissho hired a high official of the Ministry and made him executive vice-president in charge of its Tokyo office.

Takahata was probably more responsible than anyone else for plunging Nissho into politics. He was Kaneko's favourite during his time at Suzuki, and in the period of approximately one year after his return from London until Suzuki's failure, came to know intimately how Kaneko used his political connections. Probably, Takahata himself was not greatly involved in corrupt politics, but he promoted Kaifu Hachiro (who recently became infamous for his involvement in a scandal) and supported his questionable tactics.

Nissho became the exclusive agent of Boeing in 1956, but since it could not sell these aeroplanes and was about to lose agency rights, Nissho recalled Kaifu in the early 1960s from its New York office, where he had been doing extremely well in selling ships. In Japan, he did well also in selling aircraft. Boeing's aeroplanes were sold first to All Nippon Airways and then to Japan Air Lines. Using this success as a leverage in bargaining, Nissho obtained the exclusive agency right for McDonnell's military airplanes in 1964. Several years later,

Nissho won a major defense contract for McDonnell.[23]

Kaifu's success depended greatly on his approach to politicians, such as Matsuno Raizo, who as Minister of Defense was an important influence on the decision of the Defense Agency in favour of McDonnell in 1968. One of Kaifu's subordinates recalls his business tactics as follows.

When he returned from the United States, Mr. Kaifu held the view that unless he approached politicians, he could not get work done. Since it was the heyday of the Ikeda Cabinet, Kaifu approached Ikeda's secretaries, and became intimate with one of them, Tanaka Rokusuke. I accompanied Kaifu when he went to see Tanaka, and we sometimes went for drinks together. Through Tanaka, I believe, Kaifu was able to approach [Kishi's office]. Matsuno Raizo is in a line directly descending from Kishi, and relations between the two are not ordinary.[24]

Perhaps because of its strong government connections, Nissho-Iwai has also done well in Indonesia. One notable achievement was the import of liquefied natural gas (LNG). Other sogo shosha tried hard to obtain the right to import LNG, but lost to Nissho-Iwai. Where Nissho-Iwai's strength lay is a matter for speculation. Kaifu's connections with Kishi Nobusuke were probably helpful on the Japanese side (this factor is important because the LNG project required funding from the Japanese government). On the Indonesian side, Nissho-Iwai may have been more willing to accept certain questionable demands made by the head of the national oil company (PERTAMINA), Sutowo, reputedly a very corrupt official. Some questions have been raised regarding PERTAMINA's decision to charter LNG ships for the project.

Other Osaka-based companies seem to have been reluctant to resort to questionable business tactics, and to that extent their political involvements were limited. For example, in the mid-1960s, the president of Nichimen rejected a land deal involving Osano Kenji, a close associate of Tanaka Kakuei (both have recently been tried regarding the Lockheed scandal). The land deal was proposed by one of Nichimen's directors who had been a former high official of the Bank of Japan, sent in by the Sanwa Bank. (He had done a favour to the Sanwa Bank when the bank had applied for status as an authorized foreign exchange dealer.) This director favoured Nichimen's greater involvement in politics, and proposed the land deal as the first test case. The deal was rejected because the president did not want his company to go too far in that direction.[25]

Sumitomo Shoji has also managed to remain free of corruption. For whatever reason, the name of Sumitomo has not yet appeared in the history of business corruption in Japan. This tradition seems to have induced Sumitomo Shoji to adopt lofty business principles and to avoid questionable deals. Apparently, it is partly for this reason that Sumitomo Shoji has concentrated its trading in developed countries and kept a low profile in developing countries where bribery seems inevitable.

In many developing countries, bribery is often regarded as 'goodwill payments or gestures'. Consequently, this practice is sometimes part and parcel of business transactions—a practice which Japanese trading companies have not dared to challenge. Niizeki Yasutaro, one-time chairman of Mitsui Bussan, admits that the company tacitly approved bribes in South-East Asia (Thailand and Indonesia) because the salary of officials was so low that it was difficult to decline their demand for a share in the profits.[26] Also, a certain chairman of an unidentified sogo shosha, when asked whether bribes could be morally justified, replied that 'in developing countries, bribes are a natural thing. . . . It is a custom in business. If Japan alone wants to be clean, Western countries will triumph. If that happens, what would happen to the Japanese economy? You should stop arguing like a student.'[27]

On one occasion around 1966, an influential Korean came to see the president of Sumitomo Shoji to discuss a project the Japanese government was financing. The following dialogue took place between the Korean visitor and Tsuda, the president of the company.

Korean: The reason for my visit today is to discuss with you concerning the integrated steel mill the Korean government is planning at P'ohang. It will be the first integrated steel mill in Korea. I want Sumitomo to construct it. I want you to act as organizer.

Tsuda: It appears to be a very large project. What sort of plan is it? Can you explain it in more detail?

Korean: (explains the plan) ... By the way, in return for letting you undertake this project, I want you to make available for my personal use a little over ten percent of the total cost.

Tsuda: Eh?

Korean: That is, I want you to keep about ten percent of the total cost and donate it to someone in the Korean government.

Tsuda: That is impossible. Many companies will be involved in such a large project. It would be difficult to persuade them to give a large amount of that nature.

Korean: Can you try somehow?

Tsuda: It would be very difficult.[28]

The Korean came back several times, but Sumitomo Shoji declined the offer.

Some of the Osaka-based sogo shosha which approached politicians were not pioneers in this kind of business strategy; they were merely following the path laid down by Mitsui Bussan and Mitsubishi Shoji in the pre-war period. After these two companies made their comeback in the 1950s, they re-established political ties, and despite some gains made by a few Osaka-based companies, they have been in a class of their own as *seisho*. Supported by their own groups and the personal network they had developed since the early Meiji era, Mitsui Bussan and Mitsubishi Shoji have wielded much greater political power than the Osaka-based companies.

Mitsui Bussan's political influence was vividly demonstrated recently when it succeeded in converting a private petrochemical project in Iran to a 'national' project. The project was first planned in the early 1970s, but because of the uncertainty caused by the oil shock, actual construction was postponed until 1976. It was scheduled to be completed in late 1979, and production was to begin in early 1980. But political troubles began in mid-1978, and in early 1979, the construction had to be stopped. At this point, it was about 85 per cent complete.

The petrochemical complex, when completed, will be the largest in the world. Mitsui Bussan and other Mitsui companies have poured a large amount of money into it. Mitsui Bussan, the largest investor on the Japanese side, committed about 100 billion yen (about US$500 million) to this project: therefore, if the project fails, it will jolt the foundation of Mitsui Bussan.

Because the completion of the construction was postponed and because the cost of construction increased in the midst of the project, it became necessary to raise additional capital. The Iran side proposed that the joint venture company, Iran Japan Petrochemical Company, should increase its equity capital from 100 billion yen to 200 billion yen and that the increase be split equally. This made it necessary to raise the capital of an investing company set up in Japan for this project (Iran Chemical Co.). Mitsui Bussan proposed that considering the large investment already made in the past, it would be difficult for Mitsui companies to subscribe for the entire increase, so the Mitsui group should pay 5 billion yen and ask the government to subscribe for the remaining 45 billion yen. If the government could be brought in as a stockholder, the project could become a national project, and it would become easier to obtain more low interest loans from government financial institutions, as well as other government aid.

Mitsui Bussan did not get exactly what it had asked for, but it succeeded in converting the project into a national project in October 1979. How Mitsui Bussan managed to do this is a matter for speculation. The company was able to pull many strings. Firstly, one of its top executives, Yamashita Eimei, had been under-secretary of the Ministry of International Trade and Industry, and was in the position to influence its policy through his former subordinates. Secondly, around the time when the government was making the decision on the project (whether to participate in the project or not), national elections were being held. It is said that the Mitsui group made large donations to the ruling party, the Liberal Democratic Party (LDP). Mitsui Bussan denies this strongly, but it is rather difficult to believe that the LDP made the decision in favour of Mitsui Bussan and other Mitsui companies for altruistic reasons. Also, Mitsui Bussan could muster help from people for whom it or the group had done or might do favours. These people may have been in the government or, if not, in the position to influence those who were.

Mitsui Bussan's political involvements date back to its very beginning. Masuda Takashi, who came from Senshu Kaisha and headed Mitsui Bussan for the first three decades, was a protégé of the politician, Inoue Kaoru (whom the austere Saigo called head clerk [banto] of Mitsui). As mentioned in Chapter 3 Senshu Kaisha was the company Inoue founded, and it was he who brought Masuda to the company. Relations between the two remained close until Inoue died in 1915.

Although Inoue was the most important political patron of Mitsui Bussan, he was not the only one with whom Masuda cultivated close relations. Intimate relations were maintained with other political leaders from Choshu, such as Ito Hirobumi and Yamagata Aritomo, and even with some from Satsuma (who are usually regarded as anti-Mitsui and pro-Mitsubishi), such as Matsukata Masayoshi. Using these political ties, Mitsui Bussan obtained agency rights for the government-operated Miike mines and later bought them at a concessionary price. It supplied arms to the Army and the Navy by becoming an agent for arms producers in the West (Vickers in England, Carnegie in the United States, etc.), and it handled the government-operated Yahata Steel's import of iron ores from the Ta-yeh mines near Hankow (a concession Japan obtained from China by winning the Sino–Japanese War).

After Masuda left Mitsui Bussan to become director of the Mitsui zaibatsu, its political ties became somewhat weaker, but this does not mean that they ceased to be important. Political activities became an important function of the top echelon of the Mitsui zaibatsu, and Mitsui Bussan received the protection and patronage of the government as a privileged company. Mitsui Bussan continued to receive armament orders from the government, an increasing portion of which it supplied from Mitsui's subsidiary, Japan Steel Works, and other producers in Japan after the First World War. To the semi-governmental South Manchurian Railroad (the presidency of which was often held by a representative of Mitsui), Mitsui Bussan supplied the machinery and equipment needed for mining as well as railroad activities, and received from the railroad various privileges to facilitate its purchasing and transport activities in Manchuria.[29] In international finance, Mitsui Bussan obtained assistance from 'national policy' banks, such as the Yokohama Specie Bank, the Bank of Taiwan, the Bank of Chosen (which replaced the Bank of Korea in 1911), and the Industrial Bank of Japan (which was heavily involved in investment in Korea and Manchuria). In these banks, the Mitsui zaibatsu was an important voice as a shareholder and as an organization strongly backed by politicians, especially those who belonged to the Seiyukai Party for which Mitsui was an important financier.

4. THE CORRUPT POLITICAL SYSTEM

Politicians require money for election campaigning, for increasing their influence in their own parties, for giving financial assistance to their supporters in their constituencies and own parties, etc. In the pre-war period, there were politicians who were men of wealth who spent personal funds to cover their necessary expenses, but in the post-war period, such politicians have become few; most have depended upon 'votive offerings' by others. At the same time, because the number of constituents required for winning elections increased as a result of the establishment of popular suffrage, the cost of campaigning also increased sharply. For ambitious politicians who wished to become prime minister, additional money became necessary to buy votes within the party (LDP). With the combination of greater expenditures and the entry of men of less 'noble' origins into politics, the major function of influential politicians in the post-war period has become fund raising.

One effective weapon they have had has been the power of the government to affect the private sector. They wanted to 'wholesale' this power, and preferred to deal with big business, for this was the most effective way of making money for the amount of work involved. In return for passing favourable legislation and intervening with the bureaucracy on behalf of big corporations, certain politicians have asked for donations and secret funds.

Politicians require another participant in their system of corruption, namely, top ranking bureaucrats. Their cooperation has been necessary to make reasonable new legislation or budget allocations favoured by big corporations. For example, when the government had to decide one type of purchase (for example, choosing one fighter plane over another), the choice had to be justified on technical grounds; hence politicians could not decide everything by themselves. As demonstrated in Mitsui Bussan's petrochemical project in Iran, also, the decision for the government to participate depended on the support of the Ministry of International Trade and Industry. The Export and Import Bank of Japan and other government financial institutions are also in a position to make discretionary decisions.

Some top ranking bureaucrats participate in the corruption system for immediate gains, such as bribes, but this is not a typical incentive. If they cooperate with influential politicians and big corporations, when they start a second career after they retire from the government at the age of about 50, they are offered attractive jobs. They can enter the LDP and make politics their second career, or become high officials of private companies or public corporations. The latter category is called *amakudari* (descent from heaven) and is currently the most popular course for retired bureaucrats.

In terms of corruption, Japan has had an impressive list of prime ministers in the post-war period. Fukuda Takeo was arrested and tried in court in connection with a scandal he was involved in in the late 1940s as director general of the Ministry of Finance. Sato Eisaku and Ikeda Hayato were involved in a shipbuilding scandal in the mid-1950s, and barely escaped arrest thanks to the intervention of the Minister of Justice (who is empowered by the Constitution to direct or terminate investigations). Kishi Nobusuke was allegedly involved in various scandals relating to reparations, economic aid and defense contracts. Tanaka Kakuei was first arrested and tried (then acquitted) on a scandal relating to the government control of coal mines, and is now being tried in court in the Lockheed scandal.[30]

The charges against Kishi Nobusuke run the whole gamut of political corruption in Japan, but he has never been arrested. The major reason for his success in avoiding arrest seems to be that he does not touch 'hot money' directly. In the late 1930s, when he left the Ministry of Commerce and Industry to go to Manchuria, he gathered his juniors in the Ministry and told them that, 'Political contributions must be accepted only after they pass through a filter. If something goes wrong, the filter becomes the case, but the politician does not, for he drinks clear water. The politician who gets into trouble is not using the filter properly.'[31] If this has been the way Kishi has operated, it is quite in contrast with Tanaka Kakuei's maladroit manner. In the Lockheed affair, Tanaka is said to have asked Marubeni to bring cash in carton boxes to his private residence.

Sogo shosha have been involved in a number of scandals. Those in which they were actually or allegedly involved are listed in Table 8.1. The first major case was the Kongo affair of the mid-1910s, in which Mitsui Bussan bribed high officials in the Navy to win a shipbuilding contract for a British company, Vickers, for which Mitsui Bussan had been the agent in Japan. The Lockheed affair, under litigation now, is the second major case to be tried in court. According to the prosecution, Marubeni, the agent for Lockheed in Japan, took money to Tanaka (Prime Minister at the time) and obtained his assistance in selling Lockheed's passenger planes to All Nippon Airways. The airline, a private company, sought a certain concession from the Ministry of Transportation, its supervising agency, in return for acceding to Tanaka's request. Then, a scandal involving Nissho-Iwai was revealed in early 1979. According to the prosecutor's office, Nissho-Iwai gave 500 mil-

TABLE 8.1
Major Scandals in which Trading Companies
were Allegedly Involved

Case	Year	Trading Companies	Politicians and Fixers	Remarks
Kongo Affair	1914	Mitsui Bussan	High officials in the Navy	Tried in court
Indonesian Reparations	1958	Kinoshita Shoten	Kishi Nobusuke Nagano Mamoru	
Grumman vs. Lockheed	1958–9	Marubeni for Lockheed and C.Itoh for Grumman	Kono Ichiro and Kodama Yoshio for Marubeni	Lockheed's F104A Fighters won a Defense Agency Contract
McDonnell vs. Lockheed	1968	Nissho-Iwai for McDonnell and Marubeni for Lockheed	Matsuno Raizo and Kishi Nobusuke for Nissho-Iwai and Kodama Yoshio for Marubeni	McDonnell's F4E Phantom won a Defense Agency Contract
Integrated Steel Mill at P'ohang, Korea	1969	Mitsubishi Shoji, Mitsui Bussan, Marubeni, C.Itoh, etc.	Kishi Nobusuke	
Lockheed Affair	1972	Marubeni	Tanaka Kakuei, Hashimoto Tomisaburo, etc.	Being tried in court
Korean Subway	1973	Mitsubishi Shoji, Marubeni, etc.	Kishi Nobusuke	
LNG Tankers for Indonesia	1974	Nissho-Iwai	Tanaka Rokusuke and Kishi Nobusuke	

lion yen to Matsuno Raizo for his assistance in selling McDonnell's military planes to the Defense Agency in the late 1960s, but was acquitted by the statute of limitation. Recently, Kaifu, who directed Nissho-Iwai's aeroplane sales, was tried and found guilty of perjury in the Diet hearing regarding this scandal.

The other scandals listed in Table 8.1 are all allegations. Among them, the most famous is Kinoshita Shoten's involvement in Japan's reparations to Indonesia in the late 1950s. Kinoshita Shigeru, the founder of the company, was apparently successful at winning the favour of important people. In the early post-war period, he won the favour of Nagano Shigeo of Fuji Steel and Inayama Yoshihiro of Yahata Steel, and became their primary agent, which laid the foundation for his post-war success. Through Nagano and Inayama, Kinoshita came to know Kishi Nobusuke intimately, to whom he gave financial assistance for a return to politics.

Kinoshita's relationship with Kishi paid off handsomely in the 1950s. One indication of this is the fact that Kinoshita won a large reparation project in Indonesia. Probably through Kishi's associates, e.g., Kobayashi Ataru, Kinoshita established contacts with President Sukarno and became his favourite merchant in Japan. When President Sukarno expressed the desire to take back to Indonesia a fashion model he met during his tour of Japan, Kinoshita was happy to arrange it. He also met the costs of the President's spending spree in Japan. For these and other services, Kinoshita became the supplier for nine out of the ten used ships Indonesia bought with reparations. It was alleged that the average price of the used ships Kinoshita sold was higher than the price of equivalent new ships and that the mark-up was used to pay for President Sukarno's expenses for pleasure in Japan, to pay him a commission, and to buy a villa at Atami for Kishi, then Prime Minister.[32]

Most scandals in which trading companies have been involved (sometimes allegedly) in the post-war period fall into two categories. One is purchases by the Defense Agency, and the other involves Japan's reparations and economic aid. The first category includes the two so-called 'FX Wars', competitions over the sale of aircraft to the Defense Agency.[33] The first 'FX War' was fought in the late 1950s between Marubeni and C.Itoh. Marubeni won the battle, thereafter supplying Lockheed military planes to the Defense Agency. It is said that Marubeni obtained the help of Kono Ichiro and Kodama Yoshio, another Class A war criminal (Kishi Nobusuke was also designated a Class A war criminal). The second 'FX War' was fought in the late 1960s, with Nissho-Iwai winning the battle, as discussed above. Falling into the second category are Kinoshita Shoten's Indonesian deal, Mitsubishi Shoji and other trading companies' steel mill and subway projects in Korea, and Nissho-Iwai's sales of LNG tankers to Indonesia.

In the past several years, the involvement of sogo shosha in political scandals has been widely publicized, as a consequence of which we tend to form the impression that they have a monopoly on political scandals. However, if we look carefully at the history of corruption in the modern period, we see that there have been numerous scandals which trading companies had nothing to do with. As explained earlier in this section, the corruption system is such that it is difficult for big business to avoid getting involved. A political scientist, C. Yanaga, summarizes this situation around the mid-1960s as follows.

The government played an increasingly decisive role as banker, investor, planner, buyer, regulator, and controller of currency, finance, trade, industrial structure, and production. Economic managers found that they could not function effectively under these conditions merely by being managers. It became imperative for them to work with and through the state to attain their goals and even to survive. This meant that they had to establish intimate working relationships with politicians and bureaucrats.[34]

Still, the fact remains that certain sogo shosha have been involved in corrupt practices and criticism of them for breaking the law and corrupting the political process is not uncalled for. A few points which mitigate their guilt somewhat should, however, be borne in mind. First is that since, the political system itself is wrong, the public who has tolerated it is equally guilty. The constituents of Sato Eisaku in Yamaguchi Prefecture continued to send him back to the Diet even after his involvement in the shipbuilding scandal and enabled him to become prime minister. When they were asked why they kept voting for him, they replied that 'the breakwater of that port, the concrete bridge of this river, . . . all these were made possible by Mr. Sato. He is the great benefactor of Yamaguchi Prefecture.'[35] Sato's constituents were not exceptional in this kind of behaviour. The constituents of Tanaka Kakuei in Niigata Prefecture have continued to vote him into the Diet even after his involvement in the Lockheed affair was brought to national attention. Tanaka has also been a great benefactor to his constituency.

Unlike in some developing countries which are run by autocratic rulers, in Japan, it is possible for the public to put pressure on the Liberal Democratic Party and demand a cleaner political system. For example, if the LDP were to decide to make all corporate donations illegal, the political system will become fairly clean. So far, however, the public has not felt a strong need for an incorrupt government, despite off-and-on campaigns by some national newspapers and opposition parties. The majority of the public has sanctioned the political style of the LDP by voting for it in elections. Thus, when accusations are levelled at sogo shosha for participation in political corruption, the public should be denounced with even greater vehemence for tolerating such a system.

Another disturbing problem is that while bribes are illegal, political contributions are legal, despite the fact that both have similar effects. In order to illuminate the questions involved, contrast Marubeni's Lockheed affair with Mitsui Bussan's petrochemical project in Iran. In the Lockheed affair, Marubeni is accused of bribing Tanaka Kakuei. In the case of Mitsui Bussan's petrochemical project, it is not clear exactly how the company succeeded in getting government assistance, but it is highly likely that the political contributions of Mitsui Bussan and other Mitsui companies in the past and their pledges for the future were a crucial factor.

Ironically, in the Marubeni case, now being tried in court as bribery, there were no real costs to the public, because All Nippon Airways, the airline which bought the Lockheed aeroplanes, is a private company and the aeroplanes seem as good as any other. Mitsui Bussan, on the other hand, managed to obtain costly assistance from the government and thus in effect imposed financial burdens on the public. Yet, because Mitsui Bussan's operations are legal, the company has been free from public prosecution, while Marubeni is being tried for what are considered illegal activities. If both bribes and contributions corrupt the political process, why should Marubeni alone be called to account?

Marubeni broke the law, but Mitsui Bussan did not; therefore, Marubeni should be prosecuted. This, at least, is the viewpoint of the prosecutor's office. Why did Marubeni feel compelled to resort to such illegal tactics? The answer seems to be that for the same amount of money, bribes are more effective than political contributions, for bribes can be spent in any way while contributions must be declared, and funds which pass through official organs may not necessarily reach the particular individuals the donors intended. Probably, Marubeni, operating without the backing of its group (Fuyo) in selling Lockheed aeroplanes, wished to make effective use of money, while Mitsui Bussan was able to use the fact that it had previously made large contributions together with other Mitsui companies as a strong bargaining point when it negotiated with influential politicians. If this is so, the tragedy for Marubeni was that it did not have group backing. C.Itoh and Nissho-Iwai also seem to have faced the same problem.

Under the present system, political contributions are a type of investment for corporations. With contributions, they can buy government influence to enhance their business interests. Just as there are bad and good investments, there are ineffective and effective contributions. It seems that economy of scale is involved in contributions, such that only beyond a certain amount do they become effective in obtaining the desired results. So, unless companies are really large (like Nippon Steel), single contributions do not seem to be very effective. But if they form a coalition, contributions become larger and, thus, more effective. This must be the political economy of enterprise groups. If they are as cohesive as the former zaibatsu groups, since member companies tend to share the same fate, they can give large contributions on a constant basis and use these as leverage when government favours become necessary.

5. CONCLUDING COMMENTS

The approximately eighteen-month period from early 1973 was the period of ordeal for sogo shosha. They were accused by the press, leftist politicians and intellectuals, who claimed that they had caused inflation by speculation. Since the basic reason for the inflation at that time was the failure of the government's monetary policy, sogo shosha were not responsible; nevertheless, they were put in an embarrassing position. They had become too respectable to admit openly their speculative activities but at the same time, too large for such activities not to destabilize prices.

The Fair Trade Commission (FTC) has great misgivings about sogo shosha. They obtain large loans from city banks and wield considerable power as investors and creditors. In some ways, they have become *konzern*, which are not permitted under the present law. Also, they play a leadership role in the expansion and solidification of enterprise groups, which have come to function like former zaibatsu. In order to prevent an operating company such as a sogo shosha from functioning also as a holding company, the FTC put a ceiling on stockholding, but since the ceiling is rather high (net assets or equity capital, whichever is the larger), it is unlikely that it will have significant impact on the role of sogo shosha. The FTC's other concern, the large flow of bank loans to sogo shosha, was taken up by the Ministry of Finance, and now bank loans are restricted to 20 per cent of their equity. This restriction has greatly affected the mode of fund raising by sogo shosha. It will also have adverse effects on enterprise groups.

Sogo shosha are criticized for being *seisho*. They have given donations and bribes to politicians, and have also helped top ranking bureaucrats in starting their second careers. Some of their activities are illegal; others are legal but morally unjustifiable. For these activities, they may be rightly criticized. But at the same time, we must criticize with even greater vehemence the political system which depends on big business for money. Such a system could be changed if all political donations were made illegal and campaign expenses were met by government funds. Yet the majority of the public has sanctioned the present system by voting for the ruling party, the LDP. Any criticism of sogo shosha as *seisho* should be appraised against this backdrop of a corrupt political system and tacit approval of it by the majority of the public.

1. Fair Trade Commission (FTC), *Sogo Shosha ni kansuru Chosa Hokoku*, January 1974.

2. *Seikei Genron*, 10 May 1973.

3. The data on land holdings in this paragraph and that on profit from wood transactions in the following paragraph were revealed by two Socialist members of the Diet in Matsuura Toshihisa and Hirabayashi Takeshi, *Kaishime Shosha*, Gakuyo Shobo, 1973, p. 223.

4. *Ekonomisuto*, 13 March 1973, p. 28.

5. Ministry of International Trade and Industry, 'Ote Shosha no Eigyo Katsudo no Chukan Jittai Hokoku', April 1973.

6. *Ekonomisuto*, 13 March 1973, p. 28.

7. Fair Trade Commission (FTC), *Sogo Shosha ni kansuru Dainikai Chosa Hokoku*, January 1975, p. 4.

8. This criticism and the following criticism by a former MITI official are reported in Sankei Kigyokisha Gurupu, *Sekai no Fushicho*, Jiyu Kokumin-sha, 1973, p. 104.

9. FTC (1975).

10. FTC (1974), p. 10.

11. FTC (1975), p. 10.

12. Ibid., pp. 20–1.

13. The data in this and the following paragraphs are from FTC (1975), p. 16.

14. Marubeni, *The Unique World of the Sogo Shosha*, 1978, pp. 109–10.

15. FTC (1975), p. 14.

16. This is based on an interview with Tajika Tokuzo of the archives section of Marubeni. The interview took place in October 1979.

17. In a funeral address, Tanaka Kakuei stated that he had personally asked Ichikawa to take over management of Fujikoshi. See *Marubeni, A Special Issue Commemorating the late Chairman Ichikawa*, February 1974, p. 6.

18. *Nihon Keizai Shinbun*, 13 April 1966.

19. This paragraph is based on Kishi Nobusuke's recollection which appeared in Itohchu Shoji, *Itoh Chubei-o Kaiso-roku*, 1974.

20. According to Tsuneyoshi Ken of the general affairs department of C.Itoh's office in Osaka, for a few years before Kosuga retired, the relations between him and Chubei had been somewhat strained. During this time, C.Itoh's relations with Chubei were maintained by Echigo and some other directors.

21. *C.I. Monthly*, December 1951.

22. Sejima Ryuzo is widely regarded to have been the model for Iki Tadashi, the hero of Yamazaki Toyoko's novel, *Fumo Chitai*. In the novel, Iki plays a central role in establishing close relations between his company and the Defense Agency.

23. For a detailed discussion on Nissho's success in aeroplane sales, see Kakuma Takashi, *Dokyumento Nissho-Iwai*, Tokuma Shoten, 1979.

24. Ibid., p. 109.

25. This paragraph is based on an interview with Fukui Keizo, former president of Nichimen. The interview took place in February 1980.

26. *Ekonomisuto*, 15 February 1972, pp. 86 and 89.

27. Asahi Shinbun-sha, *Sogo Shosha*, Asahi Shinbun-sha, 1977, p. 30.

28. Ibid., pp. 31–2.

29. This and the following sentences are based on J. Roberts, *Mitsui: Three Centuries of Japanese Business*, Tokyo, Weatherhill, 1973, pp. 150 and 169.

30. The so-called Lockheed scandal will be explained in more detail below.

31. Quoted in Kakuma, p. 189.

32. Kinoshita's Indonesian deal is discussed in more detail in Chi-

toshi Yanaga, *Big Business in Japanese Politics*, New Haven, Yale University Press, 1968.

33. Supposedly, 'F' in FX is the abbreviation for 'fighter', and 'X' stands for 'unknown'.

34. Yanaga, p. 309.

35. Quoted in Murofushi Tetsuro, *Oshoku no Susume*, Kobundo, 1963, p. 257.

9

Conclusion

DESPITE the criticisms which have erupted recently, it is difficult to deny that trading companies have made important contributions to the Japanese economy. Japan's industrialization depended to a significant degree on foreign trade. At first, machinery had to be imported from the West, in exchange for which rice, silk, tea, and other Japanese products had to be exported. Machinery continued to occupy an important position in total imports, but as Japanese industrialization progressed, raw materials became the most important import. Trading companies procured raw materials for manufacturers in sufficient amounts by undertaking investment if it was necessary. They also marketed new products abroad aggressively, and realized exports which manufacturers alone would have been unable to carry out. In short, trading companies have been the linchpin of Japan's foreign trade.

Since trading companies have not played a significant role in industrialization in other developed countries, the question naturally arises as to what sets Japan apart from those countries. One important factor was the cultural gap between Japan and foreign countries, which separated the Japanese market from the international market. The need arose for a select group of people who could handle foreign language and international transactions to fill the gap.

The cultural gap existed in the Meiji era because Japan had been cut off from foreign contacts for about two centuries during the preceding Tokugawa period. With the Meiji Restoration, Japan became an open country, but the gap persisted for a long while. In the pre-war period, because of xenophobic nationalism, the government limited foreign influence and artificially preserved much of the cultural gap. In the post-war period, however, the country became completely open, and the gap narrowed. As a consequence, the basis for sogo shosha began to be eroded.

At this point, two factors helped to boost the position of sogo shosha in the Japanese economy. Major banks found sogo shosha to be convenient collaborators and channelled large funds to them. Sogo shosha used these funds to act as intermediaries between banks and small companies and also to buy stocks to establish their own subsidiaries or strengthen the ties of enterprise groups. They, therefore, enhanced their positions by becoming part of financial capital.

The high growth rate of the Japanese economy not only gave sogo shosha manoeuvrability but also protected them from manufacturers who might usurp their functions. Sogo shosha may be compared to the Japanese folk hero, Zatoichi, who is a master swordsman despite his blindness. He is strong because he trained his ears to detect any sound his attackers would make: only when they stop moving does he become vulnerable. If the environment in which sogo shosha operate were to become static, like Zatoichi, sogo shosha would become impotent because of the loss of manoeuvrability and the increasing inroads by manufacturers into their areas of activity.

The future of sogo shosha is uncertain. The restriction on large bank loans, which became fully effective at the end of 1979, has forced sogo shosha to look for new sources. Prior to this restriction, banks could lend any amount to sogo sho-sha, but now they can lend only up to 20 per cent of their equity capital. For sogo shosha, this means that the loans from their main banks are limited to 20 per cent of the banks' equity capital and loans from other banks must be reduced accordingly (if main banks are to be meaningful, they must be the largest lenders).

In order to make up for the reduction of bank loans, sogo shosha have begun raising funds directly in the capital market in Japan and abroad, but because of various regulations on the capital market by the Ministry of Finance, none of the alternative sources have become an effective substitute for the bank loans. If sogo shosha cannot find new sources of large funds, which appears to be a difficult proposition under the present circumstances, their financial power will be significantly curtailed.

The inroads of manufacturers into foreign trade have been restricted largely to consumer durables, such as cars and electronic equipment, but in the future, manufacturers may move into foreign trade more aggressively. For one thing, language is becoming a less significant barrier. These days a large number of Japanese can speak English, the language which has become the lingua franca of international trade, and manufacturers are less constrained in this respect. Besides, since it is likely that the slow growth of the past several post-oil shock years will become the norm for the Japanese economy in the future, manufacturers can divert their energy from production to marketing, and begin encroaching upon the functions of sogo shosha. Already, the sales subsidiaries of steel manufacturers, whose activities had concentrated on the domestic market, have begun strengthening their international staff.

In the event that manufacturers increase their involvement in foreign trade, what will then happen to sogo shosha? Despite the problems pointed out above, it is unlikely that all sogo shosha will go bankrupt or that they will become insignificant companies in the near future. What is certain, however, is that they will face greater competition in international trade from manufacturers, smaller Japanese trading companies, and foreign companies. As a consequence, the number of sogo shosha (nine at present) is likely to decline. Under competitive pressure, some might, as Ataka did, put a large amount of resources into risky operations and get into financial difficulties (and then be merged by others), or encounter greater obstacles in increasing sales, fall behind others, and cease to be sogo shosha.

Even those which survive will be compelled to place greater emphasis on non-trading activities. The Fair Trade Commission considers that sogo shosha have already become conglomerates, not simple trading companies any more, although so far, trading has been the linchpin of their various activities. In the future, however, if they wish to continue to grow, they will have to give subsidiaries greater autonomy and also move into new promising areas, irrespective of links with trading: that is, they must create new cores of activities. This is what European trading companies, such as Jardine Matheson, have done. The major distinction between Japanese and European trading companies has been that the need for diversification was postponed for the former (because of the cultural gap, etc.).

The dire prediction by Marxists and others in the early 1960s that the sun had set on sogo shosha proved to be inaccurate because they failed to take two factors into consideration. One was that they regarded sogo shosha as part of commercial capital (which Marx and other European scholars felt was bound to decline in the face of the rise of industrial capital) and overlooked the link between sogo shosha and banks. The other was that the 'general law' (the demise of commercial capital) did not apply equally to all countries because cultural difference affected its operation. Now that the financial power of sogo shosha has been curtailed and the cultural gap is diminishing, it finally seems that the sun is indeed setting on sogo shosha, at least on their trading activities.

Can other countries develop a type of institution like the sogo shosha? This would be possible if some of the conditions which gave rise to sogo shosha in Japan could be replicated. One important factor in Japan, as pointed out above, was the cultural gap. It is unlikely that this factor would carry as much weight in other countries, for today, most of the countries where the native tongue is not English include a large number of people who can handle that language. This is particularly true for former British and American colonies. Even those countries which were the colonies of Continental European countries, such as Indonesia, have de-emphasized the languages of their former colonizers, and adopted English in large measure as the major foreign language. Furthermore, because these countries do not have such strong nationalism as that which prevailed in pre-war Japan, and because international contacts are much more frequent today, any cultural gap which may exist today is unlikely to be an important factor in foreign trade.

If a significant cultural gap does not exist, the automatic growth of trading companies into sogo shosha cannot be assumed. The only way to generate this transition would be to create arbitrarily the other conditions which supported the growth of trading companies in Japan. The most effective arrangement would be to form a zaibatsu type of organization which comprises a bank, a trading company, and industrial companies. Since the bank has to be the major financier of the trading and industrial companies, it cannot be a local bank but it must be a major national bank. The trading company could use the bank as the main bank, and with its backing also borrow money from other banks if necessary. With these funds, the trading company could set up an international distribution system as well as be able to establish contacts with companies in industries where the economy of scale is not important and financial capital has not moved in directly (for example, labour intensive industries). For industrial companies in the organization, the trading company could collect information, market products and purchase raw materials.

If a trading company were able to function as a member of such an organization, how much time would pass before it became a sogo shosha? This would depend on how dynamic the industrial companies were and whether the bank could increase its financial resources commensurate with the speed at which the industrial companies grew. The Japanese experience shows that it can be a matter of less than two decades. For example, as explained in Chapter 3, Mitsubishi Shoji was established in 1918, and by the end of the 1930s, it had grown to handle a wide product line and to have an extensive international network.

For countries in which holding companies may not be established to coordinate the activities of various companies in a group, the example of Sumitomo Shoji may be more useful. The Sumitomo group does not have a holding company, yet it has remained a cohesive group, making it possible for Sumitomo Shoji to become a sogo shosha in about two decades. As explained in Chapter 4, Sumitomo Shoji was established after the Pacific War, and recorded spectacular growth in the 1950s and 1960s. Close personal ties cultivated in the pre-war period were a great help in solidifying the group, and in this respect, zaibatsu tradition was carried over. But personal ties alone were insufficient. In many instances, the Sumitomo Bank has acted as coordinator of the group and played the role of the pre-war holding company.

One might argue that if grouping is a necessary condition for the development of sogo shosha, the idea of sogo shosha should be dropped, for according to the FTC, grouping has ominous implications for economic efficiency and democracy. The FTC, which was created during the Occupation period as a replica of the Anti-Trust Division of the Department of Justice in the United States, attaches too much importance to atomistic competition and economic democracy. In the past, economists believed that economic efficiency could be maintained only if many companies competed in the same industry. This belief underlies the Anti-Trust Law of the United States and the Anti-Monopoly Law of Japan. Over time, it has become clear, however, that oligopoly does not necessarily impair economic efficiency, and, in many cases, even promotes it. This is because there is economy of scale in production, research and development, marketing and purchasing. Certainly, the strengthening of enterprise groups cannot be supported wholeheartedly because of some adverse implications for economic democracy, but barring excesses, enterprise groups are necessary in the present age of international competition. The group approach to industrialization, and the development of a sogo shosha as a member of the group can be an appropriate strategy for developing countries.

On a micro-level, the major task of top management is to keep their companies prosperous. Since trading is a simple activity in many ways, it may seem that not much skill is involved in making a trading company successful. In actual fact, however, competition in trading is fierce because the barrier to entry is low; to remain a prosperous company for a long period is not an easy task. In the history of trading companies in Japan, there are numerous companies which were once prosperous which either no longer exist today or are just barely surviving.

The first thing the top management of the present sogo shosha realized early in their history was that trading companies are people. For example, if a trading company wished to remain prosperous for a long time, it was necessary to make great efforts to recruit competent people and treat them fairly in terms of both remuneration and promotion. In the early stage of development, top management was often not completely open, because family enterprises were the dominant form of organization. As organizations became large, however, it became necessary to introduce a system of meritocracy in the selection of top management and to separate management from ownership. Also, since there was a great deal of skill necessary for trading which could not be taught in school, new recruits had to be trained on-the-job, and an appropriate incentive system set up to keep them. It was ideal if they could develop a sense of group loyalty in the process of training.

The family enterprise is not a truly modern organization, and it might be best if they were dispensed with, but in the early stage of economic development, such enterprises can play important roles. This was the case in the development of Japanese trading companies: most started out as family enterprises. After all, the family is the most cohesive social organization, and family members can be trusted. In developing countries where social integration is still in an early stage, the family could form the core of the company.

To what extent developing countries should rely on family enterprises depends in part on how fast they want to push development. In the Japanese case, growth was much faster than in the case of Western countries, but it was slow in comparison with the speed at which many developing countries are growing, or the paces they have set as targets. It was possible in Japan for family enterprises to develop gradually into modern organizations, but a comparable speed may be too leisurely today. If so, the family enterprise cannot be depended upon as a modernizer of the economy.

The evolution of Nippon Menka and Gosho, set up as joint stock companies by pooling capital from several sources, may be a more relevant example for developing countries of today. These cases show that even in the early stages of development, if the required amount of capital is too large for one merchant to risk, a trading company can be established as a joint stock company and successfully managed by professionals. Then, the family need not be the major organization principle in trading companies. In view of the speed at which developing countries want to push development, they may want to promote joint stock companies from the beginning.

One model developing countries should avoid is that of a state trading company. Trading is a competitive industry which can be best handled by private companies. In a trading company, people must work hard, and they should be rewarded for their efforts and achievements. If they mismanage, they should face the consequences. Otherwise, the trading industry cannot be efficient. The major drawback with a state trading company is that it does not encourage striving for maximum efficiency because of government interference and protection.

The state is a poor substitute for the family as an organization principle in trading companies. If the family enterprise is de-emphasized, the type of organization to be promoted should be the joint stock company. In the beginning, stockholdings cannot be dispersed, for in forming such a company, one person or a small number of persons must take the initiative and play the organizing role. At this stage, ownership has strong influence on management. If the venture is successful, as the cases of Nippon Menka and Gosho illustrate, equity capital increases, and management becomes independent. Initially, the joint stock company may have more management problems than a family enterprise because the interests of stockholders have to be accommodated, but if these problems are overcome, the road to separation of management from ownership is much smoother than in the case of family enterprises.

In the event that there are already a number of large family-dominated trading companies, instead of discouraging their growth, it might be best to use government power to force the owner families to disperse their holdings at a certain point. In the Japanese case, this was done forcibly by Occupation authorities. This was an humiliating experience for Japanese nationalists, but its impact on the development of trading and other companies was favourable. Because of the dispersion, former family enterprises, such as C.Itoh, Marubeni, Mitsui Bussan, Mitsubishi Shoji, etc., came to be run without the influence of their former owners. Those in which families retained influence lost out in competition, and no longer exist today as independent companies. Measures for dispersion need not be as drastic as in the case of Japan, but if governmental power is wisely used, it can have revitalizing effects on family enterprises.

Appendixes

1. *Mitsubishi Group**

Banking and Insurance
  Mitsubishi Bank
  Mitsubishi Trust and Banking
  Tokio Marine and Fire Insurance
  Meiji Mutual Life Insurance

Trading
  Mitsubishi Shoji

Mining and Manufacturing
  Mitsubishi Mining and Cement
  Mitsubishi Oil
  Mitsubishi Metal
  Mitsubishi Steel Manufacturing
  Mitsubishi Heavy Industries
  Mitsubishi Kakoki
  Mitsubishi Gas-Chemical
  Mitsubishi Plastics Industries
  Mitsubishi Rayon
  Mitsubishi Petrochemical
  Asahi Glass
  Mitsubishi Paper Mills
  Kirin Brewery
  Mitsubishi Motor
  Nippon Kogaku
  Mitsubishi Electric
  Mitsubishi Chemical Industries

*Members of the Kinyo-kai

Mitsubishi Aluminium
Mitsubishi Monsanto Chemical

Others
Mitsubishi Warehouse and Transportation
Nippon Yusen
Mitsubishi Estate
Mitsubishi Construction

2. *Mitsui Group**
Banking and Insurance
Mitsui Bank
Mitsui Trust and Banking
Mitsui Mutual Life Insurance
Taisho Marine and Fire Insurance

Trading
Mitsui Bussan

Mining and Manufacturing
Mitsui Mining
Mitsui Mining and Smelting
Mitsui Shipbuilding and Engineering
Mitsui Toatsu Chemicals
Mitsui Petrochemical Industries
Toray Industries
Japan Steel Works
Sanki Engineering
Nippon Flour Mills
Tokyo Shibaura Electric
Oji Paper
Toyota Motor

Others
Mitsukoshi
Mitsui Warehouse
Mitsui Real Estate Development
Mitsui OSK Lines
Hokkaido Colliery and Steamship
Mitsui Construction

3. *Fuyo Group*†
Banking and Insurance
Fuji Bank
Yasuda Trust and Banking

*Members of the Nimoku-kai
†Members of the Fuyo-kai

Yasuda Fire and Marine Insurance
Yasuda Mutual Life Insurance

Trading
Marubeni

Mining and Manufacturing
Yokogawa Electric Works
Oki Electric Industry
Canon
Kureha Chemical Industry
Kubota
Sanyo-Kokusaku Pulp
Sapporo Breweries
Showa Denko
Toa Nenryo Kogyo
Toho Rayon
Nippon Kokan
Nissan Motor
Nippon Seiko
Nisshin Spinning
Nisshin Flour Milling
Nippon Reizo
Nihon Cement
Nippon Oils and Fats
Hitachi

Others
Keihin Electric Express Railway
Showa Line
Taisei
Tobu Railway
Tokyo Tatemono

4. *Sumitomo Group**
Banking and Insurance
Sumitomo Bank
Sumitomo Trust and Banking
Sumitomo Mutual Life Insurance
Sumitomo Marine and Fire Insurance

Trading
Sumitomo Shoji

Mining and Manufacturing
Sumitomo Coal Mining
Sumitomo Metal Industries

*Members of the Hakusui-kai

Sumitomo Chemical
Sumitomo Electric Industries
Nippon Electric
Sumitomo Shipbuilding and Machinery
Nippon Sheet
Sumitomo Cement
Sumitomo Aluminium Smelting
Sumitomo Light Metal Industries
Sumitomo Bakelite

Others
Sumitomo Warehouse
Sumitomo Realty and Development
Sumitomo Construction
Sumitomo Forestry

5. *Sanwa Group**
Banking and Insurance
Sanwa Bank
Toyo Trust and Banking
Nippon Life Insurance

Trading
Nissho-Iwai
Nichimen
Iwatani

Mining and Manufacturing
Osaka Cement
Kansai Paint
Kobe Steel
Daihatsu Kogyo
Teijin
Tokuyama Soda
Toyo Rubber Industry
Nakayama Steel Works
Hitachi
Hitachi Shipbuilding and Engineering
Maruzen Oil
Unitika
Iwatsu Electric
Shin Meiwa Industry
Sekisui Chemical
NTN Toyo Bearing
Hitachi Chemical
Hitachi Metals

*Members of the Sansui-kai

Hitachi Cable
Fujisawa Pharmaceutical
Sharp
Tanabe Seiyaku
Ube Industries

Others
Ohbayashi-gumi
Hankyu
Takashimaya
Nippon Express
Yamashita-Shinnihon Steamship
Toyo Construction
Orient Leasing

6. *Dai-Ichi Kangin Group**

Banking and Insurance
Dai-Ichi Kangyo Bank
Asahi Mutual Life Insurance
Taisei Fire and Marine Insurance
Nissan Fire and Marine Insurance
Fukoku Mutual Life Insurance

Trading
C.Itoh
Nissho-Iwai
Kanematsu-Gosho
Kawasho

Mining and Manufacturing
Furukawa
Furukawa Electric
Asahi Denka Kogyo
Yokohama Rubber
Fujitsu
Fuji Electric
Nippon Light Metal
Nippon Zeon
Kawasaki Steel
Kawasaki Heavy Industries
Sankyo
Shiseido
Electro-Chemical Industrial
Niigata Engineering
Nippon Columbia
Honshu Paper

*Members of the Sankin-kai

Yasukawa Electric Manufacturing
Ishikawajima-Harima Heavy Industries
Kobe Steel
Showa Oil
Asahi Optical
Hitachi
Asahi Chemical Industry
Isuzu Motors
Iseki Agricultural Machinery
Ebara Manufacturing
Chichibu Cement
Lion Dentifrice
Japan Metals and Chemicals

Others
Kawasaki Kisen Kaisha
Korakuen Stadium
Seibu Department Store
Nippon Kangyo Kakumaru Securities
Nippon Express
Shimizu Construction
Shibusawa Warehouse

7. *Tokai Group**
Banking and Insurance
Tokai Bank
Chuo Trust and Banking
Chiyoda Mutual Life Insurance
Chiyoda Fire and Marine Insurance

Trading
Toyo Menka
Okaya

Mining and Manufacturing
Toyota Motor
Fujikoshi
Japan Rolling Stock Manufacturing
Idemitsu Kosan

Others
Toyota Motor Sales
Fujita
Matsuzakaya
Japan Development and Construction
Nippon Shinpan

*Members of the Wakaba-kai

APPENDIX 2

The Shares of Exports, Imports, Domestic Trade, and Offshore
Trade in Mitsui Bussan's Sales in the Period 1897—1932
(Unit: per cent)

Year	Exports	Imports	Domestic Trade	Offshore Trade
1897	19	62	18	1
1898	22	62	15	1
1899	33	53	13	1
1900	25	51	22	2
1901	28	50	19	3
1902	29	51	17	3
1903	34	50	14	2
1904	34	43	20	3
1905	29	47	17	7
1906	36	37	19	8
1907	35	44	14	7
1908	29	42	13	16
1909	38	34	15	13
1910	37	31	17	15
1911	35	36	18	11
1912	35	33	17	15
1913	38	33	15	14
1914	37	34	15	14
1915	35	25	17	23
1916	34	23	16	27
1917	31	18	22	29
1918	25	25	20	30
1919	19	23	24	34
1920	20	23	24	33
1921	26	22	24	28
1922	30	26	23	21
1923	27	23	25	25
1924	26	24	24	26
1925	25	23	25	27
1926	24	24	25	27
1927	24	23	28	25
1928	23	23	33	21
1929	23	22	35	20
1930	21	20	36	23
1931	21	16	38	25
1932	25	16	38	21

Source: Mitsui Bussan, *Mitsui Bussan Shoshi*, 1951, pp. 146—7.

APPENDIX 3
Mitsui Bussan's Shares in Japan's Exports and Imports
in the Period 1897–1932
(Unit: per cent)

Year	Exports	Imports	Exports and Imports
1897	5.9	14.5	10.7
1898	7.5	13.2	11.0
1899	11.3	17.1	14.2
1900	10.3	15.0	13.0
1901	8.0	13.9	11.0
1902	9.1	15.6	12.4
1903	11.0	14.6	15.3
1904	13.2	14.4	13.8
1905	15.5	17.0	16.7
1906	16.5	17.2	16.9
1907	18.6	20.7	19.7
1908	18.4	22.6	20.5
1909	20.1	18.8	19.4
1910	21.7	17.5	19.6
1911	24.0	20.5	22.5
1912	22.7	17.9	20.1
1913	23.5	17.3	20.1
1914	27.6	24.1	25.8
1915	20.7	19.4	20.9
1916	20.6	21.1	20.8
1917	20.1	18.4	19.5
1918	19.7	18.5	19.1
1919	18.7	21.0	19.9
1920	18.1	17.2	18.0
1921	16.1	10.3	12.8
1922	15.5	11.0	13.0
1923	15.6	9.5	12.4
1924	14.5	9.7	11.5
1925	12.0	9.7	10.7
1926	13.2	10.9	12.0
1927	13.3	11.4	12.3
1928	14.4	11.9	13.0
1929	11.9	11.3	11.8
1930	14.7	13.2	13.9
1931	14.7	10.5	12.5
1932	15.9	10.2	13.0

Source: Mitsui Bussan, *Mitsui Bussan Shoshi*, 1951, p. 145.

APPENDIX 4

Mitsui Bussan's Profits in the Period 1876–1939
(Unit: thousand yen)

Year	Amount	Year	Amount	Year	Amount	Year	Amount
1876	8*	1896	850	1916	19,182	1936	18,059
1877	200	1897	1,123	1917	32,187	1937	27,663
1878	120	1898	1,719	1918	36,464	1938	16,302
1879	151	1899	1,868	1919	19,864	1939	31,297
1880	43	1900	1,355	1920	16,395		
1881	−103	1901	1,687	1921	7,718		
1882	46	1902	1,533	1922	11,121		
1883	70	1903	1,668	1923	10,164		
1884	80	1904	2,211	1924	14,177		
1885	60	1905	2,347	1925	16,226		
1886	100	1906	2,188	1926	20,766		
1887	30	1907	2,052	1927	16,851		
1888	40	1908	1,364	1928	19,158		
1889	40	1909	1,971	1929	18,904		
1890	78	1910	4,504	1930	15,096		
1891	76	1911	6,015	1931	13,345		
1892	226	1912	5,361	1932	13,579		
1893	302	1913	5,218	1933	22,430		
1894	633	1914	3,960	1934	15,895		
1895	1,087	1915	7,055	1935	16,228		

Source: Mitsui Bussan, *Mitsui Bussan Shoshi*, 1951, pp. 141–2.
*Only for July to December.

APPENDIX 5
Sales in the Period 1900–1940
(Unit: million yen)

Year	Mitsui Bussan	Mitsubishi Shoji	Marubeni	Iwai	Nissho
1900	88				
1901	74				
1902	86				
1903	96				
1904	127				
1905	180			9	
1906	199			12	
1907	235			12	
1908	242			9	
1909	223			10	
1910	278			14	
1911	317			15	
1912	359			*	
1913	402			*	
1914	452			*	
1915	438			*	
1916	721			*	
1917	1,095			*	
1918	1,602			*	
1919	2,130			*	
1920	1,921	89		*	
1921	813	118	33	*	
1922	865	202	36	*	
1923	882	250	43	*	
1924	1,035	309	44	*	
1925	1,141	341	43	*	
1926	1,181	315	53	*	
1927	1,167	402	71	*	
1928	1,265	462	89	*	15
1929	1,323	439	79	*	33
1930	1,080	347	72	*	21
1931	841	278	72	*	22
1932	948	418	81	*	43
1933	1,233	568	110	*	70
1934	1,499	736	131	*	76
1935	1,773	862	132	*	80

APPENDIX 5 (continued)

Year	Mitsui Bussan	Mitsubishi Shoji	Marubeni	Iwai	Nissho
1936	1,797	992	148	200	98
1937	2,355	1,305	191	285	162
1938	2,393	1,552	197	256	168
1939	2,914	1,898	212	288	181
1940	3,446	2,278	218	310	207

Sources: Mitsui Bussan, *Mitsui Bussan Shoshi*, 1951, pp. 143–7 and 180; Mitsubishi Shoji, *Ritsugyo Boeki-roku*, 1958, p. 947; Marubeni, *Marubeni Zenshi*, 1977, pp. 212–13; Iwai Sangyo, *Iwai Hyakunen Shi*, 1964, pp. 170 and 362; and Nissho, *Nissho Shiju-nen no Ayumi*, 1968, p. 609.

*Indicates that data are not available.

APPENDIX 6
Paid-up Capital in the Period 1893–1940
(Unit: million yen)

Year	Mitsui Bussan	Mitsubishi Shoji	C.Itoh	Marubeni	Daido	Iwai	Nissho
1893–1908	1.0						
1909	20.0						
1910	20.0						
1911	20.0						
1912	20.0					2.0	
1913	20.0					2.0	
1914	20.0					2.0	
1915	20.0					2.0	
1916	20.0					2.0	
1917	20.0					5.0	
1918	100.0	15.0	10.0	5.0		10.0	
1919	100.0	15.0	10.0	5.0		10.0	
1920	100.0	15.0	10.0	5.0	1.0	10.0	
1921	100.0	15.0	10.0	5.0	1.0	10.0	
1922	100.0	15.0	7.0	5.0	1.0	10.0	
1923	100.0	15.0	7.0	5.0	1.0	10.0	
1924	100.0	15.0	7.0	5.0	1.0	10.0	
1925	100.0	15.0	7.0	5.0	1.0	10.0	
1926	100.0	15.0	7.0	5.0	1.0	10.0	
1927	100.0	15.0	7.0	5.0	1.0	10.0	
1928	100.0	15.0	5.0	5.0	1.0	10.0	1.0
1929	100.0	15.0	5.0	5.0	1.0	10.0	1.0
1930	100.0	15.0	5.0	5.0	1.0	10.0	1.0
1931	100.0	15.0	5.0	5.0	1.0	10.0	1.0
1932	100.0	15.0	5.0	5.0	1.0	10.0	1.0
1933	100.0	15.0	5.0	5.0	1.5	10.0	1.0
1934	100.0	15.0	6.2	7.5	1.8	10.0	3.0
1935	100.0	15.0	7.5	8.5	2.0	13.0	3.0
1936	150.0	15.0	7.5	8.5	2.0	13.0	3.0
1937	150.0	15.0	12.5	10.0	3.5	13.0	4.5
1938	150.0	15.0	12.5	10.0	3.5	13.0	5.0
1939	150.0	50.0	12.5	10.0	3.5	15.0	5.0
1940	300.4	100.0	12.5	10.0	3.5	15.0	5.0

Sources: Mitsui Bussan, *Mitsui Bussan Shoshi,* 1951, pp. 115–22; Mitsubishi Shoji, *Ritsugyo Boeki-roku*, 1958, pp. 3–11; Marubeni, *Marubeni Zenshi*, 1977, pp. 208–11; Itohchu Shoji, *Itohchu Shoji Hyakunen*, 1969, pp. 562–3; Iwai Sangyo, *Iwai Hyakunen Shi*, 1964, pp. 557–8; and Nissho, *Nissho Shiju-nen no Ayumi*, 1968, p. 609.

Bibliography

THIS is a select list of writings on Japanese trading companies. There are numerous writings on this topic in Japanese weekly and monthly magazines, such as *Ekonomisuto, Toyo Keizai*, and *Daiyamondo*, but they are not, in principle, included. In the case of books, journalistic as well as scholarly works are included. Under each heading, Japanese sources appear first, followed by English sources.

1. ANNUALS AND STATISTICS

Ministry of Finance, *Yuka Shoken Hokokusho Soran* [Securities Report].

Ministry of International Trade and Industry, *Boeki Gyotai Tokei-hyo* [Statistical Tables on Trade Conditions].

_____, *Tsusho Hakusho* [White Paper on International Trade].

Seikei Tsushin-sha, *Sogo Shosha Nenkan* [General Trading Companies Annual].

2. COMPANY MAGAZINES

C.Itoh, *C.I. Monthly*.

Kanematsu-Gosho, *KG Monthly* (*Kanematsu Geppo* until March 1967, and *Kanematsu Gosho Geppo* from April 1967 to January 1969).

Marubeni, *Marubeni*.

Mitsubishi Shoji, *Ryowa*.

——, *Ryowa β* (June 1977 to June 1979).

Mitsui Bussan, *MBK Life*.

Nichimen, *Gekkan Nichimen*.

Nissho-Iwai, *Nissho-Iwai Life* (*Saibi* until 1961, and *Nissho Life* from 1962 to August 1968).

Sumitomo Shoji, *Sumisho News* (*Sumisho Digest* from March 1965 to March 1973).

Toyo Menka, *Tomen*.

3. TRADING COMPANIES IN GENERAL

Arita, Kyosuke, *Sogo Shosha: Mirai no Kozu o Saguru* [General Trading Companies: Exploring Compositions for the Future], Nihon Keizai Shinbun-sha, 1970.

Asahi Shinbun-sha, *Sogo Shosha* [General Trading Companies], Asahi Shinbun-sha, 1977.

Boeki no Nihon: Tokushu—Ote Shosha Kensetsu Bumon [Trade of Japan: Special Number—Construction Divisions of the Major Trading Companies], December 1976.

Chuo Koron Keiei Mondai, Fall 1977. Special Number on General Trading Companies.

Chuo Koron Keiei Mondai, Spring 1980. Special Number on General Trading Companies.

Fair Trade Commission, 'Saihensei Katei ni okeru Boeki Shosha no Kihon Doko' [Basic Trends of Trading Companies in the Process of Reorganization], 1955.

——, *Sogo Shosha ni kansuru Chosa Hokoku* [Investigative Report on General Trading Companies], January 1974.

——, *Sogo Shosha ni kansuru Daini-kai Chosa Hokoku* [Second Investigative Report on General Trading Companies], January 1975.

Gendai Shosha Kenkyukai (ed.), *Boeki Shosha Man* [Trading Company Man], Toyo Keizai Shinpo-sha, 1980.

Haber, Daniel (tr. Tsuda, Takeshi), *Nippon no Sogo Shosha* [General Trading Companies in Japan], Saimaru Shuppan-kai, 1975.

Hiraiwa, Takeo, *Sogo Shosha no Hateshinai Kuno* [The

Boundless Distress of the General Trading Companies] , Aki Shobo, 1978.

Infure Taisaku Kenkyu-kai, *Shosha o Kokuhatsu Suru* [We Indict the Trading Companies] , Yale Books, 1974.

Jiji Tsushin-sha, *Shosha shin-Jidai* [The New Age of Trading Companies] , Jiji Tsushin-sha, 1970.

Kaido, Mamoru, *Hikaku Nippon no Kaisha: Sogo Shosha* [Comparison of Japanese Companies: General Trading Companies] , Jitsumu Kyoiku Shuppan, 1979.

Kato, Isao, *Setogiwa ni Tatsu Sogo Shosha: Sangoku-kan Boeki, Kaigai Toshi* [General Trading Companies Standing at the Brink: Offshore Trade and Overseas Investment] , Seikei Tsushin-sha, 1979.

Keiei Shigaku, Vol. 8, No. 1 (1973). Special Number on General Trading Companies.

Kikai Shinko Kyokai, *Kaigai Jigyo Katsudo to Sogo Shosha* [Overseas Business Activity and General Trading Companies] , 1975.

Kitada, Yoshiharu, and Tanihara, Norio, *Sogo Shosha* [General Trading Companies] , Shin Nihon Shuppan-sha, 1974.

'Kono Hito to Ichi-jikan, Kakushin o Motte Shosha Kisei o— Takahashi Toshihide (Kotori Iin-cho)' [An Hour with This Person: Takahashi Toshihide (Fair Trade Commission Chairman)—Regulating Trading Companies with Confidence] , *Ekonomisuto*, 29 May 1973.

Kubo, Iwao, *Sogo Shosha to Sekai Zaibatsu-gun* [General Trading Companies and World Financial Cliques] , Tokyo Nunoi Shuppan, 1975.

Mainichi Shinbun-sha, *Shosha 50-nendai no Tenbo* [Survey of Trading Companies in the Fifties] , Mainichi Shinbun-sha, 1975.

Matsui, Kiyoshi, 'Boeki Shosha-ron' [Treatise on Trading Companies] , *Chuo Koron*, August 1952.

_____ , *Boeki Shosha-ron* [Treatise on Trading Companies] , Yuhikaku, 1952.

_____ , *Kindai Nippon Boeki-shi* [History of Modern Japanese Trade] , Yuhikaku, 1959.

———, *Nippon no Boeki* [Japanese Trade], *Iwanami Shinsho* No. 162, Iwanami Shoten, 1954.

Matsuura, Toshihisa and Hirabayashi, Takeshi, *Kaishime Shosha* [Trading Companies Corner the Market], Gakuyo Shobo, 1973.

Ministry of International Trade and Industry, 'Ote Shosha no Eigyo Katsudo no Chukan Jittai Hokoku' [Interim Fact-Finding Report on the Business Activities of Large Trading Companies], April 1973.

Misonoo, Hitoshi, 'Sogo Shosha wa Shayo de Aruka' [Has the Sun Set on General Trading Companies?], *Ekonomisuto*, 23 May 1961.

Mitsui Bussan (Chosa Bu), *Atarashii Sogo Shosha-zo o Motomete* [In Search of a New Image for General Trading Companies], April 1977.

Miyamoto, Mataji *et al.* (eds.), *Sogo Shosha no Keiei-shi* [Business History of General Trading Companies], Toyo Keizai Shinpo-sha, 1974.

Nanaju Nendai ni Idomu Sogo Shosha [General Trading Companies Challenging the Seventies], Seikei Raiburari No. 3, Seikei Tsushin-sha, 1969.

Nihon Boeki-kai, 'Kosei Torihiki Iinkai no "Sogo Shosha ni kansuru Daini-kai Chosa Hokoku" ni tsuite' [On the Second Investigative Report on General Trading Companies by the Fair Trade Commission], 1975.

———, 'Sogo Shosha no Kino to Tokushitsu—Kokkai Rongi, Kotori no Mondai Teiki ni Kotaete' [The Functions and Special Characteristics of General Trading Companies—in reply to problems raised by the Fair Trade Commission], 1974.

Nishimura, Katsuhiro, *Gendai no Kaibutsu, Sogo Shosha* [Monsters of the Present Age, General Trading Companies], Keizai Orai-sha, 1972.

Oki, Yasuo, *Sogo Shosha to Sekai Keizai* [General Trading Companies and the World Economy], Tokyo Daigaku Shuppan-kai, 1975.

Onoda, Shuji, *Shosha no Inbo* [Trading Company Intrigue], Nisshin Hodo, 1979.

'Ote Shosha no Shihairyoku o do Miruka' [How Shall We View the Grip of the Major Trading Companies?], *Oru Bijinesu*, April 1974.

'Sangyo Kozo-ki no Sogo Shosha' [General Trading Companies in the Formative Period of Industry], *Keizai Hyoron*, July 1972.

Sankei Kigyokisha Gurupu, *Sekai no Fushicho: Sogo Shosha no Himitsu* [Phoenix of the World: The Secret of the General Trading Companies], Jiyu Kokumin-sha, 1973.

Sasago, Katsuya, *Shosha Kin'yu* [Trading Company Finance], Kyoiku-sha, 1979.

Seiji Keizai Kenkyusho, *Nippon no Boeki-gyo* [Foreign Trade Industry of Japan], Toyo Keizai Shinpo-sha, 1960.

Shibagaki, Kazuo, *Nippon Kin'yu Shihon Bunseki* [Analysis of Japanese Finance Capital], Tokyo Daigaku Shuppan-kai, 1960.

Shioda, Nagahide, *Nihon no Shosha* [Trading Companies of Japan], Shiseido, 1966.

_____, *Sogo Shosha* [General Trading Companies], Nihon Keizai Shinbun-sha, 1976.

Shosha Kino Kenkyu-kai, *Gendai Sogo Shosha-ron* [Treatise on Today's General Trading Companies], Toyo Keizai Shinpo-sha, 1975.

Takada, Tsutomu, *Gendai no Sogo Shosha* [General Trading Companies of Today], Nippon Jitsugyo Suppan-sha, 1975.

Tsuda, Noburu, *Sogo Shosha—Sono Kino to Honshitsu* [General Trading Companies: Their Essence and Function], Sangyo Noritsu Tanki Daigaku Shuppanbu, 1975.

Uchida Katsutoshi, *Shosha Hakusho* [White Paper on Trading Companies], Kodansha, 1967.

Uchimura, Gosuke (ed.), *Darega Shosha o Sabakeruka* [Who can Judge the Trading Companies?], Takagi Shobo, 1979.

Umezu, Kazuro, *Nippon no Boeki Shosha* [Japanese Trading Companies], Nippon Hyoron-sha, 1971.

_____, *Nippon Shosha-shi* [History of Japanese Trading Companies], Jikkyo Shuppan, 1976.

_____, *Shosha* [Trading Companies], Kyoiku-sha, 1975.

* * *

Emori, Morihisa, 'Japanese General Trading Companies: Their Functions and Roles', in Pierre Uri (ed.), *Trade and Investment Policies for the Seventies: New Challenges for the Atlantic Area and Japan*, New York, Praeger, 1971.

'The Giant Trading Companies: Japan's Secret Weapon?' *Forbes*, May 1972.

Japan Foreign Trade Council, 'The Sogo Shosha: What They are and How They Can Work for You?', 1978.

'Japan's Giant Trading Companies', *Forbes*, July 1978.

JETRO, 'The Role of Trading Companies in International Commerce', JETRO Marketing Series 2, n.d.

Shioda, Nagahide, 'The Sogo Shosha and its Functions in Direct Foreign Investment', *Developing Economies*, December 1976.

'The Trading Houses of Japan', *The Economist*, 3 June 1967.

Yamamura, Kozo, 'General Trading Companies in Japan: Their Origins and Growth', in H. Patrick (ed.), *Japanese Industrialization and Its Social Consequences*, Berkeley, University of California Press, 1976.

Yamazawa, Ippei and Kohama, Hirohisa, 'Trading Companies and Expansion of Japan's Foreign Trade', in *Papers and Proceedings of the Conference on Japan's Historical Development Experience and the Contemporary Developing Countries: Issues for Comparative Analysis*, International Development Center of Japan, October 1978.

Young, Alexander, *The Sogo Shosha: Japan's Multinational Trading Companies*, Boulder, Colorado, Westview, 1978.

4. INDIVIDUAL TRADING COMPANIES

(I) MITSUBISHI SHOJI

Chihara Shobo, *Zusetsu Mitsubishi Shoji* [Diagrammatic View: Mitsubishi Shoji], Chihara Shobo, 1979.

Daiyamondo-sha, *Sangyo Furontia Monogatari: Shosha Mitsubishi Shoji* [Frontier Tale in Industry: Trading Company, Mitsubishi Shoji], Daiyamondo-sha, 1965.

Mainichi Shinbun-sha (ed.), *Nippon no Shosha—Mitsubishi Shoji* [Japanese Trading Companies: Mitsubishi Shoji], Mainichi Shinbun-sha, 1973.

Mishima, Yasuo, 'Sekitan Yushutsu Shosha kara Sogo Shosha e: Mitsubishi Shoji' [From Coal Exporter to General Trading Company: Mitsubishi Shoji], in Miyamoto Mataji *et al.* (eds.), *Sogo Shosha no Keiei-shi* [Business History of General Trading Companies], Toyo Keizai Shinpo-sha, 1976.

Mitsubishi Shoji, *Mitsubishi Shoji, Sono Ayumi: 20-shunen Kinen-go* [Mitsubishi Shoji, Its Course: Twentieth Anniversary Number], 1974.

_____, *Ritsugyo Boeki-roku* [Record of the Promotion of Trade], 1958.

_____(Koho Shitsu), *Jisa wa Kane Nari* [Time Difference Means Money], Saimaru Shuppan-kai, 1977.

Ryoko Soko, *Meiko Shunju* [Happy Events], 1972.

Ryowa, January 1980. Special Number on Twenty-Five-Year Progress at Mitsubishi Shoji.

(II) MITSUI BUSSAN

Boeki no Nihon-sha and Domei Tsushin-sha, *Mitsui Bussan Tokushu-go* [Special Number: Mitsui Bussan], n.d.

Chucho-kai Nakamigawa Sensei Denki Hensan Iin, *Nakamigawa Sensei Den* [The Life of Venerable Nakamigawa], 1939.

Gendai Kigyo Kenkyu-kai, *Mitsui Bussan*, Gendai Kigyo Kenkyu-kai, 1962.

Iwasaki, Hiroyuki, 'Seisho Hogo Seisaku no Seiritsu' [Establishment of Protections for Privileged Merchants], *Mitsui Bunko Ronso*, 1967.

_____, 'Seisho Shihon no Chikuseki Kozo' [Structure of Capital Accumulation of Privileged Merchants], *Mitsui Bunko Ronso*, 1976.

Kasuga, Yutaka, 'Kan'ei Miike Tanko to Mitsui Bussan' [Government-controlled Miike Coal Mines and Mitsui Bussan], *Mitsui Bunko Ronso*, 1976.

Kizaki, Tetsuya, 'Shin "Mitsui Bussan" no Tanjo' [Birth of the New "Mitsui Bussan"]' *Chuo Koron*, September 1958.

Kojima, Naoki, *Shosetsu: Mitsui Bussan* [Mitsui Bussan: A Novel], Kodansha, 1969.

Mainichi Shinbun-sha (ed.), *Nippon no Shosha—Mitsui Bussan* [Japanese Trading Companies: Mitsui Bussan], Mainichi Shinbun-sha, 1973.

Matsumoto, Hiroshi, 'Nihon Shihon Shugi Kakuritsu-ki ni okeru Mitsui Bussan Kaisha no Hatten' [Development of Mitsui Bussan during the Rise of Japanese Capitalism], *Mitsui Bunko Ronso*, 1973.

———, 'Sekitan Hanbai Puru-sei no Seiritsu to Sono Keika: 1910-nendai ni okeru Mitsui Bussan Sekitan Hanbai no Tokushitsu ni tsuite' [Establishment of a Pooling System for Coal Sales and its Progress: the Special Characteristics of Mitsui Bussan's Coal Sales in the 1910s], *Mitsui Bunko Ronso*, 1977.

Mitsui Bussan, *Chosen to Sozo* [Challenge and Creation],1976.

———, *Kaiko-roku* [Reminiscences], 1976.

———, *Mitsui Bussan Shoshi* [Short History of Mitsui Bussan], 1951.

Mizukami, Tatsuzo, 'Watashi no Rirekisho' [My Personal History], in *Watashi no Rirekisho, No. 49*, Nihon Keizai Shinbun-sha, 1973.

Morikawa, Hidemasa, 'Meiji-ki Mitsui Bussan no Keiei Soshiki: Kyotsu Keisan Seido o Chushin ni' [Management Structure at Mitsui Bussan in the Meiji Era: Focusing on the Common Accounts System], *Keiei Shirin*, Vol. 9, No. 1, 1972.

———, 'Meiji Zaibatsu no Keiei Soshiki: Meiji-ki Mitsui Bussan no Shiryo o Chushin ni' [Management Structure of Meiji Era Financial Cliques: Focusing on Historical Sources Pertaining to Mitsui Bussan in the Meiji Era], *Keiei Shirin*, Vol. 6, Nos. 1–2, 1969.

———, 'Taisho-ki Mitsui Bussan no Keiei Soshiki' ,[Management Structure at Mitsui Bussan in the Taisho Era], *Keiei Shirin*, Vol. 10, No. 1, 1973.

Nagai, Minoru, *Jijo Masuda Takashi-o Den* [Autobiography of Venerable Masuda Takashi], 1939.

Niizeki, Yasutaro, 'Watashi no Rirekisho' [My Personal History], in *Watashi no Rirekisho, No. 1*, Nihon Keizai Shinbun-sha, 1957.

Sagara, Yasuhiko, *Mitsui Bussan*, Ushio Shuppan-sha, 1979.

Shimura, Kaiichiro, *Ikaseruka Semeno Taishitsu: Mitsui Bussan* [Are Aggressive Policies Successful?: Mitsui Bussan], Asahi Sonorama, 1980.

Takada, Tsutomu, *Mitsui Bussan no Sekai Senryaku* [The Global Strategy of Mitsui Bussan], Gakken Kenkyu-sha, 1969.

Takahashi, Toshitaro, *Mitsui Bussan no Omoide* [Memories of Mitsui Bussan], Kyobun-kan, 1934.

Togai, Yoshio, 'Kiito Shoken o Meguru Naigaisho no Kakuchiku' [Rivalry between Japanese and Foreign Traders over Trade Rights for Raw Silk], *Senshu Daigaku Shakai Kagaku Kenkyusho Geppo*, No. 66, 20 March 1969.

_____, *Mitsui Bussan Kaisha no Keiei-shi teki Kenkyu* [Historical Study of Mitsui Bussan], Toyo Keizai Shinpo-sha, 1974.

_____, 'Saisho ni Shutsugen Shita Sogo Shosha: Mitsui Bussan' [The First General Trading Company: Mitsui Bussan], in Miyamoto Mataji *et al.* (eds.), *Sogo Shosha no Keiei-shi* [Business History of General Trading Companies], Toyo Keizai Shinpo-sha, 1976.

Yamada, Taketaro, *Mitsui Bussan*, Bunsei-sha, 1934.

Yamamoto Jotaro-o Denki Hensan-kai, *Yamamoto Jotaro-o Denki* [Biography of Venerable Yamamoto Jotaro], 1942.

Yamamoto, Yujiro, *Mitsui Bussan: 80-nendai no Nihon Keizai o Ninau Sogo Shosha* [Mitsui Bussan: The General Trading Company, the Support and Driving Force of the Japanese Economy in the 1980s], Bunka Joho Buren, 1977.

Yamashita, Naoto, 'Keisei-ki Nippon Shihon Shugi ni okeru

Rinsun Kogyo to Mitsui Bussan' [Mitsui Bussan and Match Manufacturing during the Formative Period of Japanese Capitalism] , *Mitsui Bunko Ronso*, 1972.

Yamaura, Kan'ichi, *Mori Kaku* [The Life of Mori Kaku], Takayama Shoin, 1943.

* * *

Mitsui Bussan, *The Mitsui Story: Three Centuries of Japanese Business*, n.d.

————, *The 100 Year History of Mitsui & Co., Ltd.: 1876–1976*, 1977.

(III) MARUBENI

Boeki no Nihon: Marubeni Kabushiki Kaisha Tokushu [The Trade of Japan: Special Number—Marubeni] , 1972.

Boeki no Nihon: Marubeni Kikai Bumon no Ishiki to Kodo [The Trade of Japan: Consciousness and Conduct of Marubeni Machinery Division] , 1976.

Boeki no Nihon: Mitsui, Mitsubishi ni Semaru Marubeni–Iida Tokushu [The Trade of Japan: Special Number—Marubeni–Iida Closes in on Mitsui and Mitsubishi] , 1966.

Ichikawa, Shinobu, 'Watashi no Rirekisho' [My Personal History] , in *Watashi no Rirekisho, No. 40*, Nihon Keizai Shinbun-sha, 1970.

Mainichi Shinbun-sha (ed.), *Nippon no Shosha—Marubeni* [Japanese Trading Companies: Marubeni] , Mainichi Shinbun-sha, 1973.

Marubeni, 'Marubeni Kessha no Zenya' [The Eve of the Formation of Marubeni] (mimeographed), No. 1–4, 1964.

————, *Marubeni Shashi: Honshi-hen* [History of Marubeni: Main History Volume] , 1975.

————, *Marubeni Zenshi* [Early History of Marubeni] , 1977.

Marubeni Shoten, *Marubeni Shoten Enkaku* [History of Marubeni] , 1931.

Sase, Minoru, *Shosetsu Marubeni* [Marubeni: A Novel], Futami Shobo, 1976.

Takashimaya Iida, *20-shunen Kinen Takashimaya Iida* [Twentieth Anniversary of Takashimaya Iida], 1936.

* * *

Marubeni, *The Unique World of the Sogo Shosha*, 1978.

(IV) C.ITOH

Aono, Bunsaku, *Mirai Shosha: Kodo Suru Zuno Shudan: Itohchu no Zenbo* [Trading Company of the Future: A Complete Picture of C.Itoh, A Think Tank in Action], Noda Keizai-sha, 1973.

Boeki no Nihon: Itohchu Shoji Kikai Bumon no Ishiki to Kodo [Consciousness and Conduct of C.Itoh Machinery Division], 1977.

Boeki no Nihon: Itohchu Shoji Tokushu [The Trade of Japan: Special Number, C.Itoh], 1969.

Echigo, Masakazu, 'Watashi no Rirekisho' [My Personal History], *Nihon Keizai Shinbun*, 17 September 1975 to 14 October 1975.

Fuji Intanashonaru Konsarutanto Shuppanbu, *Sekai o Tsunagu Itohchu Shoji* [C.Itoh Covering the World], *Kigyo no Gendai-shi* No. 13, Fuji Intanashonaru Konsarutanto Shuppanbu, 1962.

Itohchu Shoji, *Itoh Chubei-o Kaiso-roku* [Memoirs of Venerable Itoh Chubei], 1974.

———, *Itohchu Shoji Hyakunen* [C.Itoh's One Hundred Years], 1969.

Mainichi Shinbun-sha (ed.), *Nippon no Shosha—Itohchu Shoji* [Japanese Trading Companies: C.Itoh], Mainichi Shinbun-sha, 1973.

Yamazaki, Toyoko, *Fumo Chitai* [The Barren Zone], Shincho-sha, 1976.

Yokota, Makoto, 'Shosetsu: Itohchu' [C.Itoh: A Novel], *Fuji Janaru*, May 1973 to October 1975.

* * *

C.Itoh, *An Outline of C.Itoh & Co., Ltd.*, 1937.

(V) SUMITOMO SHOJI

Mainichi Shinbun-sha (ed.), *Nippon no Shosha—Sumitomo Shoji* [Japanese Trading Companies: Sumitomo Shoji], Mainichi Shinbun-sha, 1973.

Sumitomo Shoji, *Sumitomo Shoji Kabushiki Kaisha-shi* [History of Sumitomo Shoji], 1972.

(VI) NISSHO-IWAI

Boeki no Nihon: Nissho-Iwai Tokushu-go [The Trade of Japan: Special Number—Nissho-Iwai], 1973.

Boeki no Nihon: Nissho Soritsu 40-shunen Kinen Tokushu [Nissho's Forty Years: A Commemorative History], 1968.

Iwai Sangyo, *Iwai Hyakunen Shi* [Iwai's First One Hundred Years], 1964.

Kakuma, Takashi, *Dokyumento Nissho-Iwai* [Report: Nissho Iwai], Tokuma Shoten, 1979.

Katsura, Yoshio, 'Sangyo Kigyo no Ikusei to Shosha—Suzuki Shoten' [Trading Companies and the Promotion of Industrial Enterprises: Suzuki Shoten], in Miyamoto Mataji *et al.*, (eds.), *Sogo Shosha no Keiei-shi* [Business History of General Trading Companies], Toyo Keizai Shinpo-sha, 1974.

——, *Sogo Shosha no Genryu: Suzuki Shoten* [The Beginning of General Trading Companies: Suzuki Shoten], Nihon Keizai Shinbun-sha, 1977.

Mainichi Shinbun-sha (ed.), *Nippon no Shosha—Nissho-Iwai* [Japanese Trading Companies: Nissho-Iwai], Mainichi Shinbun-sha, 1973.

Nishikawa, Masaichi, 'Watashi no Rirekisho' [My Personal History], *Nihon Keizai Shinbun*, 30 June 1978 to 28 July 1978.

Nissho, *Nissho Shiju-nen no Ayumi* [Progress over Forty Years at Nissho], 1968.

Shiroyama, Saburo, *Nezumi* [Rat], Bungei Shunju-sha, 1966.

Takahata, Seiichi, 'Watashi no Rirekisho' [My Personal History], in *Watashi no Rirekisho, No. 48*, Nihon Keizai Shinbun-sha, 1973.

Yakushin Monogatari: Nissho Kabushiki Kaisha [A Tale of Rapid Progress: Nissho & Co.], Kigyo Series No. 3, Nihon Kogyo Shinbun, 1963.

* * *

Katsura, Yoshio, 'The Role of Sogoshosha in Japanese Industrialization: Suzuki & Co., 1877–1927', in Herman Krooss (ed.), *Proceedings of the Business History Conference*, Indiana University, 1975, 2nd Series, Vol. 3.

(VII) TOYO MENKA

Boeki no Nihon: Tomen [The Trade of Japan: Tomen], 1973.

Boeki no Nihon: Tomen Kikai Bumon no Ishiki to Kodo [The Trade of Japan: Consciousness and Conduct of Tomen Machinery Division], 1978.

Ogino, Chuzaburo (ed.), *Kodama Ichizo Den* [Biography of Kodama Ichizo], 1934.

Toyo Menka, *Tomen Shiju-nen Shi* [Forty Year History of Tomen], 1960

(VIII) KANETMATSU-GOSHO

Boeki no Nihon: Kanematsu-Gosho Tokushu-go [The Trade of Japan: Special Number—Kanematsu-Gosho], 1972.

Gosho, *Gosho Rokuju-nen Shi* [Sixty Year History of Gosho], 1967.

Hakubun-do, *Abe Fusajiro Den* [Biography of Abe Fusajiro], Hakubun-do, 1930.

Kanematsu, *Kanematsu Kaiko Rokuju-nen* [Sixty Year Review of Kanematsu], 1950.

____, *Kanematsu Rokuju-nen no Ayumi* [Sixty Years at Kanematsu], 1960.

____, *Kanematsu Saikin no Junen* [The Last Ten Years at Kanematsu], 1959.

(IX) NICHIMEN

Fukui, Keizo, *Kaiko-roku: Waga Hanseiki* [Reminiscences: A Half Century of My Life], 1974.

Nichimen Biruma Kai (ed.), *Shosha Man kaku Tatakaeri: Nichimen no Biruma Kaiko-roku* [The People of a Trading Company Fought like This: Reminiscences of Nichimen in Burma], rev. ed., 1979.

Nichimen Jitsugyo, *Nichimen Shichiju-nen Shi* [Seventy Year History of Nichimen], 1962.

Nippon Menka, *Kita Matazo-kun Den* [Biography of Kita Matazo], 1933.

———, *Nippon Menka Kabushiki Kaisha Goju-nen Shi* [Fifty Year History of Nippon Menka], 1942.

(X) ATAKA

Ataka Sangyo, *Ataka Sangyo Rokuju-nen Shi* [Sixty Year History of Ataka], 1968.

Kunimitsu, Shiro, *Ataka Ichizoku* [The Ataka Family], Sankei Shuppan, 1978.

Matsumoto, Seicho, *Ku no Shiro* [Castle of Emptiness], Bungei Shunju-sha, 1978.

NHK, *Aru Sogo Shosha no Zasetsu* [The Setbacks of A Certain General Trading Company], Nihon Hoso Shuppan Kyokai, 1977.

Nihon Keizai Shinbun-sha, *Hokai: Dokyumento Ataka Sangyo* [Collapse: A Document of Ataka's Failure], Nihon Keizai Shinbun-sha, 1977.

Shioda, Nagahide, *Ataka Sangyo no Kenkyu* [A Study of Ataka], Daiyamondo-sha, 1977.

(XI) OTHER TRADING COMPANIES

Boeki no Nihon: Okura Shoji [The Trade of Japan: Okura Shoji], 1978.

Furukawa Kogyo, *Kogyo Hyakunen Shi* [A Hundred Year History of Mining], 1976.

Furukawa Toranosuke-kun Denki Hensan-kai, *Furukawa*

Toranosuke-kun Den [Biography of Furukawa Toranosuke], 1953.

Hanwa Kogyo, *Hanwa Kogyo Sanju-nen Shi* [Thirty Year History of Hanwa Kogyo], 1978.

Ichida, *Kurieito Hyakunen* [A Hundred Year History of Creation], 1974.

Inanishi, *Kaiko-roku* [Reminiscences], 1927.

Itoh, Teizo (ed.), *Tazuke Masajiro Den* [Biography of Tazuke Masajiro], 1935.

Itoman, *Itoman Goju-nen Shi* [Fifty Year History of Itoman], 1933.

Kuhara Fusanosuke-o Denki Hensan-kai, *Kuhara Fusanosuke* [The Life of Kuhara Fusanosuke], Nihon Kogyo, 1970.

Maruzen, *Maruzen Shashi* [History of Maruzen], 1951.

Matsushita Denki Boeki, *Sanju-nen no Ayumi* [Thirty Year Progress], 1966.

Meijiya, *Meijiya Shichijusan-nen Shi* [Seventy Three Year History of Meijiya], 1958.

Miyamoto, Mataji, 'Boeki Shosha no Genryu' [The Origin of Trading Companies], in Miyamoto Mataji *et al.* (eds.), *Sogo Shosha no Keiei-shi* [Business History of General Trading Companies], Toyo Keizai Shinpo-sha, 1976.

Morikawa, Hidemasa, 'Nippon Zaibatsu-shi ni okeru Sumitomo to Furukawa (Ge)' [Sumitomo and Furukawa in the History of Japanese Financial Cliques, Part II], *Keiei Shirin*, Vol. 3, 1966.

Naigai Wata, *Naigai Wata Kabushiki Kaisha Goju-nen Shi* [Fifty Year History of Naigai Wata, Inc.], 1937.

Nihon Kami Parupu Shoji, *Hyakusanju-nen Shi* [A Hundred and Thirty Year History], 1975.

Nozaki Sangyo, *Rokuju-nen no Ashiato* [Footprints of Sixty Years], 1953.

Sakudo, Yotaro, 'Senmon Shosha kara Sogo Shosha eno Michi: Kansai-kei Tekko Shosha no Baai o Chushin toshite' [The Path from Specialized Trading Company to General Trading Company: Focusing on The Case of Steel Trading Companies of Kansai Origin], in Miyamoto Mataji *et al.*

(eds.), *Sogo Shosha no Keiei-shi* [Business History of General Trading Companies], Toyo Keizai Shinpo-sha, 1976.

Shinko Sangyo, *Wagasha Shiju-nen no Ayumi* [Forty Year Progress of Our Company], 1976.

Shinko Shoji, *Watashitachi no Nijugo-nen* [Our Twenty Five Years], 1971.

Sugi Michisuke Tsuito-roku Kanko Iin-kai, *Sugi Michisuke Tsuito-roku* [Sugi Michisuke Memorial Record], 2 vols., 1965.

Tamurakoma, *Tsuioku* [Reminiscences], 1932.

Taniguchi, Kaichiro, *Ito Hitosuji* [With Yarn Alone], 1960.

Uchida Yoko, *Bunka ni Tsuchikau: Kabushiki Kaisha Uchida Yoko Sogyo Goju-nen Shi* [Fostering Culture: The History of Uchida Yoko, the First Fifty Years], 1960.

Watanabe, Wataru *et al.*, 'Okura Zaibatsu no Kenkyu' [Study of the Okura Zaibatsu], *Tokyo Keidai Gakkaishi*, 6 parts, 1976–8.

Yagi Shoten, *Sogyo Hachiju-nen Shi* [Yagi Shoten: An Eighty Year History], 1972.

Yamaguchi Gen, *Yamaguchi Gen Hachiju-nen Shi* [Eighty Year History of Yamaguchi Gen], 1965.

Yamamoto Kogyo, *Yamamoto-ke 80-shunen Shoshi* [Short Commemorative History on the Eightieth Anniversary of the House of Yamamoto], 1952.

5. RELATED WORKS

Ajia Shobo, *Mitsui Tokuhon* [Mitsui Reader], Ajia Shobo, 1943.

Edo, Hideo, *Sushiya no Shomon* [Testimony of a *Sushi* Maker], Asahi Shinbun-sha, 1966.

Hagiwara, Keiichi, *Senba wa Ikinobirareruka* [Can Senba Survive?], Nippon Jitsugyo Shuppan-sha, 1971.

Hoshino, Yasunosuke, *Mitsui Hyakunen* [Mitsui's One Hundred Years], Kajima Kenkyusho Shuppan-kai, 1968.

Itoh, Chubei, 'Kanji Zenpai-ron' [Essay on the Abolition of Chinese Characters], *Chuo Koron*, June 1958.

_____, 'Watashi no Shosha Hitsumetsu-ron' [Trading Companies Are Doomed to Perish: A Personal Opinion], *Daiyamondo*, Shinshun Tokubetsu-go, 1966.

'Itoh Chubei ga Kataru Shosha-ron' [Itoh Chubei's Views on the Trading Company], *Oru Bijinesu*, March 1972.

Ito, Sadao, *Kikaisho Hishi* [Confidential Notes by Machinery Merchants], Kogyo Yomimono-sha, 1940.

Iwasaki Koyata Den Hensan Iinkai, *Iwasaki Koyata Den* [Biography of Iwasaki Koyota], 1957.

Kanno, Wataro, *Omi Shonin no Kenkyu* [Study of the Omi Merchants], Yuhikaku, 1941.

Katsuta, Sadaji, *Nippon Kontserun Zensho, Vol. X: Okura, Nezu Kontserun Tokuhon* [Collected Works of Japanese Konzern, Volume Ten: A Reader on Okura and Nezu Konzern], Shunju-sha, 1938.

Kawasaki Seitetsu, *Kawasaki Seitetsu Nijugo-nen Shi* [Twenty Five Year History of Kawasaki Seitetsu], 1976.

Kindai Keiei Kenkyu-kai (ed.), *Shin Mitsui Tokuhon* [A New Reader on Mitsui], Sawa Shoten, 1971.

Kobayashi, Shunji, *Kigyo no Seiji Kenkin: Mo Hitotsu no Toshi no Ronri* [Corporate Donations to Political Parties: Another Form of Investment], *Nikkei Shinsho*, No. 249, Nihon Keizai Shinbun-sha, 1976.

Kubota, Akira, *Mitsui, Chuo Shinsho* No. 122, Chuo Koronsha, 1966.

Matsumoto, Hiroshi, *Mitsui Zaibatsu no Kenkyu* [Study of the Mitsui Zaibatsu], Yoshikawa Kobun-kan, 1979.

Minomura, Seiichiro, *Minomura Rizaemon Den* [Biography of Minomura Rizaemon], 1969.

Mitsubishi Sogya Hyakunen Kinen Jigyo Iinkai, *Mitsubishi no Hyakunen* [The One Hundred Years of Mitsubishi], 1970.

Mitsui Ginko, *Mitsui Ginko Hyakunen no Ayumi* [A Hundred Year History of the Mitsui Bank], 1976.

Miyamoto, Mataji, *Senba*, Kyoto, Mineruba Shobo, 1960.

Mochikabu Kaisha Seiri Iinkai, *Nihon no Zaibatsu to Sono Kaitai* [Japanese Zaibatsu and their Dissolution], reprint, Hara Shobo, 1973.

Murofushi, Tetsuro, *Oshoku no Susume* [Corruption Recommended], Kobundo, 1963.

Nichibo, *Nichibo Shichijugo-nen Shi* [Seventy Five Year History of Nichibo], 1966.

Nihon Keizai Shinbun-sha, *Kansai Keizai no Hyakunen* [A Century of Kansai Business], Nihon Keizai Shinbun-sha, 1980.

Nihon Menka Kyokai, *Menka Hyakunen* [Cotton's Hundred Years], 2 vols., 1969.

Nihon Menshifu Yushutsu Kumiai, *Nihon Mengyo Boeki Shoshi* [Short History of the Foreign Trade of Cotton Products in Japan], 1957.

Nishinoiri, Aiichi, *Nippon Kontserun Zensho, Vol. IX: Asano, Shibusawa, Okawa, Furukawa Kontserun Tokuhon* [Collected Works of Japanese Konzern, Vol. 9: A Reader on Asano, Shibusawa, Okawa, and Furukawa Konzern], Shunju-sha, 1937.

Ogura, Eiichiro, *Omi Shonin no Keifu* [Genealogy of the Omi Merchants], *Nikkei Shinsho*, No. 320, Nihon Keizai Shinbun-sha, 1980.

Okakura, Koshiro, *Oshoku no Seiji Keizaigaku* [Political Economy of Corruption], Rodo Junpo-sha, 1967.

Ouchi, Minoru, *Fuhai no Kozo* [Structure of Corruption], Daiyamondo-sha, 1977.

Sato, Kiichiro, 'Watashi no Rirekisho' [My Personal History] in *Watashi no Rirekisho, No. 26*, Nihon Keizai Shinbun-sha, 1966.

Sato, Noboru, *Nihon Tekko Hanbai-shi* [History of Steel Marketing in Japan], Osaka, Kyodo Kogyo Shinbun-sha, 1978.

Senba Konjaku Monogatari [Senba Stories, Past and Present], 1967.

Shibagaki, Kazuo, *Mitsui, Mitsubishi no Hyakunen* [One Hundred Years of Mitsui and Mitsubishi], Chuo Koron-sha, 1968.

Taiwan Ginko-shi Hensan Shitsu, *Taiwan Ginko-shi* [History of the Bank of Taiwan], 1964.

Takahashi, Kamekichi, *Nihon Zaibatsu no Kaibo* [Anatomy of Japanese Zaibatsu], Chuo Koron-sha, 1930.

Takamura, Naosuke, *Nihon Boseki-shi Josetsu* [Introduction to the History of Japanese Cotton Spinning], 2 vols., Hanawa Shobo, 1971.

Tamaki, Hajime, *Nihon Zaibatsu-shi* [History of Japanese Zaibatsu], Shakai Shiso-sha, 1976.

Tokyo Daigaku Shakai Kagaku Kenkyusho, *Kurashiki Boseki no Shihon Chikuseki to Ohara-ke no Tochi Shoyu* [Capital Accumulation of Kurashiki Spinning Co. and Landownership of the Ohara Family], Tokyo Daigaku Shakai Kagaku Kenkyusho Chosa Hokoku, No. 11, March 1970.

Toyo Boseki, *Toyo Boseki Shichiju-nen Shi* [Seventy Year History of Toyo Boseki], 1953.

Tsuchiya, Takao, *Kindai Nippon no Seisho* [Privileged Merchants in Modern Japan], Seikei Orai-sha, 1956.

Wada, Hidekichi, *Mitsui Kontserun Tokuhon* [Reader on the Mitsui Konzern], Shunju-sha, 1937.

Yamada, Kiyoshi, *Mitsubishi no Hito to Keiei* [Management and the People of Mitsubishi], Kigyo Bunka-sha, 1974.

Yamaguchi, Kazuo (ed.), *Nippon Sangyo Kin'yu-shi Kenkyu: Boseki Kin'yu-hen* [Research on the Financial History of Japanese Industry: Cotton-Spinning Financing], Tokyo Daigaku Shuppan-kai, 1970.

Yokohama Shokin Ginko-shi [History of the Yokohama Specie Bank], 1920.

* * *

British Economic Mission to the Far East, *Report of the Cotton Mission*, 1931.

Mitsui Gomei Kaisha, *The House of Mitsui*, 1933.

Roberts, John, *Mitsui: Three Centuries of Japanese Business*, Tokyo, Weatherhill, 1973.

Yanaga, Chitoshi, *Big Business in Japanese Politics*, New Haven, Yale University Press, 1968.

Index*

*Numbers in italics refer to tables and figures.